Electric October

Seven World Series Games,

Six Lives,

Five Minutes of Fame

That Lasted Forever

KEVIN COOK

Henry Holt and Company
Publishers since 1866
175 Fifth Avenue
New York, New York 10010
www.henryholt.com

Henry Holt ® and 🄷 ® are registered trademarks of Macmillan
Publishing Group, LLC.

Library of Congress Cataloging-in-Publication Data

Names: Cook, Kevin, 1956– author
Title: Electric October : seven world series games, six lives, five minutes of
    fame that lasted forever / Kevin Cook.
Description: New York : Henry Holt and Company, [2017] | Includes
    bibliographical references and index.
Identifiers: LCCN 2017008793| ISBN 9781250116567 (hardcover :
    alk. paper) | ISBN 9781250116574 (electronic book : alk. paper)
Subjects: LCSH: World Series (Baseball)—History.
Classification: LCC GV878.4 .C65 2017 | DDC 796.357646—dc23
LC record available at https://lccn.loc.gov/2017008793

Our books may be purchased in bulk for promotional, educational, or
business use. Please contact your local bookseller or the Macmillan
Corporate and Premium Sales Department at (800) 221-7945, extension
5442, or by e-mail at MacmillanSpecialMarkets@macmillan.com.

First Edition 2017

Designed by Meryl Sussman Levavi

Printed in the United States of America

1   3   5   7   9   10   8   6   4   2

To Cal Cook, my partner,
Lily Cook, my heroine,
and
Pamela Marin, the gamer I admire most of all

Contents

Part Three: SIX FUTURES

Prologue

Mortals

A tanned, weathered hand lifts a VHS cassette. Clacks it into a videotape player.

"Where's the remote thingy?"

A voice from the next room. "Dad, are you watching it again?"

On the TV, Red Sox pitcher Bob Stanley peers in for a sign from Rich Gedman. It's October 25, 1986, Boston vs. the New York Mets in the most-watched World Series ever. Fifty million Americans see Mookie Wilson foul off Stanley's pitch. But in this little ranch house in the Bay Area, it's not 1986 for long. The brightly colored TV screen blinks and reappears in black and white. Men in baggy flannel uniforms jog to their positions on a diamond that has bare spots in the grass. DiMaggio, Rizzuto, Berra. It's Game Four of the 1947 World Series, the New York Yankees against the Brooklyn Dodgers. The game's most popular teams had both broken attendance records, the mighty Yanks at their gleaming stadium in the Bronx and the hope-springs-eternal Dodgers at Ebbets Field, their cracker box in Flatbush. Now they faced off in the first truly modern World Series.

It was the first integrated Series thanks to Jackie Robinson, who broke baseball's color line that year. It was the first televised World Series. But some things never change. Late in Game Four the Yankees, winners of ten World Series to Brooklyn's total of none, are taking command. One more victory and they'll lead the '47 Series three games to one. And they're practically rubbing the Dodgers' noses in it. With two outs in the ninth inning Bill Bevens, the Yanks' rangy fireballer, has thrown eight and two-thirds innings of no-hit ball. He's one out from the first no-hitter in World Series history.

But Bevens is spent. He has thrown 135 pitches. His jersey soaked with sweat, he rears back and uncorks another fastball.

Pinch hitter Cookie Lavagetto swings through it. He shakes his head at himself. The pitch was high and away, right where he likes 'em, and he missed it.

Thirty-nine years later, watching the scratchy black-and-white screen, he calls to his son in the other room.

"Want to watch?"

"Sure, why not?"

Ernie Lavagetto joins his old man in front of the TV. They have seen this tape many times.

On the screen, Bevens winds up and fires, shutting his eyes as he lets the ball go.

"Another fastball," Cookie says, watching his younger self lunge at the pitch.

You can hear his bat meet the pitch with a clack that sends the ball on a long arc toward the GEM RAZOR billboard on the right-field fence at Ebbets Field, toward baseball history and the rest of his life.

This is the story of half a dozen men who shared a week that changed their lives forever. The six of them played, practiced, traveled, fought, laughed, ate and drank, won and lost with a couple of immortals whose names are still celebrated seventy years later: Jackie Robinson and Joe DiMaggio. But Cookie Lavagetto, Al Gionfriddo, and manager Burt Shotton of the Brooklyn Dodgers, and Bill Bevens, Snuffy Stirnweiss, and manager Bucky Harris of the New York Yankees were baseball mortals. They're remembered by the game's historians and trivia buffs if they are remembered at all. Small-town boys, most of them, each one a hometown hero, they spent a week in the national spotlight and then faded away, forgotten, until somebody mentioned the 1947 World Series.

The six of them played key roles in a World Series that Joe DiMaggio called "the most exciting ever." Red Barber, the radio voice of the game's golden age, swore he'd never witnessed such unlikely highs and lows, a time when the stars became supporting players while journeymen, scrubs, and substitutes played hero. Or goat. Or both.

For some the '47 Series presaged happier times. For others it was the one shining moment in a losing battle to stay in the majors. Three of them were finished in the big leagues after 1947.

One spent the rest of his days living down a near miss in the game of his life.

Two spent decades shaking fans' hands, accepting free drinks and pats on the back, telling and retelling the story of their long-ago heroics.

One died young in a disaster as bizarre as the '47 World Series.

Two—the managers—endured endless what-ifs about the moves they made that fall in Brooklyn and the Bronx.

This is the story of how seven ballgames shaped the rest of their days. It's a true tale of fame, friendship, teamwork, memory, and life's biggest challenge: how we deal with the cards that fate deals us.

As Barber put it, "For human stories, you'll never beat this one."

Six Lives

Young Old Burt

Burton Edwin Shotton was born in 1884. Professional base-ball was only fifteen years old. Mark Twain, who finished writing *The Adventures of Huckleberry Finn* that year, described baseball as America's "very symbol of the drive, and push, and rush and struggle of the raging, tearing, booming nineteenth century!" Like Huck Finn, young Burt imagined a wider world than the small-town Midwest of his youth. The son of a sailor who manned the freighters plying Lake Erie, he grew up in Bacon's Corners, Ohio, just west of Cleveland. As a teenager, Burt loaded iron ore onto those freighters. On weekends he earned extra nickels as a substitute barber. Free hours he played sandlot ball. Most turn-of-the-century Americans were more like Theodore Roosevelt—more bullish on boxing and college football—but dockworker Burt Shotton daydreamed about baseball, about slashing doubles and stealing bases like Jesse Burkett and Bobby Wallace of the major-league Cleveland Spiders.

Soon Burt was fighting his way up through baseball's bush leagues. Turns out he had speed to burn, enough speed to beat out infield singles and lead minor-league teams in stolen bases. He slowed down just long enough to marry a fan of one of those teams, the Steubenville (Ohio) Stubs. Mary Daly, a plump, bubbly brunette as old-fashioned as he, became Mrs. Burt Shotton in 1909. They would spend more than half a century together.

Burt made his big-league debut that season, then bounced back to the minors for a season before joining the St. Louis Browns to stay in 1911. That last-place Browns club was skippered by his old Spiders hero Bobby Wallace, a Hall of Fame player who proved to be a fretful washout as a manager, winning 57 games and losing 134 before he was replaced early in the 1912 season. Two years later, Browns owner Robert Lee Hedges hired another young manager, Branch Rickey. Shotton starred for Rickey, stealing more than forty bases four years in a row, with batting averages from .269 to .297. He played shallow in center, making shoe-top catches that turned bloops into outs, racing back to snag long fly balls. Like every speedster he got nicknamed "Barney" after Barney Oldfield, the first one-hundred-mile-an-hour race car driver. A 1915 poll of big-league players chose three All-Star outfielders: Ty Cobb, Tris Speaker, and Burt Shotton.

Like most big-league stars, Shotton resisted overtures to jump to the upstart Federal League, which placed a team in St. Louis, the Terriers, to vie with the major-league Browns and Cardinals. But some players made the leap. Future Hall of Famers Chief Bender, Three-Finger Brown, and Bill McKechnie joined Federal League clubs. Aging shortstop Joe Tinker of "Tinker to Evers to Chance" fame jumped to the outlaw league's Chicago Whales, whose owner built a new ballpark that would later become known as Wrigley Field. After the Federal League folded in 1915, the owners of the Baltimore Terrapins franchise brought an antitrust lawsuit against the National and American leagues. That suit went all the way to the U.S. Supreme Court, which ruled that because baseball was a sport, not a business, it was immune to federal antitrust laws. Justice Oliver Wendell Holmes Jr. wrote that "personal effort . . . is not a subject of commerce." In effect, the court granted major-league owners monopoly power over their players, an ownership right that lasted until the players' union finally beat them in court half a century later.

After the Federal League collapsed, St. Louis Terriers owner Philip De Catesby Ball, a wealthy ice maker, bought the Browns and brought manager Fielder Jones with him, to replace Branch Rickey. But Ball kept Rickey on the payroll, bumping him to the front office. One of Rickey's first moves as the Browns' business manager was to give his favorite speedster a raise to $3,500, worth about $80,000 today. Shotton still spent the winter working in Ohio, cutting hair at a combined cigar store and barbershop. But his knees had begun to ache, and sciatica sapped his speed. His last decent season was a sixteen-steal campaign in 1919, the year the major leagues faced a new threat to their survival.

The 1919 Chicago White Sox, underpaid and angry at owner Charles Comiskey, conspired with gamblers to throw the World Series to the Cincinnati Reds. Baseball owners reacted to the "Black Sox" scandal by naming Judge Kenesaw Mountain Landis as the first commissioner of baseball, giving him nearly unlimited power to restore public faith in the game. Landis had already pleased the owners by siding with them in the Federal League case. Now he banned eight of the "Black Sox" for life. Among those excommunicated was Shoeless Joe Jackson, who'd batted .375 in the 1919 Series and was one of the game's biggest stars. To Judge Landis, a man with the charm of a grumpy iguana, baseball's reputation mattered more than any man's career.

In the twenties a livelier ball and the rise of home-run hero Babe Ruth helped make baseball America's true national pastime. By then, Shotton looked older than his years. He'd begun going gray when he was a rookie—too much thinking, teammates said. Yet as his speed faded, Shotton's quick mind set him apart. By 1922 he was a squinting, thirty-seven-year-old pinch hitter for the St. Louis Cardinals. The following year Branch Rickey, who was now the Cardinals' skipper, made Barney Shotton his right-hand man.

Rickey's name may evoke images of the Brooklyn Dodgers of the 1940s, but in 1923 he was not yet the grand Mahatma of later legend. In fact, Shotton was among the first to see genius in his forty-one-year-old boss. He spent hours following Rickey around. "Burt, try this," the manager told him. "Watch this." "Burt, you must never forget this."

An Ohioan like Shotton, Rickey started out as a flop. Serving as a backup catcher for the 1907 New York Highlanders, he set a record that still stands. One sunny Friday, thirteen Washington Senators tried to steal a base on him. Branch Rickey threw none of them out. In 109 seasons since then, more than 160,000 big-league games, no catcher has ever allowed so many stolen bases.

The Highlanders released him. Rickey paid his way through law school and discovered that he was better suited to running and promoting a ball club than playing for one. While other teams took the field in blank flannels, he put a picture on his Cardinals' jerseys, a pair of redbirds perched on either end of a bat, the original version of the logo the team still wears.

Rickey's quirky, questing intellect led him to doubt every tradition, to seek every edge. It was Rickey who outfoxed richer clubs by inventing the farm system and using it to stockpile talented prospects in places like Houston, Syracuse, and Fort Smith, Arkansas. It was Rickey who hired the game's first statistician, Rickey who transformed spring training from lazy weeks of long toss and jumping jacks to a modern program featuring batting tees, sliding pits, and pitching machines, Rickey who touted each innovation in his Sunday-go-to-meeting baritone. Shotton felt lucky to earn a little of his favor.

Shotton watched his mentor squat behind the plate at the team's spring camp, nearly busting the seams of his business suit, tying yellow twine to poles he planted at the corners of home plate. Rickey had invented a sort of virtual strike zone like the ones seen on TV today.

"Throw to the strings!" he told his pitchers.

Pitchers who laughed at the thought of throwing to a twine zone got traded or released. Branch Rickey had no time for unbelievers.

A keen judge of talent on and off the field, Rickey sent Shotton to oversee the Cardinals' minor-league camp in 1923, hoping the aging outfielder would "show me something." Shotton promptly memorized the names, positions, strengths, and flaws of all 122 players in camp.

Rickey was a farmer's son who'd promised his fervently Methodist mother he would never set foot in a ballpark on a Sunday. Through the years he chose several players to sub for him as "Sunday manager," and Shotton was his favorite. Rickey would tell him which pitcher and lineup to use but let Burt run the show once the game began, and the plan worked. Shotton proved himself a strategist on the field and a diplomat off it. When the Cardinals' winning percentage improved on Sundays, he kept that fact to himself.

At thirty-eight he looked forty-eight, his long face as severe as Judge Landis's except for the smile lines by his eyes. Reporters called him "good old Burt," a modest man who was good for a quote that took the edge off the thunder they heard every day from Rickey. One day he told the writers that he, Sunday manager Burt Shotton, had discovered the secret to managing a winning team: "Have good players."

A year later he retired as a player and joined Rickey's coaching staff. Good old Burt tutored outfielders and base runners, and coached third during games. There was something grandfatherly about him even then, the gray-haired, kindly-voiced gent clapping his hands and calling "Let's go" from the third-base coach's box.

In March 1924 the Cardinals made a bumpy hour-long bus trip from their training camp in Bradentown, Florida, to Tampa for a spring-training game against the Washington Senators. Four-time batting champ Rogers Hornsby led the Cards off their bus at Tampa's Plant Field, where the baseball diamond overlapped a horse-racing oval on the Florida State Fairgrounds. This is the day when the threads that lead to the 1947 World Series would cross for the first time. Spring training in Florida was only a dozen years old. It was in Bradentown—not yet shortened to Bradenton—that Rickey built the first batting cages to train hitters for preseason games in what had become known as the Grapefruit League.

Why not the Orange League or the Seashell League? The spring circuit owes its name to a stunt by Brooklyn manager Wilbert Robinson in 1915. Robinson, egged on by his players, boasted that he could catch a ball thrown from an aeroplane. The players put down their bets and talked pioneer aviator Ruth Law, "Florida's Fabulous Feminine Flyer," into tossing a ball from five hundred feet over the field. But Law left the baseball in her hotel room that day. At the last minute, a member of her ground crew gave her a grapefruit instead. Soon Robinson was circling under the missile, backpedaling and calling, "I got it!" The impact drove him to the ground in a gush of pulp and juice. Thinking a baseball had pierced his chest, Robinson squirmed and cried, "Oh God, it's killed me!" Once his players finished laughing and collecting on their bets, they told everyone they knew, and Florida's spring schedule became the Grapefruit League.

Several hundred fans turned out to see the Senators' star pitcher Walter Johnson take the mound against a Cardinals club led by Rogers Hornsby on March 22, 1924. That afternoon's duel of immortals was also a clash of longtime losers. Of the sixteen major-league ball clubs only the Senators, Cardinals, and Browns had never won a pennant. But while the Cardinals were coming off three straight winning seasons (thanks to Hornsby and Rickey), the Washington Senators, also known as the Nationals, Americans, Federals, Capitals, Woefuls, and Awfuls, hadn't finished better than third in the eight-team American League in more than a decade. Their best weapon, Johnson's legendary speedball, had been losing steam for years. The Big Train, as Johnson was called, was now thirty-six years old and hadn't won twenty games since 1919. Newspapermen joked that Washington was forever "first in war, first in peace, and last in the American League."

Both clubs' fans applauded Rogers Hornsby as he stepped to the plate in the first inning, his jug ears poking out under his short-billed cap. The regal Rajah didn't drink or smoke or chew tobacco, but he chewed gum so hard that you could hear his jaw working five paces away. Burt Shotton shouted encouragement from the third-base coach's box, but Hornsby ignored him. To Hornsby, Shotton was "Rickey's boy," despite the fact that leathery old Burt was almost forty.

Hornsby disdained Rickey's newfangled ideas. Batting cages? Strike zones made of twine? It was all horseshit to him, a term newsmen rendered as "hooey" or "folderol." He swore he could top his Triple Crown stats of 1922, when he'd hit .401 with forty-two homers and 152 RBIs, with no help from fenced-in hitting cages or a picture of a bird on his shirt.

That afternoon, Hornsby grounded out to Senators second baseman Bucky Harris. He tipped his cap to the pitcher. Johnson gave him a nod. Just a couple of matinee idols at an out-of-town rehearsal. Hornsby jogged to the visitors' dugout, found a seat on the bench, and spent the rest of the inning watching Harris, the "boy wonder" player-manager everyone in baseball was talking about.

The kid was boyish all right. How wonderful remained to be seen. Hornsby suspected that the boy wonder angle, like most baseball stories, was horseshit.

CHAPTER 2

The Fabulous Breaker Boy

Stanley Raymond Harris came from sleepy Port Jervis, New York, Rip Van Winkle's hometown. He was five when his father, a semipro pitcher, moved the family to Pennsylvania coal country. He was twelve when his father walked out on the rest of them. While older brother Merle played minor-league baseball, Stanley dropped out of elementary school to support their mother.

He worked as a breaker boy in a coal mine, grabbing chunks of anthracite as they skidded down a chute, separating coal from slate. Dirty, dangerous work. The steel-mesh conveyor belt at the bottom of the chute caught other boys' fingers and tore them off. Some breaker boys lost arms or legs or their lives in the mines, but Stanley survived intact, playing shortstop on a church-league team on Sunday, his only day off work. He and his friends built the local diamond themselves. They used burlap feedbags to approximate the canvas bags packed with sand or sawdust that served as bases in the big leagues. The church leaguers repaired broken bats with glue and duck tape. Stanley's mother taught him how to sew mangled baseballs back together.

He was fourteen when his boss at the mine raised his pay from twelve to eighteen cents an hour. Catherine Harris wept the day her son handed her a silver dollar.

Soon he made a semipro team. "I got a lucky hit in my first money game," he recalled. "The ball hit a pebble and bounced over the third baseman's head." Years later a nearly identical bad-hop single would turn the tide in a World Series, but the near-term changes in Stanley's life had to do with his work and his name. First, he quit the mine in hopes of becoming a professional ballplayer like his brother Merle. Then an old-timer, spitting tobacco juice, asked, "Kid, you got a nickname?"

"Yes sir. They call me Bucky," he said, thinking of another sport, one he played in the winter. "I was playing a rough game of basketball when a couple of fellows jumped on my back. I shook them off and shot a basket, and they gave me that name. They said I bucked like a little bronco."

"Keep on bucking," the veteran said. "You'll have to fight for everything you get in this world."

In 1915 Detroit Tigers manager Hughie Jennings took pity on the boy. Jennings, an old semipro teammate of Bucky's father (and big-league teammate of outfielder Wee Willie Keeler and grapefruit catcher Wilbert Robinson), summoned the teenager to the Tigers' spring camp in Texas. Bucky's mother bought a five-cent map so they could locate the small town of Waxahachie. She was saddened to see that it was a thousand miles away. Her son had never traveled farther from Pittston, Pennsylvania, than Wilkes-Barre, a journey of eight miles. Bucky packed a cardboard satchel and rode the overnight train to Texas, where he weighed in at 115 pounds and stared wide-eyed at Ty Cobb, his new teammate. Eighteen-year-old Bucky spent a week flailing at batting-practice fastballs, kicking grounders during infield drills. He wrote mournful letters to his mother: *Ty Cobb told me to get off the field.* And then he beat some of the letters home to Pittston after the Tigers released him.

A year later Jennings gave him another shot, this time with the minor-league Muskegon Reds. The scrawny nineteen-year-old batted

.166. In the field, he recorded more errors than putouts. Released again, Bucky Harris joined a party of local baseball fans on a trip to New York to see Babe Ruth and the Boston Red Sox play Wilbert Robinson's Brooklyn Robins—precursor to the Dodgers—in the 1916 World Series. Dazzled by the big city, with no idea how to order off a menu or tip a waiter, he kept his mouth shut.

He returned to the Pennsylvania Coal Company's mine in Pittston while dreaming of New York—"the richly dressed women and their escorts, the soft lights, fine linens and tables crowded with silver"— and his days with Cobb and the Tigers. He wrote letters to all the baseball men he'd met, pleading for a tryout. Nobody wrote back. Finally he heard that the second baseman of the minor-league Reading Pretzels was about to be suspended for an on-field brawl. Harris phoned Reading manager George Wiltse, who said, "Yeah, yeah" and took down his name. Two days later Wiltse sent a telegram: REPORT TO BINGHAMTON AT ONCE. But the telegram was addressed to Merle Harris, Bucky's older brother, who was better known in the pro ranks.

"You go," said Merle, who had spent years scuffling in the minors. "You're the one who phoned him."

With his brother's blessing, Bucky rode the Empire State Express to Binghamton, where he introduced himself to Wiltse. "I'm Harris," he said.

The manager looked him over. "You ain't Merle."

"Mister Wiltse, you need a second baseman. I just need a chance."

The manager shrugged. "You'll do till I dig up somebody else."

Bucky finished the season with the Pretzels. While other players spat chaw on their buddies' shoes or made eyes at baseball Annies in front-row seats, he studied veteran infielders' footwork, and how base-stealers used hook slides to elude tags, and how pitchers almost always threw their best pitch on 3-2 counts. He batted .250 that season with eleven doubles, improved his baserunning and his footwork in the field. An ivory hunter noticed.

Big-league scouts were known as ivory hunters, their treks to places like Pittston or Paducah likened to safaris because the hotels weren't much more than huts and there wasn't much game to be found in the bush. One day in 1919, when Bucky was playing for the Buffalo Bisons, catcher Joe Casey pointed out a clipboard-wielding gent in the seats behind home plate. "Play good today, Bucky," Casey said. "That man's from the Washington Senators."

Harris got a couple of hits. The scout praised him in a telegram to owner Clark Griffith, and Griffith rode the rails from Washington to Buffalo to scout the kid himself.

The Senators' owner, known as the Old Fox, saw a wiry infielder who weighed 130 pounds in his sweat-soaked flannel uniform. A few days before, Bucky had knocked down a line drive with his bare hand. The ring finger on that hand—his "meat hand," as opposed to the glove hand—swelled to three times its size. He taped it to his pinkie and played anyway. With a big-league owner coming to scout him, "I was resolved to stay in the game if my finger fell off."

He went six-for-six that day, stole two bases, and handled fourteen chances at second base. He was pulling the tape off his fingers after the game when Griffith clasped him by the wrist. "Let's see that finger, son," he said.

Bucky winced. "It's sprained is all."

That night his manager called him aside. "Griff thinks you're a gamer, playing with a busted finger," he said.

Griffith bought his contract for $4,500. All of a sudden Bucky Harris, all 130 pounds of him, was a big-leaguer.

He made his major-league debut that summer, smacking a single off the Yankees' Carl Mays. After the game, Bucky tried not to show how thrilled he was while Griffith thumped his back and pumped his hand.

"Damn it, son," the owner said, noticing Bucky's still-swollen finger. "Is that thing no better?"

Griffith sent him to a hospital for an expensive new procedure, an X-ray that showed three fractures in Harris's finger. Bucky swore he'd play through the pain but the Old Fox, who doubled as the club's manager, benched him as Washington slogged to the end of another losing season.

"Save your strength, boy. Save it for next year," he said.

Bucky Harris became Griffith's pet project. Here was a fatherless boy who was eager to play hurt, a scrapper who'd do anything short of murder to help the lowly Senators. The following season, Bucky's first full year in the majors, he hit just one home run and got caught stealing more than he stole, but he led the American League in one category: getting hit by pitches. By his own description he was still "green enough for the cows to eat," but he never backed down from anybody, not even one of his idols.

During a game in Detroit that year, six-foot-one Ty Cobb slid snarling into second, where Bucky slapped a hard tag on him. Cobb, who had no memory of the kid from spring camp five years before, was notorious for spikes-first slides that had crippled a few infielders. He bounced up and barked, "Try that again, *busher*, and I'll carve you like a turkey."

Bucky showed him the ball. "Next time, old man, I'll throw this between your eyes."

Cobb liked that. A busher with backbone! The next time he slid into second, safe on a double, he gave Bucky Harris a nod that said, *Kid, you're all right.*

The ex-busher relished big-league life—$3.50 a day meal money when a dinner of steak and ice cream cost 85 cents! Soon he weighed in at 140. Going into the final game of the 1920 season with a batting average of .295, dying to bat .300, he went three-for-three. "You've put in a fair day's work," Griffith said. "I'm taking you out of the game." He was sure three hits would boost the rookie's average to .300, but without a statistician or a pencil and paper in the dugout, Griffith was guessing.

"Give me one more crack up there," Harris pleaded. "This pitching is my meat." He doubled in his last at-bat to lift his average to .300. Had he skipped that last time up he would have finished at .299.

During the next two seasons he repeated as the major-league leader in getting hit by pitches, leaning over the plate, daring pitchers to throw inside. Griffith cheered every time a baseball thudded off Bucky's body. In 1923, when Donie Bush became the Senators' manager, the owner chose Bucky to be Bush's roommate on road trips, a vote of confidence for the young second baseman. Which was more than Bush got. After another losing season, Griffith fired Bush and tried to hire Eddie Collins, the White Sox' star second baseman, as the Senators' player-manager.

"If I get Collins, he'll be our second baseman," Griffith told Bucky. "Would you be willing to switch to third?"

"I'll play anywhere you want," Bucky said, and the Old Fox prized him more than ever. When Collins decided to stay in Chicago, Griffth sent a special-delivery letter to Harris.

Bucky was reading the letter for the second time when his telephone rang. With a shivering hand, he reached for the phone.

"Well, how about it?" Griffith asked. "You're only a kid, but I'm gambling on you having the right stuff. You've been hustling since you were knee-high to a duck. You've built a strong body from a frail one. Now tell me, are you ready to manage the Washington Senators?"

"I'm ready."

He had just turned twenty-seven years old.

The newsprint in the *Washington Post* wasn't dry before the move had a nickname. Writers called it "Griffith's folly." They predicted that other teams' fans would wave diapers at the youngest manager in major-league history. But with the owner in his corner he could ignore the sportswriters, at least for now. The new player-manager's first worry was how to deal with the team's veterans. Who was he to tell Walter Johnson how or when to pitch?

Johnson set the tone for the season to come. When Bucky went to see him, the broad-shouldered, kindhearted king of major-league hurlers looked down at his new manager and said, "I'll work my head off for you." That spring the thirty-six-year-old Johnson set an example by outworking his younger teammates—and manager—in preseason drills. He defended Harris to writers who called the "boy wonder" too boyish for the job.

"I'm for giving a fellow a fair chance," the Big Train said.

The writers agreed, then began sniping at Bucky the moment spring training began. How could a shavetail like him presume to manage the great Johnson? Or Sam Rice, Roger Peckinpaugh, and the club's other elders? How did he like being called tadpole, tyke, moppet, nipper, whippersnapper? Didn't he hear other clubs' bench jockeys bawling like babies every time he came to bat?

"I hear them," he said.

And?

"I try to keep my crying to myself."

The writers liked that one. And here was one of the first lessons he learned as a manager: the more he entertained reporters with a quip or an off-the-record comment, the less they bothered Johnson and the other players.

On the day Johnson took the hill against St. Louis in that spring of '24—the day Rogers Hornsby, Branch Rickey, Burt Shotton, and the rest of the Cardinals rode the bus to Tampa's Plant Field—Johnson was in the shape of his life. His speedball looked quick as ever. Rickey cheered his Cardinals from the visitors' dugout while Shotton flashed signals from the third-base coach's box. To no avail. Johnson allowed one harmless single in four shutout innings. He retired Hornsby on a grounder and a pop-up. When a liner up the middle banged off shortstop Peckinpaugh's glove, Peck scrambled for the ball and flipped it to second baseman Harris for an out.

After Johnson left the game for a leisurely shower, Washington's bullpen gave up five runs. The fans barely noticed—it was only spring training—but Bucky, pounding his glove at second base, barked at the men who played with (and for) him. "*Wake up!*" he said. "*We are here to win!*"

St. Louis loaded the bases in the ninth. Hornsby walked, forcing in a run. The Senators' lead was down to two runs. With two out and the tying run at second, the Cardinals' Jim Bottomley slapped a grounder up the middle. Bucky gobbled it up and threw to first to win the game.

Jogging off the field, he passed the Cardinals' third-base coach. If they spoke or shook hands that day—short, spunky Bucky Harris and loyal old Burt Shotton—there is no record of it. But they would meet again.

CHAPTER 3

Zenith

Six and a half months later, Bucky Harris led his lowly Senators into the World Series. On the first Sunday of October 1924, fans filled every seat and some of the aisles at Washington's Griffith Stadium, a mile from the White House. A barbershop quartet crooned "Take Me Out to the Ball Game" atop the home dugout while President Calvin Coolidge beckoned player-manager Harris to the flag-draped presidential box. The smiling president shook hands with the game's "boy wonder" and handed him a baseball, the game ball that Harris walked to the mound and placed in Walter Johnson's glove.

Jogging to his position at second base, Bucky spent a moment taking in the sights and sounds of a capital city the papers were calling "a town gone mad for baseball." It was a day no fan, sportswriter, bettor, or Senator ever expected to see.

Back in March the youngest manager in major-league history had called a team meeting. "Far be it from me to tell you fellows how to play ball," Bucky told Johnson and the others, most of them older than their newly appointed boss. "What I'm asking is that you go out and make me a good manager."

Modesty was the right policy. If you read the experts' preseason predictions, you knew the rookie skipper's team was expected to finish no better than fifth in an eight-team American League featuring the Detroit Tigers of Ty Cobb and .403-hitting Harry Heilmann; the St. Louis Browns with Gorgeous George Sisler, twenty-game winner Urban Shocker, and Baby Doll Jacobson; and the defending world champion Yankees with their bigger-than-life right fielder. Babe Ruth was appetite incarnate. Coming off an MVP season in which he batted .393 with a league-best forty-one home runs (to the Senators' team total of twenty-six) while topping the league in hot dogs gobbled, illegal Prohibition-era booze guzzled, and baseball Annies bedded, the twenty-nine-year-old Bambino led a Yankees club that was odds-on to make its fourth straight World Series. As Yanks owner Jacob Ruppert boasted, "Our boys will win their fourth straight pennant as sure as the sun rises and sets."

One reporter dismissed Walter Johnson as "a great, heroic, pathetic figure." Yet the Big Train, restored by his preseason training regimen—plus Bucky's vow never to use him as a relief pitcher—went on to beat Cobb and the Tigers for his twelfth win against six losses on the first day of August. Two weeks later Johnson shut out Tris Speaker's Indians to run his record to 14-6. Two weeks after that he spun a seven-inning no-hitter against Sisler's Browns to go 17-6. Before long he would be 23-6 as Washington's Woefuls found themselves leading New York by a nose. "You're pitching your head off for sure," Bucky told him.

"Just doing my job," Johnson said.

The young skipper told the press he'd "brook no meddling" from owner Clark Griffith, but he stood by when Griffith fired pitching coach Jack Chesbro and hired Al Schacht in his place. Chesbro was and still is the majors' last forty-game winner, while Schacht was a flake, a former pitcher who had turned himself into a novelty act—"The Clown Prince of Baseball." He once took the mound on horseback, wearing a wig and a calico dress. Schacht and his partner in shenanigans, Senators coach Nick Altrock, were hailed (and mocked) as baseball's leading clowns, whose pratfalls and fake fights gave fans a show even when the home team lost. In one routine they played a pair of belly dancers. Another cast Schacht as a matador wooing Altrock, a stubble-cheeked senorita with a rose between her teeth. Griffith loved them (they helped at the gate), but Bucky put a stop to their sideshow as the club closed in on its first pennant—between innings, at least. "Once the game starts," he told them, "you must be as serious as the players."

In September the muggy capital sweated over every inning while Washington nursed its slim lead over the Yankees. As Bucky went to bat in the first inning of a late-season game against Boston, the umpire called time. Several local businessmen brought a token of thanks to the boy wonder manager, a diamond-studded baseball. Moments later, with his new trophy locked safely in Griffith's office, Bucky lashed a plain old horsehide ball for a triple.

With two weeks left in the season, the pennant race a dead heat, the Senators rode the B&O Railroad through Cincinnati, Indiana, and southern Illinois to a crucial series against the St. Louis Browns, who'd beaten them five times in a row. "Here's something to test our courage," Bucky said. He asked his team, "Can we shake off the thought that we can't beat the Browns? Can we break the jinx?"

Washington won the opener to take a one-game lead in the standings. A day later they trailed 11–7 while coach Altrock hid in the tunnel between the clubhouse and the dugout, struck down by an acute case of pennant fever. When his comic partner Schacht urged him to sit on the bench, Altrock cried, "No! I can't stand it!" He peeked out just in time to see a Senators pitcher fling a sure double-play ball into center field. After that Altrock whimpered, "I'm through with baseball. It's killing me."

Next came a pivotal series in Chicago. Altrock lay on the bench with a towel over his head, pestering Schacht for the play-by-play.

"One man on base for the Sox," Schacht said. "Uh-oh, there goes another."

"No! What now?"

"It's worse!" Schacht said. "Now they've got four men on."

By then the Senators were baseball's favorite underdogs. In Boston, Fenway Park fans cheered for them to beat the seventh-place Red Sox and put the damn Yankees in their place. "Ask any school-child to describe Washington," the *Boston Globe* reported, "and he will tell you it is the capital of the American League, located on the Potomac directly behind first base."

On the season's penultimate day, with Washington leading by two games with two to play, the Fenway faithful gave Bucky Harris a standing ovation as he stepped to the plate against the Red Sox. His Senators won to clinch Washington's first pennant, setting off a cele-bration that began with Bucky's players smashing a water cooler and hurling bats, gloves, caps, and jerseys onto the field. Walter Johnson, who had waited seventeen years for this moment, stood on the mound with tears in his eyes.

In Washington, First Lady Grace Coolidge listened to the game on the radio. She relayed the good news to the president, who sent Bucky a telegram: HEARTIEST CONGRATULATIONS. A *Washington Post* reporter heard "thousands of automobile horns" blaring at the good news from Boston. "Wherever men and women gather, the one topic of conversation, the source of elation, is the unparalleled feat of Bucky Harris and the ball tossers."

Bucky told his men they should eat, drink, stay up late, and enjoy themselves before the now-meaningless final game of the regular sea-son. The next day he let coach Altrock pitch against the Red Sox at Fenway Park. Fans and even umpires laughed as Altrock lobbed his glove to the plate with the ball in it.

Next day the victors rode a morning train to Washington's Union Station, where a parade led them to the Ellipse, the small oval park just south of the White House. "Pennsylvania Avenue has seen many parades," the *New York Times* reported, "but none to vie for the nature and spirit of the one held today." At the Ellipse, where government clerks once played "a game of base-ball" while President Lincoln looked on, Bucky followed Walter Johnson up rickety wooden steps to a reviewing stand, where they shook hands with the president.

Calvin Coolidge smiled up at the Big Train, then spoke at length about his love for baseball's Senators. "On Tuesday morning, when I finished reading details of the decisive battle at Boston and turned to affairs of government," he told a crowd of more than eighty thousand, "I found on top of everything else on my desk a telegram from Congressman John F. Miller of Seattle, which I shall read. 'Respectfully suggest it is your patriotic duty to call a special session of Congress so members may have the opportunity to sneak out to see Walter Johnson make baseball history. Can't speak for the New York delegation but hereby pledge all others to root for Washington and serve without pay or traveling expenses.'"

The president presented Bucky a silver trophy inscribed TO STANLEY HARRIS BY THE CITIZENS OF WASHINGTON D.C. IN RECOGNITION OF HIS WINNING FOR WASHINGTON ITS FIRST PENNANT OCTOBER 1, 1924. Turning back to the crowd, Coolidge said, "To those who devote themselves to this enterprise in a professional way, and by throwing their whole being into it raise it to the level of an art, the country owes a debt of gratitude."

Bucky shook hands with the president, accepted the trophy, and handed it to Johnson. Years later he remembered that day as "my best day. The best honor, the best handshake. Baseball gave me the opportunity America holds for all."

The World Series was four days away.

Fans fought over tickets to the 1924 Series pitting the Senators against the New York Giants. Scalpers hawked three-dollar seats for what the *Post* called "fabulous sums" of up to fifty dollars. The National League champion Giants would be appearing in their fourth consecutive Fall Classic. They'd won two of the past three, trumping Ruth and the Yankees in 1921 and '22 before losing to the Yanks in '23. Bucky's

Senators were the first team from outside New York to reach the World Series in four years.

Giants manager John McGraw was a frowning pug of a man. Reporters had dubbed him baseball's Little Napoleon. At fifty-one he was Bucky's height but thicker, heavier, and nearly a quarter century older. His résumé featured ten National League pennants, three World Series titles, and friends who included Arnold Rothstein, the mob boss who was notorious for fixing the 1919 World Series. According to one of the Giants' coaches, "McGraw eats gunpowder for breakfast and washes it down with warm blood."

McGraw told his cronies that the Senators' young manager was a "punk kid" who needed to be put in his place. Bucky liked hearing that. "I know as much baseball as that old buzzard," he told Griffith. The callow mine boy who'd been dazzled by New York in 1916 had grown up in the past eight years. There was no coal dust on him now. "I would have cracked under the strain had I been the nervous type," he said. Instead, the pressure turned this undersized lump of coal into something sharper and harder.

Bucky was more analytical than McGraw—more modern. In an era when starting pitchers were expected to finish every game whether they gave up a run or two or seven or eight, "I determined to take out any pitcher when a club began to hit him hard." He explained his idea with a proverb: "A stitch in time saves nine," in this case the Washington nine.

Fred Marberry, a young Texan on the Washington pitching staff, "had a wonderful fastball and the heart of a lion," Bucky said. Marberry was known as Firpo for his resemblance to the Argentine boxer Luis Firpo, who had knocked the great Jack Dempsey out of the ring in their 1923 heavyweight title bout. Dempsey tumbled through the ropes and conked his head against a reporter's typewriter, then charged back into the ring to knock out Firpo. A year later, it was Fred "Firpo" Marberry who demonstrated how to finish off an opponent. Under Bucky's direction, Marberry became the first modern relief pitcher. Bucky used him to save tight games, replacing a tiring starter with a fireballer who finished his delivery with a pirouette, his fingers reaching toward first base while his back foot pointed to third. His rise as a reliever foreshadowed a trend that came decades later and continued into the twenty-first century. In 1924, major-league pitchers threw 1,198 complete games. In 2016 big-league pitchers recorded only 83 complete games, a number that shrinks every year as managers turn the late innings over to ninth-, eighth-, and even seventh-inning specialists. The lineage of today's elite relievers traces directly to Bucky Harris, whose hard-earned view of late-inning fastballs was that he had a hell of a time hitting them. According to stats guru Bill James, Firpo Marberry was "the first pitcher aggressively used to protect leads rather than being brought in when the starter was knocked out. Thus, Marberry is in my opinion the first true reliever."

Washington's run to the '24 Series finally made Walter Johnson a national hero. He had long been held in the highest regard by his teammates, opponents, and the long-suffering Washington fans, but now, after seventeen seasons toiling for a mediocre club (and racking up 377 wins), Johnson stood squarely in the limelight. Will Rogers hailed the Big Train in his newspaper column: "He has played so fair and so good and given his all to the game. The man, woman or child in the United States who don't love Walter Johnson and admire him as a man is not a good American."

The fresher, stronger, rejuvenated Johnson brought his best steam into the '24 Series. Bucky had handled him with care all season, bringing in Marberry to finish seven of the Big Train's twenty-three victories, which saved wear and tear on his aging right arm. After Bucky plopped the presidential baseball into his glove, Johnson struck out a dozen New York Giants in Game One. Unfortunately for him, the owner had outfoxed the home team by changing the dimensions of the ballpark. Griffith's franchise lost money year after year; now, with the Senators suddenly selling out every contest, he capitalized by adding a bank of temporary bleachers in front of the left-field fence at Griffith Stadium. In the second inning of the opening game, the Giants' George "High Pockets" Kelly lofted a fly ball into the temporary seats for a solo home run. Two innings later Bill Terry did the same. If not for Griffith's greed, Johnson might have taken a 1–0 lead into the ninth. Instead the Senators had to scratch out a ninth-inning run to tie the game at 2–2. Thirty-five thousand fans howled themselves hoarse as Johnson dueled Art Nehf into the eleventh and twelfth innings. Then New York scored twice on a pair of walks, two singles, and a sacrifice fly. A Bucky Harris RBI single in the bottom of the twelfth cut the Giants' lead to 4–3. Bucky got as far as third but was still there at the end of what he called a "heartbreaking" loss.

The "boy wonder" homered in the second game to get Washington even, matching his regular-season total of one home run. The league champions continued trading victories in three games in New York, with Johnson allowing six runs in a Game Five loss that left the lantern-jawed ace so dejected he couldn't speak when Bucky asked how he was feeling. There was nothing to say. Bucky left him alone.

Early in the Series, a reporter turned up a human-interest story: Bucky Harris's father was now working as a detective in New Jersey. Tom Harris told the writer how he'd walked his son to the train station back in 1915 and had given him a few dollars for his journey to the Tigers' camp in Waxahachie, Texas—a heartwarming fantasy given that Tom had ditched the family years earlier. Bucky refused to meet his father or to give the writer a comment. He never said a word about Tom Harris until many years later, when a friend asked why he didn't go to his father's funeral. Bucky had a three-word answer: "He left Mother."

Meanwhile Schacht and Altrock, the coaches who doubled as pre-game jesters, pranced in their ball gowns and bullfight costumes, sometimes stripping to their underwear to mime a famous prizefight or donning fake beards to do a bit from *The Merchant of Venice*. "There is talk that I am Jewish," Schacht once told the press, "just because my father was Jewish, my mother is Jewish, I speak Yiddish and studied to be a rabbi. Well, that's how rumors get started." Nobody outside the clubhouse knew that the clowns loathed each other and sneaked real punches into their routines. When their staged fights got too rowdy, Bucky broke them up, winning cheers from fans who thought he was part of the act.

In Game Six, with Washington trailing the Giants 1–0 in the fifth inning, Bucky came to the plate against Art Nehf. The Senators had runners at first and third with two out. As player-manager, he needed to communicate with his players even while batting or running the bases. Stepping out of the batter's box, he flashed the steal sign to Earl McNeely, the runner at first. McNeely stole second base on the next pitch. Then Bucky laced a single to plate Washington's only runs in a 2–1 win that sent the Series and the season to a seventh game.

And he had a surprise in store for the old buzzard in the other dugout.

"I intend to outsmart McGraw," he told Griffith. Everyone expected Bucky to start sixteen-game winner George Mogridge in Game Seven, but he kept picturing the Giants' Bill Terry at the plate. Bucky thought that Terry, the young left-handed first baseman who'd homered off Johnson in Game One, was more dangerous than High Pockets Kelly or Hack Wilson, the Giants' right-handed power hitters. Terry had batted only .239 during the regular season, but his average was .500 through six Series games. (He would go on to a Hall of Fame career and hit .401 in 1930, the National League's last .400 average.) Still, McGraw didn't think Terry could hit left-handed pitching. He always benched the kid against lefties, which got Bucky thinking.

On October 10, the fans in Griffith Stadium were shocked to see Curly Ogden take the mound for the Senators in Game Seven. Ogden was a journeyman, a nine-game winner who would soon retire with a forgettable career record of eighteen wins and nineteen losses. But he threw with his right hand. By starting Ogden, Bucky invited McGraw to start Terry at first base. McGraw complied, stepping into Bucky's buzzard-trap.

Ogden was a decoy. "My beard pitcher," Bucky called him.

With the right-handed Ogden on the hill, McGraw penciled Terry into the Giants' lineup, batting fifth. But Ogden faced only two batters. After that, Bucky trotted from second base to the mound and gave Ogden a pat on the back pocket. He waved to the bullpen and here came Mogridge, the lefty.

In the next inning, McGraw, smelling a rat, let Terry bat. Terry grounded out to Bucky Harris.

At that point every managerial move—every bloop single or close call—stood to remake the biggest day in Washington's sporting history. In the top of the sixth, with the Senators ahead by a run, the Giants got runners to first and third with nobody out. Bill Terry started toward the plate. McGraw called him back. This was the moment Bucky had hoped for. He watched McGraw send up Irish Meusel, a right-handed pinch hitter, and remove Terry from the game. Bucky answered by bringing Firpo Marberry in to face Meusel. While Firpo fired his warm-up pitches, the young player-manager kicked some dirt around second base, keeping his mind on the game and not on the president of the United States, who was on his feet, waving his arms, leading the crowd in cheers as the hopes of Washington baseball boiled down to a last desperate hour.

Meusel's sacrifice fly tied the game at 1–1. Hack Wilson singled and then, disastrously, Senators first baseman Joe Judge kicked a ground ball for a two-base error. Shortstop Ossie Bluege booted the next grounder and the Giants were up 3–1.

Washington loaded the bases in the eighth, with Bucky Harris at the plate. He tried to surprise the Giants by hopping forward in the batters' box and slapping Virgil Barnes's pitch toward third. His grounder looked like an easy play for third baseman Freddie Lindstrom until the baseball hit something—a pebble, most likely, though some suspected the hand of God or even His big toe, while Giants fans would blame poltergeists. The ball took a crazy hop over Lindstrom's head. Two runs scored. Bucky would always dismiss his Series-changing single as a lucky hit, but lucky or not the score was tied. He chose that moment to reverse a policy he'd followed all year.

"This was the time to call upon Johnson."

Some fans wept with joy as their hero took the mound in the top of the ninth. An announcer with a megaphone strode onto the field.

"*Johnson*," the man bellowed. "Now pitch-ing for Wash-ing-ton, *Wal-ter Johnson!*"

Bucky got chills watching his ace warm up as cheers filled the stadium. The cheers died when Giants second baseman Frankie Frisch lashed a triple to center. Bucky signaled for a walk to Ross Youngs, bringing High Pockets Kelly to the plate—another maneuver that would leave him ripe for second-guessing. Youngs was a peppery outfielder with a little power—he'd hit a career-high ten home runs that year—but meanwhile Kelly had belted twenty-one homers to go with his league-high 136 RBIs. Kelly had homered off the Big Train in Game One, a fly ball into Griffith's temporary seats that Bucky dismissed as a fluke.

Johnson got two quick strikes on Kelly. "As Walter made ready to deliver his third pitch, I said a little prayer," Bucky recalled. Kelly swung through a fastball.

Game Seven went into the eleventh inning. With two on for the Giants, Johnson fanned Kelly again. The score stood frozen at 3–3 into the bottom of the twelfth, when the Senators' Muddy Ruel popped a foul ball practically straight up. Giants catcher Hank Gowdy threw off his mask, settled under the ball, and tripped on the mask. The ball fell untouched. Ruel whacked the next pitch to deep left for a double. Walter Johnson reached on an error. With two on and one out, Bucky said another prayer. The capital held its breath as Earl McNeely smacked a grounder to third baseman Lindstrom. A double-play ball. Until—

By some miracle McNeely's bouncer struck the same spot Bucky's lucky hit found four innings earlier, perhaps the same magic pebble. The ball bounded clear over Lindstrom's head into left field while Muddy Ruel, one of the slowest runners alive, rumbled around third base. Left fielder Meusel charged the ball. Calvin and Grace Coolidge and thousands of others craned their necks to see the play at the plate.

But there was no play. Seeing Ruel halfway home, Meusel corralled the baseball and toted it to the infield while delirious Washington fans twirled handkerchiefs and hurled hats, scorecards, briefcases, and seat cushions into the sky. Thousands poured onto the field. Bucky Harris zigzagged to safety in the home dugout, where Walter Johnson wrapped him in a bear hug.

President Coolidge described that day as one of the best of his administration. Judge Landis called the '24 Series "the zenith of baseball," the best of the game's twenty-one World Series to date, twenty of which were on the level. Damon Runyon, reporting from Washington for the *New York American*, observed, "The blood pressure of the citizens of Washington is at this moment, without doubt, the highest ever registered by medical science." Runyon had been around but had never witnessed such a scene. "The writer has seen many demonstrations, many riots," he wrote. "He saw Paris celebrating the armistice. He has watched New Orleans rollicking through its Mardi Gras. None of them approached Washington's celebration of its baseball victory. The thing went on all night. . . . The people tramped the streets hour after hour, laughing and shouting and tooting horns. They cheered and cheered until one marveled at the vitality of the human voice."

Bucky Harris fought his way through the glad-handing, backslapping crowd. The "boy wonder" manager had led his club to a miracle victory while batting .333 in the Series, clouting two home runs, and scoring seven times. Marveling at the workings of fate, he told a reporter, "Six years ago I was working in a coal mine." Each of the victorious Senators would receive a bonus of $5,959.64 (about $85,000 in today's dollars), a sum equal to 33,109 hours of mine wages, or thirteen years' work with Sundays off.

Later, after hours of joyous riots, handshakes, and interviews, Bucky sat in his office in the clubhouse, sifting through a stack of telegrams. Congratulations, mostly. Requests for more interviews. Employment offers: Would he like to sell stocks or bonds in the off-season? Automobiles? Oil wells? Would he like to endorse a brand of tobacco? A candy bar?

Near the bottom of the stack was a telegram from Pennsylvania.

At first it looked like the rest. CONGRATULATIONS on the top line. Then he read on.

CONGRATULATIONS.

THE HAPPIEST DAY OF MY LIFE.

On the line below that, the telegram was signed, MOTHER.

CHAPTER 4

Cookie and the Flea

The boy stood beside a huge oaken vat, stirring black slurry with a paddle the size of an oar. Flies buzzed around him, drawn to the sweet stink of crushed grapes. Harry Lavagetto, eleven years old, thought hell might be like this.

It was the summer of 1924 in Oakland, California. Harry's father, a garbageman named Luigi, had a lucrative sideline: thanks to a Prohibition loophole, he and other vintners could make up to two hundred gallons of wine per year for "home use." Luigi home-used plenty, sitting up late listening to the radio, getting soused. A fish-on-Friday, Mass-on-Sunday Catholic like everyone else on the block, Luigi liked to say that his hobby was practically God's work. Hadn't Jesus turned water into wine? Luigi did the same with California grapes.

Harry thought his father might be forgetting a couple of ingredients. It also took yeast and a boy's sweat to make the wine his father drank and sold on the black market, sometimes sharing with Prohibition agents who ignored the two-hundred-gallon limit as long as they got a few gallons for themselves.

Luigi Lavagetto and his wife, Adelaide, both born in Italy, spoke

Italian at home. Adelaide worked at a cannery for twenty-five cents a day while her husband rode a horse-drawn garbage truck six days a week, clambering on and off to hurl loads of trash into the back. Their sons worked to help pay the bills. Eddie, the oldest, did odd jobs and served as part-time father while Harry, the youngest, stirred grapes in the converted garage that served as a wine room.

Harry loathed grapes and flies. And he wasn't so sure about his name. Born Enrico Atillio Lavagetto, he found himself standing in front of an elementary-school teacher one day, nodding while she mispronounced his name. It sounded un-American, the teacher said. "Enrico, that's Italian for Henry or Harry," she said. "Why don't you choose—do you want to be Henry? Or Harry?" So he took a guess.

The boy grew tall and strong and handsome, with a quality that set him apart from other *bello* boys. He was lucky. Or charmed. His mother said he always seemed to struggle until the Good Lord smiled on him and made the right thing happen. Harry wasn't so sure, but maybe his mother had a point. For instance, there was the hotbox where he spent hours stirring grapes, wishing he could get out and play ball—

To take his mind off the heat and the stench, he taped up the handle of a broomstick and used it as a bat. Tracking flies in flight, smacking them with quick swipes of the stick, Harry became the sultan of fly swatting. Soon there were bugs all over the floor. For the rest of his life he swore that smacking flies in his father's wine room taught him how to hit a moving target.

His father cursed the boy's American ways. "Luigi was a tough guy, and an alcoholic," one relative says. "The more he drank, he more abusive he got." He was hardest on Eddie but railed at Harry, too, in his faltering English—American boy Harry and this game of his, baseball. His sons learned not to bring friends to the house. Who wanted to be there while the old man loaded himself with homemade wine and started singing? It was awkward, *imbarazzante*. Harry threw himself into school and sports at Oakland Technical High School. He starred for the baseball, basketball, and track teams and joined the glee club, warbling his heart out for a voice coach who took him aside one morning.

"I'm glad you joined," she said. "A popular boy like you—it sets a fine example." Unfortunately, he couldn't carry a tune. "I'd like you to mime the songs. Move your mouth, but don't actually sing."

The Bay Area was a baseball outpost in those days. The major leagues' western frontier was two thousand miles away in St. Louis. Like most kids living outside big-league cities, Harry played sandlot ball and followed the local minor-league and semipro clubs. In his case that meant local nines like the Alameda Elks, Benedetti Florists, and Piggly Wiggly Pigglies as well as the Oakland Oaks and San Francisco Seals of the Pacific Coast League, one rung down from the majors. Some said the difference between the PCL and the big leagues was more like half a rung. With Oakland-born catcher Ernie Lombardi launching a Hall of Fame career for the Oaks while future Yankees Lefty Gomez and Frankie Crosetti starred for the Seals, the local Coast League clubs of Harry's youth may have been no worse than major-league doormats like the Boston Braves. The Oaks would send Ernie Lombardi and Irish Meusel to the big leagues only to be outdone by the Seals, whose alums included Paul Waner, Earl Averill, and soon a Bay Area boy named DiMaggio who might have been the best who ever set foot on a diamond.

Like Harry Lavagetto, Giuseppe Paolo DiMaggio went by an Americanized name. He, too, grew up using an oar-shaped piece of wood as a bat, only for him it was in fact a broken oar from his father's fishing boat. Joe DiMaggio dropped out of San Francisco's Galileo High School to play semipro ball before joining the Seals in 1932 at the age of seventeen. A year later he batted .340 with twenty-eight homers while setting a quirky PCL record: the teen sensation recorded a base hit in sixty-one consecutive games. Had anyone ever done such a thing? Records were spotty, so nobody knew.

Harry, two years older than DiMaggio, graduated from Oakland Tech in 1930. After starring for the semipro Moffat Packers he tried out for the Seals, but his nerves got the best of him. At the plate he fouled off batting-practice slowballs. In the field he kicked a couple of grounders and threw a couple more over the first baseman's head. "Sorry, son," said the manager, sending Harry away. Luigi told his boy to forget baseball and think about the family. There was a job on the trash truck waiting for him. Reluctantly, Harry agreed. It was time for him to grow up and go to work. But first, he told his father, he'd play one last ballgame.

That summer a squad of major leaguers barnstormed up the coast, thumping semipro clubs to raise money for charity. Harry hooked on with a semipro squad that would be the big leaguers' next victim in Emeryville, just north of Oakland. He warmed the bench while the local nine fell behind. They were down by two runs when he got a chance to pinch-hit. Two outs, bases loaded. He lashed a double off the right-field fence to win the game for the underdogs. "My greatest moment," he called it. "That one swing changed my life." Victor "Cookie" Devincenzi, the owner of the Oakland Oaks, offered him a $100 signing bonus and $125 a month to jump from semipro ball to the Pacific Coast League. As a local paper noted, "His father was prominent in the Eastbay Scavengers' Association, and the younger Lavagetto was expected to make that his career. But he turned his back on the garbage trucks and signed with the Oaks."

Older players wondered what Devincenzi saw in the skinny kid with the goofy grin. "Cookie's boy," they called him. By the end of his first season, Enrico Atillio "Harry" Lavagetto had another new first name. He was known as Cookie.

He batted .312 for the Oaks in 1933, impressing a scout from the Pittsburgh Pirates. Meanwhile Devincenzi was up to his jowls in debt, a common plight for minor-league moguls. After the season ended, he sold his twenty-year-old infielder and namesake to the Pirates and used the cash to save his franchise from foreclosure. In the paperwork for the deal, Devincenzi trimmed two years from Lavagetto's age to make the Pirates think they were getting a prodigy. The *Oakland Tribune* called Cookie "the Coast League's sensation of 1933 along with Joe DiMaggio of the Seals." The two men's paths were destined to cross again and again.

A strong spring training earned Cookie a spot on Pittsburgh's major-league roster in 1934. Old-timers like Honus Wagner saw something special in the rookie. The legendary Pirates shortstop was now a coach for the team, and he gave Cookie tips about defense, demonstrating by moving around second base in slow motion, which was all the limping, sixty-year-old Wagner had left. All-Star third baseman Pie Traynor joined them, doing his bit to ease the rookie's transition to the majors. But Cookie was more than ready to take the next step. Against the St. Louis Cardinals on the second day of the season, he homered off future Hall of Famer Burleigh Grimes to win the game.

Despite his good looks and Pepsodent smile, sportswriters tagged Lavagetto as "swarthy," newspaper code for players of Italian, Spanish, or Greek heritage. At bat he hunched over the plate, choking up on the bat. He hit three home runs as a rookie and none the next season, focusing on bat control rather than power. That approach seemed to work in 1935, when he batted .290 as a part-time player. Cookie swung hard with a fierce right-handed swipe that twisted him toward third base, making him one of the slowest batters out of the box on his way to first. His lunging swing cost him some infield singles, the leg hits that boost quicker guys' batting averages, but Cookie wouldn't give it up. He was eager to try every fielding tip Wagner, Traynor, and the other veterans suggested, but hitting is more personal than fielding and harder to change. Marginal players like Cookie couldn't afford to revamp their swings and go oh-for-twenty while they adjusted. "I was never much more than a slump from getting sent home," he recalled. So he kept lunging, trusting his instincts and the good fortune he'd always counted on.

"A fair chance is all I want," he told Traynor, who had taken over as manager. But the longer he played at the game's highest level, the more he saw fate's hand—or was it God's?—giving some players a push and tripping up others. For regular guys like him, he thought, the biggest thing is to hang in there, keep plugging away, and give the spotlight a chance to find you.

After three big-league seasons he was a part-timer with unsightly statistics: a .249 average with a total of five home runs to go with thirty-three errors. In December 1936 the Pirates traded him to the Brooklyn Dodgers for pitcher Big Ed Brandt. Cookie had been happy in Pittsburgh, a city that was friendly compared to rough-and-tumble Brooklyn, where even the Italians cursed him out if he lollygagged crossing the street. To make matters worse, the Dodgers' new manager was Burleigh Grimes, the spitballer Cookie had greeted with a homer for his first big-league hit three years before. Grimes was a tough old bird known for his grudges. He'd once beaned a hitter who was still in the on-deck circle.

Cookie reported to Grimes on his first day as a Dodger. The manager sized him up and nodded, looking peeved. Finally Grimes said, "Maybe I'll forgive you."

Al Gionfriddo felt like crying when the Pirates traded Cookie. Little Al was a Pennsylvania coal miner's son, like Bucky Harris. The seventh of Rose and Paulo Gionfriddo's thirteen children, he may as well have had "little" inscribed ahead of "Albert Francis" on his birth certificate. Neighborhood kids called him *Il Pulce*, the Flea. Quick as a bug, he became a sandlot legend in Dysart, Pennsylvania, ninety miles from Pittsburgh, but nobody saw Al as much of a prospect, not at his size.

He grew up listening to the Pirates on KDKA radio, hearing announcer Rosey Rowswell describe a Waite Hoyt curveball as "the old dipsy-doodle" and call a Lavagetto double a "doozie maroonie." Rowswell called Pirate homers by blowing a slide whistle and shouting, "Hurry up Aunt Minnie! Raise the window, here she comes!" to the sound of breaking glass. Rowswell claimed his aim in life was "to educate fans to love the Pirates as much as I do."

Al Gionfriddo's aim in life was to join Cookie Lavagetto, the Pirates' only Italian player, in the lineup at Forbes Field. After Pittsburgh shipped his hero to Brooklyn, he had a hard time rooting for the Pirates. He saw that baseball was a business as well as a game, run by wealthy men to whom players were as disposable as miners were to coal barons.

Gionfriddo (pronounced *Gee-n-FREE-doe*) stopped growing at five foot six but compensated for his size with extra energy. A local sportswriter called him "an amazing little package of dynamite." A teammate said he was "the fastest, most aggressive player in any league." Still, his father, Paulo, like Luigi Lavagetto and Giuseppe DiMaggio, scoffed at his son's ambitions. "A man needs a man's job!" he'd say. He reconsidered in 1940, when a Pirates scout offered eighteen-year-old Al a contract for sixty-five dollars a month, double Paulo's wages after more than twenty years' work in the mines.

"Play," Paulo said. "Go play!"

Brooklyn manager Grimes moved Cookie Lavagetto from second base to third. Settling into a full-time role for the first time, Cookie batted .282 with eight home runs in 1937. A year later he was a National League All-Star, rubbing shoulders with DiMaggio, Bob Feller, Lou Gehrig, Johnny Mize, Hank Greenberg, Ernie Lombardi, and Lefty Gomez at the All-Star Game in Cincinnati. Nineteen thirty-nine was better yet: a .300 average, ten homers, and eighty-seven RBIs. New York Giants manager Bill Terry—the same Bill Terry who'd bedeviled Bucky Harris's Senators in the '24 World Series—couldn't find a way to get him out. "We pitch him high, we pitch him low," said Terry. "He hits 'em high, he hits 'em low!" At Ebbets Field, Dodgers fans serenaded their third baseman with whistles and kazoos, singing, "Hey lookie lookie, here comes Cookie!"

Brooklyn was just the place for a quirky character with a knack for the key hit. "Cookie walked funny and always needed a shave," a writer on the Dodgers beat recalled. "His shirt would be hanging out of his pants, and he wore his hat at a kooky angle." Cookie said he liked to keep his teammates loose. "I enjoyed wearing one sock up, the other down. I don't know why, I just enjoyed it." He never revealed one reason he tugged his shirttail out of his pants: he was allergic to wool. The moment a game ended he would yank his jersey off his back. The skin beneath was red and raw. Harking back to his Catholic upbringing, Cookie couldn't help wondering if his jersey was a hair shirt, a punishment for . . . what? His luck had been so good so far, maybe it was bound to turn. Who was he, a trashman's son, to have fans chanting his name? His father had called him a fool for playing a boy's game, but now that Cookie was making $12,000 a year, Luigi was his son's biggest fan. Or maybe second-biggest. There was also an Ebbets Field regular, a mustachioed Brooklyn restaurateur named Jack Pierce, who indulged a cheerful obsession with Cookie Lavagetto. Home games found the fiftyish Pierce dressed in his customary suit and tie, unfurling a horse blanket emblazoned COOKIE on the roof of the visitors' dugout. Settling into his seat behind the dugout, he unpacked his gear: a dozen or more balloons inscribed COOKIE; a tank of helium to fill the balloons, which he released with cries of "*Cook-eee!*" as they wafted over the field; business cards stamped COOKIE, BEST THIRD BASEMAN IN THE LEAGUE, which he tossed in all directions when Cookie came to bat; and a bottle of scotch or champagne for the slow times between Lavagetto at-bats. As *Collier's* magazine put it, "He is of the unalterable opinion that Cookie Lavagetto is the greatest ballplayer who ever lived." Pierce was so committed to his fandom that he often took two taxis to Ebbets Field, one for him and his friends and one for his balloons, banners, helium tank, booze, and an ice bucket. He was so devoted to his hero that he kept filling COOKIE balloons and yelling "*Cook-eee!*" even after Cookie left the team to join the navy.

Cookie Lavagetto wasn't the first ballplayer to join the fight against Hitler and Hirohito. More than five hundred major leaguers and thousands of minor-league players served in the armed forces during

World War II. In December 1941, Bob Feller drove from his Iowa home to Chicago to enlist after hearing the news of Japan's attack on Pearl Harbor. Hank Greenberg, Pee Wee Reese, Phil Rizzuto, Ted Williams, and other stars soon joined the war effort, but Lavagetto was among the first to volunteer. Unlike Williams and others who waited to be drafted, Cookie couldn't wait to fly in combat. He had earned his pilot's license in the off-season, buzzing over New York and New Jersey with teammate Dolph Camilli to the consternation of Dodgers president Larry MacPhail, who fined each of them five hundred dollars for risking their necks. When a navy recruiter told Cookie in the winter of 1941–42 that he was a prime candidate to fly a navy plane, he said, "Show me where to sign." Instead, his superiors sent him to Hawaii to serve his country by playing third base for a team of navy all-stars. By 1945 he was firing across a sunny infield to first baseman Stan Musial.

Headlines back home hailed him as a patriot. Columnist Bob Considine wrote, "My lid's off to a good, game guy who, with a minimum of fanfare and under no compulsion, is doing his bit." But Cookie wasn't buying it. For the rest of his life friends and fans praised him for his wartime service, but he only shrugged and said he got cheated. He'd dreamed of shooting down Messerschmitts, not playing exhibition games with Musial and other big leaguers like Army Air Forces sergeant DiMaggio, who was also stationed in Hawaii. Referring to his last stint playing ball at the Livermore Naval Air Station near Oakland, Cookie said, "Yeah, I fought the battle of Livermore."

Musial lost one prime season to his World War II service. DiMaggio, Reese, Rizzuto, and Williams all lost three. Aviation machinist mate Lavagetto lost four. An All-Star when he enlisted, Cookie was thirty-three when he reported to the Dodgers' spring camp in 1946. "I'm an old guy now," he told a friend. "They're only keeping me around because I was in the service." His knees ached. His swing was slower. But each team was allowed to keep three to five extra players who had served in the war, and the Dodgers' new boss wasn't about to miss a public-relations opportunity like bringing Cookie Lavagetto back to Brooklyn.

The new boss was Branch Rickey, who had jumped from St. Louis to Brooklyn in 1943. He'd replaced his friend Larry MacPhail as Dodgers president when MacPhail, a World War I veteran, resigned in order to rejoin the army as a colonel. Past sixty years of age, Rickey was too portly and creaky for the war effort but as talkative as ever. Introducing the first pitching machine at the Dodgers' spring camp in 1946, the game's great visionary and windbag announced, "This thing can throw twenty-five hundred baseballs a day. That equals twenty pitchers working nine innings. And it takes only one man to operate it!" Designed to save pitchers' arms from spring-training wear and tear while giving hitters a steady stream of hittable pitches, Rickey's contraption was called Iron Mike or sometimes Overhand Joe. "The batsman can be served six to ten good pitches per minute," Rickey said. "After long practice from the pitching machine, he may finally come to know the strike zone."

The machine beaned a few batters and sent others ducking for cover, but Cookie's run-in with Overhand Joe was his own fault. He was goofing around with the machine when its steel arm shot forward, smacking his right elbow. He laughed it off, but the bruise lingered. He had trouble throwing the ball the next day. His elbow ached, and he didn't feel so charmed anymore. Superfan Jack Pierce kept sending up COOKIE balloons, but Lavagetto felt embarrassed—he couldn't range more than two or three steps to his left or right, and his sore-arm throws went to first on a humpback arc. "I'm washed up," he told his wife.

He wasn't the only one who thought so. One day he came off the bench to rap a key pinch-hit single. He rode a bus home from Ebbets Field, as he often did. Stopping to buy an evening paper, he noticed the vendor's Brooklyn Dodgers cap.

"How'd Lavagetto do today?" Cookie asked.

"Got a hit," the newsie said. "He's okay in a pinch, but the guy must be married to the owner's daughter. He's too old to play!"

Al Gionfriddo followed Cookie into World War II service. Eager to prove himself during basic training, he attacked an obstacle course and tore a stomach muscle. He pleaded for another chance. Instead the army declared him 4-F. Gionfriddo reported to the Pittsburgh Pirates' Class A club in Albany, where farm boy teammates mocked his Eye-talian name until his heritage came in handy. That was the afternoon the Albany Senators hosted the Wilkes-Barre Barons, whose all-Cuban battery didn't bother with signals. Figuring their opponents didn't know Spanish, the catcher called out *"bola rápida"* or *"cambio."* As Al recalled, "Being of Italian descent, I could understand enough to know what was coming." He began signaling his teammates, who socked doozie maroonies all over the lot. The newly popular outfielder went on to bat .329 that year, legging out twenty-eight triples to set an Eastern League record that still stands.

In 1944 the Pirates called him up for a late-season tryout. That off-season he married his high school sweetheart, Arlene Lentz, and they found an apartment in Pittsburgh. He batted .284 with a pair of homers and a dozen steals to make the *Sporting News* All-Rookie team in 1945, his only season as a big-league regular. A year later, with hundreds of war vets returning to the majors, there was less room for a pint-sized slap hitter who played above his pay grade. Ralph Kiner, a navy vet, replaced Al in the Pirates' outfield and led the National League in homers while Gionfriddo watched from the bench. One day he doubled over, writhing in pain. Rushed to the hospital for an emergency appendectomy, he missed the last two months of the season. He made a few dollars working as a fireman, then caught on with a barnstorming club skippered by seventy-two-year-old Honus Wagner. Wagner's big leaguers were expected to thump all comers, but they lost a shocker to an all-Negro team led by the Brooklyn Dodgers' minor-league sensation Jackie Robinson.

Gionfriddo began the 1947 season as a scrub for a Pirates club starring Kiner and Hank Greenberg. On May 3 Pittsburgh traded him to Brooklyn for five Dodgers: hard-throwing Kirby Higbe, a twenty-two-game winner in 1941 and 1946 All-Star; Hank Behrman (11-5 with a 2.93 earned run average the year before); Dixie Howell; Gene Mauch; and the immortally named Calvin Coolidge Julius Caesar Tuskahoma McLish, a future All-Star who credited his father for his name. "There were eight kids in the family," Cal McLish explained. "I was number seven and my dad didn't get to name a one before me, so he evidently tried to catch up."

The trade was quite a haul for the Pirates and a literal haul for Gionfriddo. It happened because pitcher Higbe, a South Carolinian, had sworn he'd never take the field with "a nigger" like Jackie Robinson. Branch Rickey didn't want Higbe upsetting his "great experiment" of bringing Robinson to the majors, so he shipped Higbe and the others to Pittsburgh for backup outfielder Gionfriddo—and a hundred thousand dollars in cash. That was almost enough to pay the combined salaries of Joe DiMaggio and Ted Williams. In Rickey's view, he was delivering a message to the other Dodgers: You'll play with Robinson or I'll get rid of you. In the same bold stroke, he made off with a load of Pirate gold.

Gionfriddo boarded a train in Pittsburgh, lugging a couple of satchels. One held his clothes, glove, and toiletries. The other held one hundred thousand dollars in cash. In New York, he handed that satchel to Rickey and got a pat on the back in return. There was no doubt in either man's mind about the relative importance of the player and his luggage.

The smallest player in the big leagues became the odd man out in a 1947 Brooklyn outfield featuring Carl Furillo, Pete Reiser, and Dixie Walker. Gionfriddo got all of five at-bats in his first month as a Dodger. He sat in the dugout with his old hero Lavagetto, now a creaky veteran hoping to hang on for another year. Neither of them played much, but Cookie was admired as a four-time All-Star, war vet, and handy pinch hitter. Everybody liked Cookie, with his off-kilter cap and quick smile. Cookie would relax in the dugout, flipping through a newspaper, knowing the club wouldn't need him till the late innings, if at all. Gionfriddo sat nearby, the last man at the end of the bench, unnoticed by all but his unofficial fan club, a clutch of Brooklyn bobby-soxers who cheered Al when he shagged flies before a game. Smitten with his dimpled chin and soulful peepers, they wrote to one of the Brooklyn papers:

> The undersigned herewith wish to announce the formation of the Johnny Gionfriddo—He's Our Baby in the Left Field Bleachers—Singing and Marching Club. Please print a LARGE picture of our hero in your sports page. A picture without a cap, please, and very clear. Also one in civvies, if possible. And, too, some pertinent information about his age, height and marital status, if any. Naturally we hope he is single. Incidentally, we have decided to call him Johnny instead of Al, because we think it suits his personality better. Thank you, Mr. Editor, youses is a kind and sweet man.

The paper obliged with a photo and vital statistics: Al Gionfriddo stood five foot six, weighed 160, and was happily wed to Arlene, his bride of three years, now expecting their first child.

Riding the bench beside Cookie, still batting .000 in June, Al knew the Dodgers might ship him to the minors any day. A has-been like Cookie was a king compared to a never-was like him. Even if Rickey kept him in Brooklyn, how could he prove he belonged? Al could chase down a fly ball, beat out a single, swipe a base, but he wasn't going to come off the bench and hit a home run. Without another world war or a plague that struck down the Dodgers' outfield, he was as good as finished at the age of twenty-five. Sitting with Arlene in their Flatbush apartment, Al prayed for his wife and the baby she was expecting. Sitting in Brooklyn's half-deserted dugout when the starters took the field, he mumbled to himself, asking Jesus, the Blessed Mother, and the saints to give him a chance to help the team.

Not a homer or a hit, just a chance. He was raised to believe in miracles, but his prayers went unanswered all summer and into the fall. The Flea would finish the season with a batting average of .177, no home runs, and only eleven base hits, making him the worst Dodger and perhaps the last man you would ever expect to change baseball history.

CHAPTER 5

Bev and Snuffy

Floyd Bevens hailed from Hubbard, Oregon, a Willamette Valley town with a population of 283. "A grand place to be a boy," he called it, though country-boy Floyd's mother sometimes joked ruefully that her Hubbard cupboard was bare after her husband went to town just before the baby was born. Like Bucky Harris's father, berry farmer John Bevens left his family and never came back.

Edna Bevens's youngest boy was too sickly to help his siblings do chores. Floyd's hand-me-down overalls hung on him scarecrow-style while he chased hogs, chickens, and goats around the berry patch until they slaughtered a few in the fall and had meat for a month or two. The first holiday he recalled must have been in 1923 or '24, the Christmas when a neighbor boy got a BB gun. The neighbors were kind enough to give Edna's children a few minutes with the gun. Each Bevens kid got to fire it once. That was Floyd's Christmas present, one shot of a BB gun.

When he was fourteen his mother sent him to live at a dairy farm down the road. He got breakfast and supper in exchange for his labor, plus a blanket to keep warm while he slept in a hayloft. Floyd missed his family and hated waking at three thirty or four a.m. to milk cows before school, but that chore built up the wrists that helped him land a summer job at the Paulus Brothers Cannery. "I used to stack thirty thousand cans a day, four at a time," he recalled. "Pick up two in each hand, set them on the conveyor belt, pick up two more . . . over and over, all day long. Boy, those cans got heavy. My thumbs would just about break off." By the time he went out for baseball at Hubbard High School, he was a strapping six-footer with a fastball that scared batters and stung catchers' hands right through their mitts. A father-less boy with a little bit of a mean streak, Floyd Bevens was born to play good old country hardball.

Hubbard High students played an annual ballgame against the faculty and staff. One longtime staffer, a fellow who'd given Floyd a nasty spanking years before, had barely stepped into the batter's box when a fastball caromed off his skull. Floyd also beaned a coach he didn't like. Both times he got away with it, no questions asked. He was learning how baseball talent can make a boy special.

As a star forward for the basketball team, he jogged onto the floor one night for a big game against Independence High. Hubbard's boys came out of the locker room in shiny new warm-up suits that they stripped off as an announcer called their names.

"*Floooyd . . . Bevens!*"

Expecting cheers, Floyd tore off his sweat suit and heard . . . nothing. Then gasps and laughter. He had forgotten to put on his uniform under the warm-up suit. For a long moment he stood there in his jockstrap. Finally he ran for the locker room, where he hid out before returning to the court and another round of laughs. For years he would blush remembering that moment, but when Hubbard won the game behind leading scorer Bevens, all was forgiven. Because talent makes a boy special.

He struck out twenty-three batters in a single high school game. After high school he pitched semipro ball, fanning half the men he faced. He also returned to work at the cannery, where Mildred Hartman joined the workforce in 1936. Floyd spent his days on a catwalk twenty feet above pretty Mildred, loading cherries and strawberries onto the conveyor belt. Now and then he'd toss down a berry to get her attention. Before long they were going out for ice cream. He opened the ice-cream parlor door for her, treated her special. He felt relaxed with Millie, an Independence High grad who mentioned that she'd been in the gym the night he stripped off his pants. When he asked her to marry him, she said that at least she'd had a hint of what she'd be getting.

There was a three-day waiting period for marriage licenses in Oregon, but Floyd and Millie were in a hurry, so they drove to a courthouse over the border in Stevenson, Washington, got their license, said their vows, and stayed overnight in a hotel, a first for both of them. They made it back to Hubbard in time for work on Monday.

New York Yankees scout Joe Devine made an ivory-hunting trip to the Willamette Valley in the spring of 1937. He saw a six-foot-three-inch beanpole making semipro sluggers look silly. Devine signed Floyd Bevens for five hundred dollars and handed him a train ticket to El Paso, Texas, where the kid won sixteen games in his first professional season. He missed Oregon but enjoyed road trips through Texas and Arizona badlands he'd never dreamed of seeing, and his minor-league salary of seventy-five dollars a month more than doubled his wages at the cannery.

Millie's young husband was a good enough athlete to play the outfield when he wasn't pitching. One day he lost a fly ball in the desert sun. He threw up his hands, his feet slid out from under him, and the ball struck the bill of his cap. Miraculously, the ball bounced straight up and fell into his glove. From then on his teammates called him Bill. *Bill* Bevens, not Floyd, renamed for the heroic bill of his cap. He always said he was lucky the ball didn't come down a little lower, or he might have spent the rest of his life as Nose Bevens.

On the mound, Bevens was liable to knock you on your ass before he got around to walking you or striking you out. He never quite corralled his fastball. Early in his career he'd shout, "Look out!" if a pitch was sailing at a hitter's head. One of his minor-league managers told him to keep his mouth shut on the mound. Hitters were afraid of fast-ball pitchers with scattershot arms, the manager said. "So you keep the fear of God in 'em." After that, Bevens enjoyed being "effectively wild." It wasn't his job to warn batters, it was their job to hit or duck.

When he was right he could dominate. Bill Bevens threw two no-hitters for the low minors' Wenatchee Chiefs in 1939. Promoted to the Binghamton Triplets the following year, he got a raise to $175 a month. By comparison, Joe DiMaggio made headlines by signing for $32,500 that season, or $5,500 a month. (Ballplayers, like school-teachers, get paid only during the months when they work.) But Bill didn't need thousands of dollars to live high on the hog. With his meals, lodging, and travel paid for by the club, he dined on steaks and ice cream and still sent most of his pay home to Millie. He filled out to 210 pounds, beginning a lifelong fight against a potbelly that threat-ened to throw his delivery off-kilter.

Bevens won fifty-eight games in his first four minor-league sea-sons, once fanning seventeen in a single game. Still the Yankees let him labor in the minors for seven years. Each October he returned to Hubbard and worked in the cannery. His wrists, half again the size of another man's wrists, were so strong that he could lift a manhole cover with one hand. But strength wasn't enough. Victories weren't enough. From 1937 to 1944 he pitched more than a thousand innings at El Paso, Binghamton, and five other whistle-stops. The Yankees didn't seem to care. "What's a guy supposed to do? They're never going to bring me up," he grumped to his wife. How much longer was he supposed to ride buses that broke down half the time and sleep in fleabag hotels with snoring, farting roommates, winning ballgames nobody noticed? He was a father now—Millie had given birth to a son, Larry, soon after their marriage. "Maybe it's time I came home and stayed home," Bill said.

The Yankees finally brought him up in May 1944, after World War II had depleted their pitching staff. He reported to manager Joe

McCarthy, who grunted and turned away. A couple of days later Bevens made his major-league debut, coming in as a reliever with the Yankees trailing Detroit 4–2 in the seventh and runners on first and second. The gangly right-hander peered up at a Yankee Stadium crowd that was more than twenty-five times his hometown's population. The first batter he faced, light-hitting infielder Jimmy Outlaw, mashed a fastball for a three-run homer. The next two batters singled. Ten minutes into his big-league career, Bevens's earned run average was infinite. He settled down after that, escaping with no more damage. But it was too late—the Yanks demoted him to Newark. He phoned his wife to say he might be finished.

"You mustn't give up," Millie said.

He won a dozen games for the Newark Bears, earning another promotion in August. This time he stuck. The rest of the way he won four games and lost only one, impressing McCarthy so much that the manager penciled Big Bill Bevens into his starting rotation for 1945.

Anyone who expected the farm boy to gawk at New York was disappointed. "He may have been dazzled, but he'd never show it," says his son Larry, who came with his mother to join Bill in Manhattan. "He wouldn't give those city guys the satisfaction." Like most ballplayers, Bevens's teammates loved to hunt and fish. In the spring of '45 a few of them—shortstop Frank Crosetti, second baseman Snuffy Stirnweiss, a couple of others—invited the new guy to join them on a snipe hunt. They would split up and spend all night tracking the rare, nocturnal New Jersey snipe. When they reconvened at dawn, whoever had bagged the most snipe would be King of the Yanks.

Well, some city slickers might fall for an old trick like that, but not Bevens. He spent the night in a motel while the others passed a flask, shivering, thinking they'd put one over on him.

He settled into a 1945 Yankees rotation with veterans Hank Borowy, Tiny Bonham, Monk Dubiel, and Bill "Goober" Zuber, winning three in a row down the stretch to run his record to 13-6. He spun a one-hitter against Boston and soon received a letter from an advertising agency.

Dear Mr. Bevens:

As you probably know, our client, General Mills, Inc., makes considerable use of Major League Baseball players' endorsements of the "Breakfast of Champions" in connection with its Wheaties advertising. We are recommending the names of several players to our client and would like to include your name, providing that you actually eat and enjoy Wheaties. For your endorsement we are in a position to offer you $150.

He said yes and kept the letter for the rest of his life.

Bevens's thirteen victories led a 1945 Yankees club that finished fourth behind the pennant-winning Tigers. He pitched even better in 1946, going 16-13 with a 2.23 earned run average that was fourth-best in the league. Even then he felt unlucky. Eight of his thirteen defeats were by a single run, including a pair of 1–0 losses. Still, at age thirty he was practically a star. Not like DiMaggio, maybe, but then there was only one Joe DiMaggio. The Yankee Clipper, who returned from the army that season to universal acclaim, had his own dressing quarters in the stadium, a private sanctum for the hero other Yankees hailed, with the usual clubhouse tact, as the Dago. DiMaggio's salary had risen to $43,750, or about $550,000 in today's dollars—a far cry from modern salaries but still a lofty sum that few of his teammates could even dream of. Bevens himself had seen his pay rise to $10,500, worth about $135,000 today. He figured it was more than his no-account father had made in a decade. Yet even the best times failed to dislodge the chip on his shoulder.

Bevens suspected that manager McCarthy and general manager Larry MacPhail wanted to ship him back to Newark. He thought the big-city writers and fans saw him as a hick. He worried that the club's returning servicemen looked down on him for playing through the war years, like hundreds of other married men who weren't drafted. Still he began to feel more like a Yankee as the months passed. Teammates like Stirnweiss and Phil Rizzuto slapped him on the butt and called him Bev. Too straitlaced to join the team's bachelors when they went out on the town—Bevens may have been the Yankee least likely to wake up drunk in a whorehouse—he got along best, perhaps, with second baseman Stirnweiss, who would have tied for that distinction. Snuffy was "good people," Bev said. Like Bevens, Stirnweiss was a happily married straight arrow who fretted that fans and some of their teammates doubted him because he'd had his best years during the war. Unlike Bevens, who sweated through two or three jerseys in a typical start and tended to stomp around cursing his luck if a bloop hit fell in, the second baseman looked half asleep even while turning a double play.

Their oil-and-water personalities blended into friendship after Bevens challenged Stirnweiss one day. Bevens had been trying to pitch his way out of a jam. He was going into his stretch, looking back at the runner on second, when he saw Stirnweiss behind the runner, moving his lips with his eyes shut. Bevens got out of the inning and was jogging off the field when he pointed at Stirnweiss. "You were praying, you sonofabitch," he said.

Snuffy smiled. "And it worked."

George Henry Stirnweiss came by his name the old-fashioned base-ball way. He had a quirk. As the *Sporting News* put it, "He is a sufferer from sinus trouble." Sniffling for air from the time he was a boy, he claimed the name Snuffy forever by using snuff to clear his sinuses.

He grew up in the Bronx, near brand-new Yankee Stadium, hearing the crowds roar when Babe Ruth smacked a homer. In the summer, when school was out, he liked to join his father, a New York City policeman, on his daily rounds. In those days there were still dairy farms half a mile to the north, but the South Bronx was almost as shoulder-to-shoulder as it is today. Patrolman Andy Stirnweiss's beat snaked through the teeming 44th Precinct, where he tipped his cap or waved his baton to the grocers and bakers and tobacconists and fishmongers he passed every day. His son attended P.S. 83 and served as an altar boy at St. Dominic's Church, where the other altar boys teased him for being the straightest straight arrow in town. Georgie Stirnweiss was so pious that he never once sneaked a sip of sacramental wine. Any other boy might get roughed up or at least pelted with pebbles for acting all holier-than-thou, but everybody liked Georgie. Nobody could outrun him, guard him on the basketball court, tackle him on the football field, or strike him out. Asked how he got so fast, the boy explained that he got to school by taking a shortcut through a scary cemetery, running like the devil all the way.

In 1930, the year he turned twelve, George got the shock of his life. His father, promoted to the vice squad, now led raids on bathtubgin mills, speakeasies, and brothels populated by women the newspapers described as "Negresses." Such duty brought temptations, and Officer Stirnweiss apparently gave in. He was one of six cops suspended for taking payoffs, as part of an investigation of Nathan Blodinger, a mobster the *Brooklyn Daily Eagle* called "a Lower East Side 'uncle.'" The scandal made headlines and lasted into 1931.

Busted from the vice squad, demoted, and disgraced, Patrolman Stirnweiss left the force and became a taxi driver—with a difference. Keeping in touch with "Uncle" Blodinger and his friends, he drove mobsters and bootleggers around the Bronx. Perhaps he played middleman between the crooks and his friends on the force. If not, the mobsters must have been sensational tippers, because Andrew Stirnweiss somehow paid the rent on the family apartment on Van Nest Avenue; paid his sports-star son's tuition to Fordham Prep, a private Jesuit high school that shared a campus with Fordham University; and had money left over to buy a country home in Connecticut.

How did his son react? Snuffy Stirnweiss seldom spoke of his father and never mentioned the headlines of 1930 and '31. An all-city football and baseball star at Fordham Prep, he was soon one of the most sought-after high school athletes in the country. On the gridiron he played quarterback, halfback, and punter, returning punts and kickoffs, dodging tacklers with sprinter speed. The 1936 Fordham Prep yearbook showed blond, square-jawed Stirnweiss dressed in a tuxedo for his senior picture. "Conceded by all to be one of the great-est athletes in the 100-year history of the school," the yearbook called him "universally loved . . . her athlete supreme."

His classmates, his parents, and the future Green Bay Packers coach Vince Lombardi—one of Fordham University's famed "Seven Blocks of Granite"—all urged him to go to Fordham. He surprised them by accepting an athletic and academic scholarship to the University of North Carolina, where he became the first player to captain both the football and baseball teams. The disappointed Fordham coach Jim Crowley called Stirnweiss one of the best football players alive. "He can kick sixty yards under pressure," Crowley said, "and he's a jackrabbit with that ball. I got the creeps every time we had to punt to him."

The Bronx boy relished his time in North Carolina. He acquired a slight southern accent as well as a slightly skewed nose. The leather football helmets of the day, lacking face masks, provided little more protection than a swimming cap. Three or four broken noses surely contributed to the sinus troubles that earned him his nickname. Those flimsy helmets also played a part in the Hollywood future of his Carolina teammate Jack Palance, who went on to a fifty-year career as a tough guy in the movies. Half a century later, after the craggy Palance won an Academy Award, he joked that Snuffy Stirnweiss "gave me my career—because he broke my nose in football practice."

Drafted by the Chicago Cardinals of the National Football League, Snuffy was tempted to play pro football. He was in the trainer's room at Kenan Stadium one afternoon when a Yankees scout, Paul Krichell, stopped by.

"You'll crack an ankle or bash a head playing football," Krichell told him. "Or you can sign with the Yankee organization. Baseball's a great game, George."

"So's football," Snuffy said.

The scout smiled. "But it's great to be young and a Yankee."

Snuffy's father agreed. In the end he pleased the old man by signing with their home-borough ball club.

Within a week Andy Stirnweiss was dead. His dying was as sudden as the scandal of 1930–31: emergency appendectomy, infection, funeral. After that Snuffy worried that he'd die young, too. Over the years, upset stomachs often doubled him over. Ulcers, a doctor said. He drank milk while his teammates drank beer.

In 1942, his second season with the minor-league Newark Bears, Stirnweiss set a league record by stealing seventy-three bases. Between games of a doubleheader one day, he ran a seventy-five-yard dash in 8.2 seconds; the world record was 7.5. He took a breather and then zipped around the bases in 14 seconds flat—nearly as fast as contemporary speedster Dee Gordon, who circled the bases in 13.89 seconds in 2014, or the Negro Leagues legend Cool Papa Bell, who was clocked at 13.5. (Bell may once have beaten 13 seconds, and legend has it that he could turn the light off in a hotel room and be under the covers before the room got dark.) The *Sporting News* claimed that Newark's phenom "steals bases like no one since the days of Ty Cobb." And he did it by running on legs that were so short and muscular that he couldn't cross one leg over the other when he sat.

A friend described the bookish, devoutly religious Stirnweiss as "the nervous type," but he didn't seem nervous to nineteen-year-old Jayne Powers, a tall, blond fashion model who sat behind the home dugout at Newark's Ruppert Stadium. Jayne was cheering for the Bears one day when a batboy handed her a note:

> Please don't think me too forward or rude. If you do please tear this up, but seeing you today I'd enjoy nothing more than meeting you. Again please don't think me forward if you find it convenient I'd like to call you. George Stirnweiss #2.

They married a year later.

A bleeding ulcer kept Snuffy out of World War II. Jayne told him he worried too much. Despite his glittering minor-league stats, he felt inadequate.

In 1943 the Yankees held spring training in Asbury Park, New Jersey. Florida was too far away, especially with wartime travel restrictions in place. With fan favorite Phil Rizzuto in the navy, Stirnweiss took over at shortstop. Manager McCarthy predicted stardom for him, but Snuffy worried that McCarthy and everyone else saw him as a poor stand-in for Rizzuto.

With Rizzuto, DiMaggio, Ted Williams, and other stars serving in the armed forces, one sportswriter mocked wartime baseball as "the tall men against the fat men at the company picnic." The *New York Times*, comparing wartime ball to its deadball-era antecedents, when teams scratched for runs rather than waiting for big innings, predicted a banner year for the rookie: "Just as the horse has come back in this gas-restricted era, so has the stolen base. Its modern trailblazer is a stockily built athlete named George Stirnweiss, better known as Snuffy."

He ran wild against the war-depleted American League of 1944. You can look it up: George "Snuffy" Stirnweiss led the league with 205 hits, 125 runs, sixteen triples, and fifty-five steals while batting .319, fourth-best in the league. He was fourth in the voting for the Most Valuable Player award. *Time* magazine called him "the apple of McCarthy's eye." Even Babe Ruth, now forty-nine and retired for a decade, told reporters he liked Snuffy. "That little short shit's okay," Ruth said.

While teammates tomcatted around town during road trips, Snuffy stayed in his hotel room, reading and listening to the radio. Whenever the club hit a new town, he sent Jayne a telegram and a dozen roses.

He had an All-Star season in 1945, the last of the war years, dueling the White Sox's Tony Cuccinello for the batting title. Going into the season's final day, Cuccinello led the league with a .308 average to Stirnweiss's .306. Chicago's game got rained out, leaving Snuffy with the stage to himself on the last day. He doubled off Boston's Randy Heflin in the first inning and beat out an infield hit in the third. In the press box, a writer used a scratch pad to compute

Stirnweiss's batting average. The newsman hurried to McCarthy with the news. "Georgie boy's got it," he said. "He's ahead by a point."

The manager told Snuffy he was done for the day. "We can sit you now," McCarthy said. "You've got it locked up."

The second baseman shook his head. "No, I want to stay in." He wanted to win the batting title the right way—swinging the bat, not sitting on the bench. He felt the way Bucky Harris had felt in 1920, when he wanted to hit .300.

Snuffy flied out in the fourth inning and grounded out in the sixth. The batting crown looked lost until the Yanks scored twice in the eighth, bringing Snuffy to the plate one more time. He punched a single through the infield to claim his crown the right way, .30854 to .30846.

Oddly enough, a crucial part of that season-ending drama was based on bad math. The reporter who divided Stirnweiss's 194 hits by his 629 at-bats in the third inning had made an error. In fact Snuffy still trailed Cuccinello by a fraction of a point. Had he taken McCarthy's advice and stayed on the bench, he would have lost the batting title by the slimmest margin ever, .30846 to .30843.

In addition to the 1945 batting crown, Stirnweiss led the American League in runs, hits, triples, and stolen bases. No New York Yankee has since matched his twenty-two triples. No other Yankee would crack double figures in homers, doubles, and triples in the same season until Curtis Granderson did it in 2011. He knew some folks were saying he'd racked up his numbers on the cheap against 4-F competition; still, he was stung when general manager Larry MacPhail mailed him a 1946 contract for fifteen thousand dollars, a token raise. With no agent or players' union on his side, he protested in the only way a player could, by returning it unsigned. MacPhail eventually offered a bump to sixteen thousand dollars and Snuffy autographed the deal in his usual dignified fashion, *Geo. Stirnweiss*.

With the wartime travel restrictions lifted, the '46 Yankees held spring training in the Panama Canal Zone, where the weather was a good deal balmier than in Asbury Park. Joe DiMaggio was back in center, loping effortlessly to track down fly balls no one else could catch. Phil Rizzuto and second baseman Joe Gordon reclaimed their prewar positions, leaving no room in the middle infield for the batting champion. Snuffy ceded the leadoff spot in the lineup to Rizzuto and shifted to third base when he played, which wasn't always. His numbers tumbled from .309 with ten home runs to a punchless .251 without a single homer. *Baseball Digest* promptly dismissed Snuffy Stirnweiss as "a war-time freak, a 'Cheese Champ.'" That line ate at him worse than any ulcer.

As it happened, Gordon scuffled, too, batting only .210. The hot-tempered MacPhail accused him of "laying down" and decided to trade him. Cleveland was interested.

MacPhail went to DiMaggio. "Who do we want from Cleveland?"

Joe D suggested Allie Reynolds, a fireballing Oklahoman who was part Native American. "Get the big fuckin' Injun. I can't hit him."

MacPhail made it happen. His off-season trade of Gordon for Reynolds left second base open in 1947, giving Stirnweiss another chance. When a newsman asked Snuffy if he was excited about the coming season, he answered with a question of his own. "Am I a 'cheese champion' or a true ballplayer? Time will tell."

The other Yankees tried to buck him up. "Snuff, you're our second baseman," Rizzuto said. The altar-boy son of a crooked cop was everybody's friend. Still he stewed about his role on the club.

Rizzuto, Bevens, pitcher Joe Page, and a few other Yanks liked to finish spring training with a bang. Before returning to New York, they decamped to Maine for a hunting trip and took Stirnweiss along. They tromped through the woods, drinking beer and farting and telling jokes, making enough noise to alarm any deer within miles. Snuffy, the worrywart, admitted he was afraid of bears. If a bear charged them, he said, he wasn't sure he could shoot it in time. "What if we see one?" he asked. "Maybe we should run." That gave the others an idea. First, they paid a guide to track and shoot a six-foot black bear. Then they waited for Snuffy to fall asleep. They dragged the carcass into the outhouse by their cabin, propping it so that it would fall onto the next person through the door.

Next morning, Snuffy went to answer nature's call. In one account he "screamed a noiseless scream and, pushing the bear carcass away, raced back to the cabin, his feet barely touching the ground. He charged through the cabin door without opening it. The door shattered into millions of splinters. His mouth was moving, but nothing was coming out as he kept pointing to the outhouse. 'Spit it out, Snuff. What are you trying to tell us?' they asked. He was unable to answer as everyone was beside themselves with hysterics."

Always a good sport, Snuffy told that story on himself for years, laughing every time. If nothing else, getting pranked by Rizzuto and the others proved he was a real Yankee.

CHAPTER 6

They'll Manage

Baseball has always had as much to do with relationships and connections as with runs, hits, and errors. For Burt Shotton and Bucky Harris those connections traced back through their mentors Rickey and Griffith, all the way back to the day when Griffith, then managing the 1907 New York Highlanders, kicked dirt while his catcher, Rickey, allowed thirteen stolen bases.

Harris's heroics in the 1924 World Series made him a hero to the Old Fox and a celebrity in the nation's capital. While other players sold insurance or worked odd jobs in the off-season, the boy wonder manager wrote columns for the *Washington Post* and penned a quickie biography, *Playing the Game: From Mine Boy to Manager.* He joined Redmond & Company, an investment firm, where his duties consisted largely of shaking hands and talking baseball. Still only twenty-eight, he had a gift for running a twentieth-century ball club. Harris not only pioneered the use of relief pitchers and kept Walter Johnson fresh by limiting his innings and using him only as a starter; he also roomed on the road with team trainer Mike Martin, who updated him on which players were nursing injuries and/or hangovers. Like Shotton,

Harris chatted easily with reporters, who could count on him for a quote.

As Harris led the 1925 Senators into another pennant race, Shotton coached third base for the Cardinals and managed in Rickey's place on Sundays, at least until May, when St. Louis owner Sam Breadon canned Rickey. "I'm making Hornsby the manager," the owner said. When Rickey protested that getting fired "will ruin me," Breadon said, "No, I am doing you the greatest favor one man ever did for another." While firing him as manager, he offered Rickey a new position. As the sport's first modern general manager, Rickey would serve as liaison between the manager and the owner. He would oversee scouting, trades, contract negotiations, press relations, and, most important, the farm system. Before long Rickey had built the St. Louis minor-league chain into a powerhouse numbering thirty-two teams and more than six hundred players. Over the next nine seasons his farm system would bear fruit in the form of five pennants and three World Series titles.

Rickey urged Breadon to hire Burt Shotton instead of Hornsby, but Breadon had made up his mind. The great Rajah went on to claim his second Triple Crown with a .403 average, thirty-nine homers, and 143 RBIs, but the team finished fourth.

In that same season, his second as Washington's player-manager, boy wonder Harris led the 1925 Senators to another World Series, this time against the Pittsburgh Pirates. Once again the Series came down to an ultimate game. The sky opened up just before Game Seven, drenching Judge Landis's flag-festooned box while the commissioner shook his craggy head. No, he said, there would be no rain delay. And the weather seemed to obey him. As an announcer strode onto the field, calling the starting pitchers' names through a megaphone—"For Pittsburgh, Aldridge, *Vic Aldridge!* For Washington, Johnson, *Walter Johnson!*"—the sun appeared between clouds. A banjo trio dared the fates by playing "Let It Rain." As if on cue, it did.

Aldridge allowed four quick runs, staking the Big Train to a lead Bucky was sure he could hold. But the Pirates scored three in the third. The score was tied at 6 in the top of the eighth when Senators shortstop Roger Peckinpaugh homered to give Washington a one-run lead. Peck, Bucky's sure-handed double-play partner, had just been announced as the American League's Most Valuable Player, but he was off his game in the rain. He had already muffed a seventh-inning pop-up, and in the bottom of the eighth, with Washington now ahead by a run, Johnson induced a grounder by Max Carey—an easy force-out, it seemed, until Peckinpaugh's throw to second pulled Bucky off the bag. It was the Most Valuable Player's eighth error of the World Series, a record that still stands.

Bucky had Firpo Marberry in the bullpen, but he chose to let Johnson duel the Pirates and the elements. "The outfielders were out-lines, vague and shadowy" in the rain, wrote Damon Runyon. "Twice Walter Johnson asked for a delay that he might get sawdust to scatter around the pitching mound. The base lines were channels of mud." With rain dripping from his chin, Johnson gave up a two-run double to the Pirates' right fielder Kiki Cuyler. A half inning later the Pirates were world champions and the Senators' boy wonder was 1-1 in Series play.

When the Senators' train home reached Union Station in Washington, a Western Union delivery boy handed Bucky a telegram. It was from the American League president, Ban Johnson, who accused him of leaving the Big Train in the game "for sentimental reasons." Harris had cost his team and league the Series, Johnson wrote, with "the crudest blunder in the history of baseball."

Bucky never liked second-guessers. He wired the league office: SENTIMENT, HELL. WE WENT DOWN WITH OUR BEST.

A grateful Griffith gave him a three-year contract for one hundred thousand dollars. At a time when only Ruth, Cobb, and a few others made more, that was superstar money. Bucky's historic two-year run with the Senators had endeared him not only to Griffith and the team's followers but also to the city's social set. One pretty debutante liked to sit in her father's box at Griffith Stadium, making eyes at the player-manager. Mary Elizabeth Sutherland, known as Betty, was the glamorous daughter of former U.S. senator Howard Sutherland. She pestered friends to get them both invited to a dinner party held by Mary Louise "Texas" Guinan, the sassy hostess and movie cowgirl who greeted patrons of her New York speakeasy with a hearty "Hello, sucker." Guinan made sure the young manager and the nineteen-year-old socialite sat next to each other that night, helping launch the unlikeliest romance of the season.

Betty's parents disapproved of Bucky Harris. What could their beautiful daughter see in an athlete with an eighth-grade education? But over nights of courting, sitting in the Sutherlands' parlor listening to the radio, he won them over. Expensively dressed in his tailored business suits, comfortable in any setting, earning three times as much as the kind of senator who didn't play ball, Betty's beau could discuss world affairs like a diplomat. Now and then he quoted a friend of his, the president.

In 1926 Betty Sutherland posed for a *Washington Post* photographer in a designer suit and pillbox hat. With plucked eyebrows and strong, regular features, she was "a dazzling figure in Washington society," according to the *Post*, a swimmer, tennis player, and expert equestrienne who had grown up in her father's mansion on R Street, ten blocks from the White House.

Soon Betty was featured in another article in the *Post*. "President and Mrs. Coolidge attended the wedding this afternoon of Stanley Raymond (Bucky) Harris, manager of the Washington baseball team, and Miss Mary Elizabeth Sutherland, daughter of former Senator Howard Sutherland," the newspaper reported that October. "After a short reception the couple departed for New York to attend the first two games of the World's Series. They will go to Atlantic City for a short stay, after which they will sail for an extended trip to Europe." A follow-up story noted the reaction of Bucky's boyhood friends to seeing him in a silk top hat: "The rotogravure picture of the blushing bridegroom created a sensation in Pennsylvania mining circles among Bucky's old pals of the pits." Some of his players would rib him as Glamor Puss, an insult he laughed off by calling it a compliment for an old mine boy. He bought a house on Wyoming Avenue, and in 1927 Stanley Raymond Harris, fifteen years removed from his eighteen-cents-an-hour job in the Pennsylvania Coal Company's Mine No. 9, became the first professional athlete to be listed in the Social Register of Washington, DC. He and Betty dined at the White House. "It was a long cry from a dirty-faced boy in the coal mines" to toasting the Senators' upcoming season with Calvin and Grace Coolidge, he recalled. "Baseball had given me the opportunity America holds for all."

Burt Shotton never got within sniffing distance of a high-society dinner party, or wanted to. After retiring as a player in 1923, he began his managerial career in 1926, when Rickey dispatched him to run the minor-league Syracuse Stars. Shotton's 1927 Stars won 102 games, earning him a shot at a major-league job. Unfortunately for him, that job was with the Philadelphia Phillies, who couldn't beat an egg. They went 43–109 to finish 51 games behind Rickey's pennant-winning Cardinals. His club improved the next year, winning 71 against 82 losses, before falling back to 52–102 in 1930. Cursed by their home field, the cozy Baker Bowl, where the right-field fence was only 280 feet from the plate, Shotton's Phils lost like the latter-day Colorado Rockies. They led the league in hits and challenged the first-place Cards in several other offensive categories, but finished a distant last in pitching. After three more losing seasons, a Philadelphia writer wondered why Shotton still had a job, calling him "one of the most successful failures known to baseball."

The Phillies fired him in 1933. Shotton spent a season as a coach for the Cincinnati Reds under general manager Larry MacPhail, then told his wife his managing days were over. "Mary, I've had enough," he said. Now fifty years old, with two teenage sons and a pair of prize bloodhounds waiting for him in Florida, he went home for eight months of hunting, fishing, and golf. He was happy the first month, itchy after that. When Rickey called with an offer to manage the Rochester Red Wings, the Cardinals' top farm team, he hurried north to pilot a woeful Red Wings roster to a seventh-place finish. That led club president Warren Giles to claim, "Barney Shotton is one of the best managers in the game." Shotton and Bucky Harris were where they belonged—in dugouts, clubhouses, hotel rooms, and Pullman cars, moving through the game's managerial ranks toward their meeting in New York a decade and a half later.

The glow from 1924 and 1925 didn't last long for Bucky Harris. After the Senators finished more than twenty games out of first place in 1927 and 1928, Clark Griffith fired the boy wonder. Harris moved on to Detroit, where he managed the Tigers to five straight second-division finishes. Fired again, he led the 1934 Boston Red Sox to a record of 76-76, a thirteen-win improvement over the previous season despite a career-worst campaign by the team's foul-tempered ace, Lefty Grove, who fell from a league-leading twenty-four victories in '33 to only eight for Bucky. Yet when Sox owner Tom Yawkey saw a chance to bring player-manager Joe Cronin from Washington to Boston, he dropped the ax on Harris.

Bucky saw his own opportunity in this turn of events. He phoned the Old Fox, who had just traded away his manager. "Hello, Griff, this is your little boy," he said. "I'm out of a job. Have you any ideas?"

"I was just about to phone you," Griffith said. "Catch the next train to Washington."

Reinstalled as manager in his adopted hometown, Harris spent eight seasons on the hot seat. The best club of his second term in Washington, the 1936 Senators, came in a distant third behind the Yankees of Lou Gehrig, Bill Dickey, and the rookie DiMaggio. His other Senators clubs of the 1930s and early '40s did worse.

The columnist Red Smith told a story about the way he and other sportswriters tried to help the convivial, quotable Harris, a man they admired. Smith recalled a long summer in the late '30s when every move Bucky made backfired. In those days radio stations re-created out-of-town games off telegraph dispatches. (A young sportscaster named Ronald Reagan called ballgames that way for WHO in Des

Moines, Iowa, knocking blocks of wood together to mimic the crack of the bat.) In Washington, *Post* columnist Shirley Povich shared the microphone with announcer Arch McDonald. Povich, Bucky's best friend in the press corps, was in the booth one night when the Senators, down by two runs in the ninth, got runners to first and second with nobody out. Conventional wisdom called for a bunt, but Washington had Cecil Travis coming up and he was hitting .356. Harris let him swing, horrifying Povich, who pictured Clark Griffith sitting by his radio, spitting mad.

The wire read TRAVIS SWINGS, MISSES.

"Don't say that," Povich told announcer McDonald.

"What?"

"Do you want to get Bucky fired?"

After a few seconds of frantic miming over the mic, McDonald gave in. "Travis misses an attempted bunt," he told listeners.

Again Bucky let Travis swing away. The wire read TRAVIS SWINGS, MISSES.

Povich pleaded: "Arch, *please!*"

"Travis fouls off another bunt attempt," McDonald announced.

Travis lined the next pitch for a game-tying triple, saving Bucky's job for another day.

Larry MacPhail wanted to bring Burt Shotton to Brooklyn in the fall of 1938. MacPhail, now running the Dodgers, "thinks Shotton is the best manager in baseball," columnist Jimmy Cannon wrote. Shotton had been out of the majors for five years, winning pennants with the minor-league Columbus Red Birds, while Burleigh Grimes had mismanaged Brooklyn through two losing seasons. In the end MacPhail chose a hard-nosed young player-manager over the aging Shotton. Leo Durocher, the Dodgers' thirty-three-year-old shortstop, would lead the Dodgers to seven winning seasons in the next eight, including a National League pennant.

While Durocher's Dodgers went to the 1941 World Series, Shotton took Columbus to an American Association pennant and the minor leagues' Little World Series, where his Red Birds thumped a Montreal Royals team managed by Clyde Sukeforth. The *Sporting News* named Shotton its Minor League Manager of the Year. A season later he was back in the majors as a coach for the Cleveland Indians. Shotton owed that job to a recommendation from Roger Peckinpaugh, Bucky Harris's old double-play partner, who had managed the '41 Indians before moving up to the front office to let shortstop Lou Boudreau, baseball's latest boy wonder, take over as player-manager. Boudreau was just twenty-four years old and remains the only major-league manager younger than Bucky Harris of the 1924 Senators. Shotton coached third base, but his prime task was to mentor Boudreau. When the Tribe lost five in a row and fans called for Boudreau's head, reporters asked Shotton if he was ready to take over.

He said, "No. I don't want his job. All I want is to see this boy successful."

Boudreau survived to manage the Indians for the rest of the decade, winning a World Series and going on to manage three other teams in a Hall of Fame career. Cleveland papers of the time referred to Shotton as Boudreau's "loyal aide," two words as apt as his name.

Bucky Harris, fired again by Griffith in 1942, landed in Philadelphia, where a friendly reporter hailed him for "injecting a will to win into the Phillies that has made them a real and respected factor in the National League pennant race." It was wishful thinking. Owner Bill Cox dismissed Harris when the seventh-place Phils fell to 39–53. "A terrific shock," Bucky called his firing. The plot thickened when he revealed a secret: Cox liked to bet on baseball. Calling the owner "an all-American jerk," Bucky told reporters of a recent visit to the owner's office, where Cox's secretary asked a caller, "What are the odds on Phillies-Brooklyn this afternoon?" When she hung up, Harris stammered, "This, er, phone call—do you mean the president of the Phillies is betting on ballgames?"

"Why, yes," she said. "I call every morning and get the odds for Mr. Cox."

Bucky's revenge was Cox's undoing. After twenty-four Phillies players signed an ultimatum saying they'd refuse to play unless Bucky was reinstated, the owner apologized. Judge Landis, eternally sensitive to any whiff of gambling, banned Cox for life. "I feel vindicated," Bucky said. His players' support was "good enough for me. The stand they have taken on my behalf flatters me no little." Volunteering to step down, he urged the Phils to give their new manager, Freddie Fitzsimmons, "their level best." And with that, Bucky Harris faded away. But not for long.

Burt Shotton served as a coach for Lou Boudreau in Cleveland during the war years. He made every list of candidates to manage the Dodgers should Larry MacPhail fire Leo Durocher, and MacPhail fired Durocher more times than either man could count, but always sobered up in the morning and hired Leo back.

In 1945, Shotton retired. He was about to turn sixty-one, and he decided that his time had come. "I'm not rich or famous," he told the only reporter who took down his farewell, "but I have the satisfaction of knowing I've always done a fine job in exchange for my baseball pay." He promised his wife he would never don a uniform again. "Shotton's position in the esteem of baseball men is well established," wrote Cleveland sportswriter Ed McAuley, "but there isn't much doubt he means what he says about withdrawing from the pastime."

Still he kept his hand in, signing on as an all-purpose scout for the Dodgers after Branch Rickey replaced Larry MacPhail in Brooklyn's front office. By then, in the interborough intrigue that would mark the next decade, MacPhail had joined millionaires Dan Topping and Del Webb in a syndicate that bought the New York Yankees for $2.8 million. Installing himself as president and general manager, the so-called roaring redhead set the stage for a postwar battle between the Dodgers and Yankees, Brooklyn and the Bronx.

Leland Stanford MacPhail was a banker's son from Cass City, Michigan. A University of Michigan Law School classmate of the far less affluent Branch Rickey, he served in the army during World War I. Captain MacPhail became something of a legend after he and some other officers tried to kidnap Kaiser Wilhelm. Some months after the armistice, they posed as newspapermen coming to interview the exiled German emperor in his office in the Netherlands, and their plan was to seize the kaiser and slip him out of the country to face a war crimes tribunal. But the kaiser didn't come to the office that day. MacPhail swiped an imperial ashtray and kept it on his desk for the rest of his turbulent career.

As Cincinnati's general manager in 1934, MacPhail flew the Reds to Chicago, the first team flight in baseball history. A year later he presided over the major leagues' first night game. Night baseball had been a curiosity, a gimmick limited to minor-league backwaters. Portable lights exploded, leaving fielders fumbling for live balls in the dark while glass from blown-out bulbs crunched under their spikes. MacPhail swore he could do better, and on May 24, 1935, President Franklin Delano Roosevelt pressed a solid-gold telegraph key in the White House, igniting banks of 1,500-watt bulbs that washed Crosley Field in noonday light. Pundits expecting a debacle witnessed MacPhail's latest triumph. Three years later he staged the first night game at Ebbets Field. The visiting Reds, his old team, sent chubby-cheeked left-hander Johnny Vander Meer to the hill. Vander Meer had spun a no-hit game in his previous start. On the night of June 15, 1938, he no-hit the Dodgers to become the first and only major-league pitcher to throw two no-hitters in a row.

MacPhail was fifty-five when he took over the Yankees. Still as drunken, dyspeptic, and brilliant as ever, he hired a seasoned baseball man to be his assistant general manager: Bucky Harris. Bucky had been running the Detroit Tigers' top farm club with an eye toward becoming the Tigers' general manager, but MacPhail brought him to New York at a higher salary to help evaluate the players returning from World War II. "Bucky is joining us strictly in an administrative capacity," MacPhail told reporters. Harris was glad to hear him say it. "I have worn that uniform long enough," he announced. "I don't intend to put it on again." Privately he called baseball's flannels and garish socks his "monkey suit."

Within a year, Joe McCarthy resigned as the Yankees' manager, after too many run-ins with MacPhail. Player-manager Bill Dickey and coach Johnny Neun took the reins through the rest of the 1946 season, the Yanks' third straight without a pennant, but neither was a long-term solution. MacPhail considered them "interim guys." So who would manage the Yankees in 1947? Leo Durocher was under contract in Brooklyn, but there were persistent whispers about his antics off the field. In a *World-Telegram* column headed MACPHAIL DISCUSSES MANAGER RUMORS, Joe Williams asked, "Who's going to manage the withered Yankees in 1947? Even Larry MacPhail, and with convincing sincerity, says he doesn't know. But there's one sure bet you can make: It won't be Bucky Harris."

MacPhail bought Harris a drink one evening that fall. "Bucky," he said, "there's only one man I think can win with this club next year."

Harris knew where this was going. "Larry, I don't want to manage the Yankees," he replied. "I like the front office."

But MacPhail knew how to get what he wanted. Citing his age and questionable health after decades of binge drinking, he said he doubted his liver would hold out much longer. "I'm not going to stay on as general manager forever." If Harris agreed to manage the club for a year or two, "you can become general manager when I move on."

They shook on it. Bucky signed a two-year contract for seventy thousand dollars—far less than the Dodgers were paying Durocher.

"The veil of mystery has finally lifted on the identity of the Yankee manager for 1947," the *Times* reported. "It will be Stanley Raymond (Bucky) Harris. The Yankee prexy made the disclosure yesterday in the club's Squibb Tower offices to a roomful of scribes, radio broadcasters and press photographers. . . . Bucky, one-time 'boy manager' of the Senators but reaching fifty next Friday, will receive a yearly stipend of $35,000. . . . MacPhail spent considerable time defending the manner in which he made the selection."

Bucky stood beside his florid boss at the press conference, looking over the room with his slate-gray eyes while MacPhail declared,

"I want to assure you—and Bucky will corroborate me on this— that Harris was not my original choice for manager. He told me he was not interested in the job and wanted to work in the front office." Confirming rumors that Durocher had been a candidate, he said, "Durocher did send word to me that he was interested in the Yankee job. I replied that if Leo were free to act, he could come and see me. He never came." MacPhail also revealed that Joe DiMaggio had been the first Yankee to phone Bucky Harris his congratulations. Turning to Harris at their press conference, he asked, "Have I permission to say that Joe DiMaggio will play center field for the Yankees next year?"

"He better," Bucky said.

No one outside his family knew that Bucky was fighting personal demons as he took the game's top managerial post.

"He tried hard to be a good father," recalls his son Stanley S. Harris, who went on to be a federal judge in Washington, DC. "When I was little and he was managing the Senators, he'd grab me by the hand and take me to work with him. I had my own little Senators uniform." Later, young Stanley made straight As at Washington's Woodrow Wilson High School. As a member of the Wilson High golf team, he won a match against a kid from Roosevelt High, the future baseball commissioner Bowie Kuhn. "I was in college by the time he joined the Yankees," Stanley said of his father, "but we stayed in touch. He said he had no desire to manage the team. He only went along because MacPhail dangled the front-office job a year or two down the line. But he was greatly troubled. His family life was breaking up."

Betty Harris, now forty-one, had spent twenty years as a baseball wife, a life she had come to loathe. "The game is tough on marriages," said Stanley. "Dad was on the road so much . . . my mother became an alcoholic." The Harrises kept up appearances, swimming and dining together at the exclusive Congressional Country Club, but Bucky's storybook marriage lay in ruins as he agreed to manage the '47 Yankees.

Meanwhile, Burt Shotton, whose home life was as placid as

Florida's Kissimmee River, spent the winter of 1946–47 fishing for bass. He had a grown son selling cars in Winter Haven, another tending cats and dogs and parakeets as a veterinarian in Orlando. He took Branch Rickey fishing when the Mahatma came through Florida on his way to spring training in Havana, Cuba. They chatted about the Dodgers' minor leaguers—not just the outfielder Edwin "Duke" Snider and first baseman Chuck Connors but also the fiery infielder every fan, reporter, player, coach, manager, and man on the street would be talking about as the 1947 season approached, the one Rickey wanted to bring up from Montreal. The black one.

CHAPTER 7

The Year All
Hell Broke Loose

On the chilly morning of Tuesday, April 15, 1947, Jackie
Robinson rolled out of bed in the McAlpin Hotel in Manhattan, across
Sixth Avenue from Macy's. His wife, Rachel, and their infant son slept
while Robinson shaved, showered, and dressed in his best suit and
tie. Rachel was awake by the time her husband put on his camel's-
hair topcoat. She would follow him to Brooklyn once the babysitter
arrived.

They kissed. "See you after the game," he said. "And just in case
you have trouble picking me out, I'll be wearing number forty-two."

The drama of Opening Day had been building for months. Like
many baseball upheavals of the time, it was Branch Rickey's doing.
The portly Dodgers president had spent the war years scouting and
signing players to stock Brooklyn's farm system. Unfortunately for
him, the Cardinals system he'd built in the 1920s and '30s was deeper.
A 1946 Cardinals club led by Stan Musial, Enos "Country" Slaughter, and twenty-one-game winner Howie Pollet, all signed during
Rickey's reign, had swept Brooklyn in a best-of-three playoff to beat
the Dodgers out of the National League pennant. Still wearing the

birds-on-a-bat logo Rickey had designed, the Redbirds went on to win the World Series.

Rickey's quest to get past the Cardinals and bring the Dodgers their first Series title was personal as well as professional. Pushed out of St. Louis by owner Sam Breadon, he saw himself as the savior of Brooklyn baseball. The Dodgers had reached the Fall Classic only once in the past quarter century, and that was when Larry MacPhail was running the club. Cookie Lavagetto called that 1941 Dodgers team the best he ever played on. In Game Four of the '41 Series, the first-ever Yankees-Dodgers Subway Series, they trailed the Yankees two games to one. With two out in the ninth inning, New York's Tommy Henrich was the only batter that stood between Brooklyn and a crucial victory. He ran the count to three and two. Then Dodgers reliever Hugh Casey broke off a curve that Henrich would call "the sharpest-breaking pitch he ever threw." Henrich swung over it. Strike three! Jubilant Dodgers fans threw their hats in the air, hats that drifted down in funereal silence as Henrich hustled to first. Catcher Mickey Owen had let the third strike get by him. "I saw that little white jackrabbit bouncing" past the catcher, Henrich recalled, "and I thought, *Let's go.*" Dodgers fans looked on in horror as the Yanks rallied for four runs to win.

Brooklyn fell again the next day to drop the Series, reinforcing their sorry reputation. The proud Yankees had won a dozen pennants and nine World Series. The New York Giants boasted thirteen pennants and four Series crowns. Brooklyn's record: three and none. Year after year the Ebbets Field faithful warned, "Wait till next year!" But next year never seemed to come.

In the mid-1940s, Rickey hatched a new plan to outsmart his rivals. Ensconced in a dimly lit office on Montague Street in bustling Brooklyn Heights, he sat at a half-ton mahogany desk in front of a blackboard on which he had written the name of each player in the Brooklyn organization, all the way down to the Olean (New York) Oilers of the Class D Pony League. At some point it occurred to him that every one of those hundreds of players was as white as the chalk he used to write their names. All the while a wealth of talent in the Negro Leagues went untapped. Several years earlier, Pittsburgh Pirates owner William Benswanger had wanted to sign Josh Gibson, the so-called black Babe Ruth of the Homestead Grays, but Judge Landis nixed the idea. After the flinty Landis died in 1944, Albert "Happy" Chandler, a former U.S. senator and governor of Kentucky, succeeded him as commissioner. Rickey suspected Chandler's heart was kinder than Landis's, and he intended to take advantage of it.

In August 1945, Rickey summoned a twenty-six-year-old Negro Leaguer to Brooklyn. Dodgers coach Clyde Sukeforth led Jack Roosevelt Robinson into Rickey's office, where a stuffed elk head loomed from one wall, along with portraits of two of the Mahatma's favorite leaders, Abraham Lincoln and Leo Durocher. An illuminated aquarium stocked with tropical fish bubbled in the corner. Rickey sat in an upholstered swivel chair. "His piercing eyes roamed over me with such meticulous care, I almost felt naked," Robinson recalled in his memoir, *I Never Had It Made*. Rickey saw a young man whose skin had been compared by newsmen to tar, coal, ebony, chocolate, coffee, Shinola, midnight, and the ace of spades. One writer labeled him "the blackest black man, as well as one of the handsomest." Robinson knew that the Dodgers had scouted him for his color and attitude as well as for his wheels and bat. He knew this meeting was an audition but thought Rickey wanted him to join the Brooklyn Brown Dodgers of a new United States Negro Baseball League.

But Rickey was thinking bigger. He was thinking that a black Brooklyn Dodger could break baseball's color line. "Are you the man to do it?" That was his first question. There was more to it than hitting and fielding, he said. "What will you do when they call you a black son of a bitch?"

Rickey got to his feet. He said he knew Jackie Robinson was no shrinking violet. During the war Lieutenant Robinson had been court-martialed for refusing to move to the back of an army bus at Fort Hood, Texas—eleven years before Rosa Parks would refuse to sit in the back of a bus in Alabama. Rickey told him truthfully that he wasn't sure Robinson could handle the task ahead. Leaning down into the younger man's face, he asked, "What will you do when they call you a nigger? When they *spit in your face?*"

Robinson sat with his fists clenched. "Mr. Rickey, do you want a ballplayer who's afraid to fight back?" he asked.

"No!" Rickey shouted. "I want a player with guts enough *not* to fight back!"

In Sukeforth's recollection, Robinson sat still for several minutes before he spoke. "If you take this gamble," he said in his high, nasal voice, "I promise you there will be no incident."

Assigned to the Dodgers' top farm club in 1946, Robinson led the Montreal Royals to the International League pennant, won the batting title with a .349 average, scored 113 runs in 124 games, stole forty bases, and incited no riots. The following January, Commissioner Chandler chaired a secret meeting of team owners with only one question on the table: Should they allow Brooklyn to bring Robinson to the majors? The Dodgers voted yes; the other fifteen clubs voted no. According to one attendee, "You wouldn't believe what some of those owners said. One said that if Robinson played they'd burn down the Polo Grounds the first time the Dodgers came in." Rickey reminded the commissioner that he had the power to overrule the owners. In the end Chandler, a longtime parishioner at St. John's Episcopal Church in segregated Versailles, Kentucky, told him, "I'm going to meet my Maker someday, and if he asks me why I didn't let this boy play and I say it's because he's black, that might not be a satisfactory answer. So bring him up."

Of course Branch Rickey, the man behind "baseball's great experiment," wasn't acting solely or even mainly for heroic reasons. While he may be remembered as a social progressive, he was above all a *baseball* progressive. Yes, the pious Mahatma hoped to strike a blow for racial equality, but that would be a bonus. Rickey's main aim was to get a star player cheap and to draw a new population of fans to his ballpark. He was playing *Moneyball* 1940s-style.

The 1947 Dodgers spent part of spring training at Fort Gulick in the Panama Canal Zone, where manager Durocher got wind of a mutiny in the making. A dozen Brooklyn players, led by Georgia-born outfielder Dixie Walker, an Ebbets Field favorite known as "the People's Cherce," swore they'd never take the field with a nigger. As Durocher recalled, "Mr. Rickey had some kind of pipe dream that as soon as the players recognized how much Jackie could help us, they were going to demand that he be brought up. What happened was the opposite." Lying awake in his bunk one night, Durocher decided to "nip it in the bud, step on them hard." He woke his coaches, told them to round up the team and assemble in the mess hall.

Durocher had come up as a Yankees teammate of Babe Ruth, who despised him. Ruth dubbed the banjo-hitting shortstop "the All-American Out." He told teammates to keep an eye on the kid, saying, "He stole my watch out of my locker." Durocher called the Babe a liar but kept working the shady side of the street. As Brooklyn's player-manager in 1939, he fleeced rookies out of their paychecks in clubhouse poker games. The only things you could trust about the balding, lying, glimmer-eyed Durocher were that he'd outdrink you, out-cuss you, and outdress you in his sharp suits and two-tone shoes, and he'd do anything to beat you.

It was after midnight when he entered the mess hall in his silk pajamas and canary-yellow bathrobe. The Dodgers leaned on refrigerators and sat on freezers and chopping blocks, rubbing sleep from their eyes, a few puffing cigarettes. "I hear some of you fellows don't want to play with Robinson," Durocher said. "I hear you have a petition."

Cookie Lavagetto wished he were back in his bunk. He had already signed Dixie Walker's petition. Lavagetto had nothing particular against Robinson, but he was a get-along guy. When his friend and teammate Walker brought his petition around, Cookie autographed it. He started having second thoughts about a minute later.

Durocher went on. "Well, boys, do you know what you can do with that petition? You can wipe your ass with it. I'm the manager of this ball club, and I'll play an elephant or a fuckin' zebra if he can do the job, and to make room for him I'd send my own brother home."

They knew he meant it. Back in 1940 Durocher had made room for rookie Pee Wee Reese by benching the club's veteran shortstop, Leo himself.

"There's more coming up behind him," he said of Robinson and other Negro League players. "They're hungry, they're good athletes, and there's nowhere else they can make this kind of money. Unless you wake up, they'll run you right out of the ballpark. So I don't want to see your petition. This meeting's over. Go back to bed."

That shut down the mutiny but not the drama. Durocher was set to write Robinson into his Opening Day lineup when Commissioner Chandler called him into a disciplinary hearing. Official charge: consorting with gamblers. Unofficial charge: conducting a torrid extramarital affair with the actress Laraine Day, whose jilted husband had sued Durocher for alienation of affection. Day's husband called the Dodger manager a "love pirate" who "clandestinely pursued the love" of Laraine while posing as a friend. Lurid Leo-and-Laraine tales incensed Brooklyn's 125,000-strong Catholic Youth Organization, giving Yankees boss Larry MacPhail a pretext to attack. MacPhail tarred Durocher with charges of "underworld associations." True enough—Leo's movie-star pal George Raft, who specialized in mobster roles, served as his guide to the world of real-life crime bosses Joe Adonis, Bugsy Siegel, and Meyer Lansky. Raft bragged that he and Leo were so close that they "use each other's suits, ties, shirts, cars, girls." The Dodgers shot back that MacPhail was no better; his friends included "known gamblers" like a bookie he'd hosted in his owner's box that very spring.

Brooklyn boiled. One beat writer sent a terse report: *Log of the good ship Dodger. Men grumbling. Still enough food to keep squad alive and Rickey talking.*

A week before Opening Day, Chandler suspended Durocher for the entire 1947 season. Radio announcers broke into music and news programs with the story: *Leo's Out!* Phones in the Dodgers' offices rang until the lines jammed. Durocher's suspension, the most drastic punishment a major-league manager had ever received, shocked

Rickey. It has puzzled baseball historians for seventy years, but it made political sense. At the same time Chandler was sticking his neck out to support the Dodgers and Jackie Robinson, he appeased MacPhail and other owners by coming down hard on Rickey's manager. The move also preempted charges that Happy Chandler wasn't as tough as his predecessor. As the *Sporting News* saw it, "Leo's suspension is a warning that the man running things is as severe a czar as the late Judge Landis."

With Durocher banished, Clyde Sukeforth skippered the Dodgers on April 15, as Robinson made history.

Vendors hawked I'M FOR JACKIE buttons outside sold-out Ebbets Field on Opening Day. Rachel Robinson hurried from the McAlpin Hotel to catch a taxi after her babysitter arrived. She stood with her hand in the air while empty cabs flew by—not the only black person, then or now, to have trouble catching a cab. That day's *New York Post* called her husband "the first colored boy to don major league flannels." Radio announcer Red Barber gave the rookie a coy introduction. "Jackie," he said, "is very definitely brunette."

Rachel arrived in time to see her husband go oh-for-three in his debut, a victory over the Boston Braves. The Dodgers won again the next day. Still nobody saw Sukeforth, a former catcher with a perpetual squint from a hunting accident, as more than an interim manager, least of all Sukey himself. "I wasn't any world-beater even before I got shot in the eye," he said.

Rickey was entertaining reporters one day, rolling his swivel chair toward the window, pretending he was about to jump. "Help! I'm falling!" he said, waving a sheet of paper. "One of the names typed on this page can save me. One of them can manage Brooklyn this year. Help me pick the right man, or down I go!" Everyone figured Joe McCarthy had to be on the list, but the longtime Yankees manager wanted no part of Brooklyn's experiment. Rogers Hornsby, another candidate, had doubts of his own. "It won't work out," the aging Rajah said. "It's going to be more difficult for the Negro player to adjust to the life of a major league club than for the white players to accept him." Sukeforth may have been on the list, too, but he told his boss he wasn't cut out to be a manager.

"Well, Clyde," said Rickey, "if you're not the man for the job, who is?"

Sukeforth had a man in mind. No one knows if that name was on Rickey's list or if there were any names on his sheet of paper. It would have been like Rickey to wave a blank page and claim it held the Dodgers' future. All anyone knows for sure is that Rickey took Sukeforth's advice. He fired off a telegram to Florida: BE IN BROOKLYN TOMORROW MORNING. SEE NOBODY. SAY NOTHING. RICKEY.

The recipient, a tall, bespectacled part-time scout, told his wife it was probably nothing much. "Rick wants to see me about some players. I'll fly up there and be right back."

Burt Shotton packed an overnight bag and headed for the airport.

The Yankees opened the 1947 season with Joe DiMaggio limping. Three months before, surgeons had removed a three-inch bone spur from his left heel, and the wound festered. This is the injury Ernest Hemingway immortalized in *The Old Man and the Sea*, in which the old man, Santiago, hails "the great DiMaggio who does all things perfectly even with the pain of the bone spur." Doctors tried everything to relieve the Yankee Clipper's pain. They sewed maggots into his heel to devour the diseased tissue. Trainers taped him up until DiMaggio said he felt "like a mummy." As the *New York Times* put it, his plight "seems to be giving more prominence to the human heel than it has received since the days of Achilles."

The Yankees' real Achilles' heel, if they had one, could be found in the front office. That's where Larry MacPhail railed against his enemies, fueling his ire with White Horse scotch. "With one drink, he's a genius. With two drinks, he's insane. And rarely does he stop at one," Red Barber said of MacPhail, who had hired Barber in 1934 to call Cincinnati Reds games on the radio and took him along to Brooklyn four years later.

Under Bucky Harris the '47 Yankees were the bookies' second or third choice behind the defending American League champion Red Sox, who had finished seventeen games ahead of them the year before. DiMaggio's bone spur kept him out of the lineup until the fifth day of the season. He homered the next day, then went almost a month without a home run as the Yanks fell to fourth place. Harris urged his slumping second baseman Snuffy Stirnweiss to ignore the talk that he was a "cheese champ" who could only hit lousy wartime pitching. "That's newspaper bullshit," he said. A week later the Yankees tumbled to fifth place. A month after that, Bill Bevens lost to the White Sox, dropping his record to 3-8, with an unsightly 4.94 ERA. Like any scuffling pitcher, Bevens felt cursed. Every fastball he threw on the corner the ump judged a ball. Every broken-bat bloop fell for a hit. The lumbering right-hander feared the worst when Harris cornered him in the team hotel.

Harris held up his hands. "Don't worry, I'm not sending you down," he said. Bevens must have looked relieved. "I might yet, but probably not, if you do what I tell you," Harris went on.

"What's that?"

The little manager peered up at him. "Trust your fastball. Show me nobody can hit it."

With Rickey's telegram in his pocket, Burt Shotton dozed on a morning flight from Florida to New York. Rickey picked him up at LaGuardia Field. They barely spoke while the Mahatma drove to Manhattan, where the Dodgers were about to play the Giants at the Polo Grounds in Harlem. Then Rickey pulled over and climbed out of the car. "I need to get a haircut," he said. "You know the way to the ballpark. I want you to manage the Dodgers."

Shotton was shocked, but he hid it. This was bizarre behavior even for Rickey. "You don't argue with Rick," he said later, "for the very good reason that he does all the talking." Shotton slid behind the wheel and pulled into traffic. It took him about five minutes to prove

Rickey wrong in one particular: the new manager didn't know his way to the Polo Grounds. He hadn't set foot there for more than a decade. He found himself driving across the George Washington Bridge to New Jersey and barely made it to the park for the game.

He had no contract, no mandate, no hotel room to sleep in that night. Entering the visitors' clubhouse in the same two-tone shoes, slacks, sweater, and tie he'd put on that morning in Florida, he hung his jacket and fedora on a hook. Turning to look over his team, Shotton squinted through his gold-rimmed specs at Pee Wee Reese and Jackie Robinson, sour-faced Dixie Walker, smiling Sukey, scrawny pitcher Ralph Branca, brawny rookie Duke Snider, pinch hitter Lavagetto, and the rest. And he smiled. According to the *Times*, the new skipper "appeared like something whisked out of a magician's closet by Professor Branch Rickey." Keeping his pledge to stay out of uniform, Shotton wore a jacket and bow tie in the dugout from that day on. He and the Philadelphia Athletics' eighty-four-year-old Connie Mack were the only big-league managers to work in street clothes. (They would also be the last.) The Dodgers lost 10–4 with Robinson hitting his first home run while Giants second baseman Bobby Thomson clouted two. During Red Barber's postgame radio show, Shotton told Barber that his overnight bag wouldn't be enough. "I must ask Mary to send me some clothes," he said. Mary Shotton shipped her husband several suits and bow ties, plus thermal underwear for New York's cold nights.

He could have used a suit of armor. Within a week, Shotton was embroiled in the most tumultuous season in modern history. "There has not been another time like it," Barber wrote in his chronicle *1947: When All Hell Broke Loose in Baseball*. "Baseball became a force that year, not only in sports but in the overall history of this country." World War II was won, the United States was on top of the world, and baseball had surpassed boxing, horse racing, and college football as the country's favorite sport. Attendance at major-league parks would set a new record of 19,874,539, doubling prewar totals, with the Yankees and Dodgers leading the way. The Yanks ruled their borough as if by divine right, winning or at least contending with the ease of their leading man. Newspaper polls ranked DiMaggio ahead of the president and the pope in American hearts. Even on a bum heel he exemplified *sprezzatura*, the art of making greatness look easy. Meanwhile the "bums" of Brooklyn, like the hapless Chicago Cubs of later years, lost loveably. In the '40s you could stroll the two hundred blocks from Brooklyn Heights to Coney Island and barely miss a pitch as Barber's play-by-play spilled from car radios and open windows. With Jackie Robinson in their lineup, the Dodgers suddenly dominated headlines in all five boroughs and from coast to coast.

The Philadelphia Phillies and their manager, Ben Chapman, barked insults at Robinson and his team of "nigger lovers." The world-champion Cardinals, led by outfielder Enos "Country" Slaughter, out of Roxboro, North Carolina, matched the Phils' invective, calling Robinson "shoeshine boy" and worse. Slaughter sharpened his cleats in hopes of spiking him. It's worth noting that their slurs were nothing new. Bench-jockeying was all about driving opponents to distraction. DiMaggio and other Italians got heckled as dagos, guineas, and wops. Hank Greenberg was razzed as a kike. Brooklyn-born pitcher Albert Zachary, who was thought to look Asian, was called Chink Zachary. Baseball nomenclature also singled out a turn-of-the-century outfielder named William Hoy, who'd been rendered deaf and mute by a childhood bout of meningitis. Hoy batted .288 over fourteen seasons, stealing 596 bases to rank nineteenth among base-stealers in major-league history. To this day he is known as Dummy Hoy.

Yet there was something different about the color line. There was no fear of a wave of deaf-mute ballplayers breaking into the big leagues, but Robinson represented a genuine threat. If he succeeded, how many more black ballplayers would win jobs away from white men?

Robinson worried his teammates, too. In addition to Dixie Walker, pitcher Kirby Higbe, and the conflicted Lavagetto, the anti-Jackie camp included second baseman Eddie Stanky, a Philadelphian who pulled Robinson aside that spring. "You're one of twenty-five players on my team, but I want you to know I don't like you," Stanky said.

Robinson took the high road, saying, "I appreciate you telling me to my face."

April's headlines, newsreels, beanballs, and bench-clearing rhu-barbs didn't seem to budge Burt Shotton's blood pressure. Upon arrival he announced that he didn't know the players well enough to do much managing. "As soon as I think I know something about the club and can help, I'll start to work. Till then I'll just watch," he told reporters. Sitting in the dugout, his bow tie a little crooked, he tapped a rolled-up scorecard on his knee as Brooklyn took an early lead in the National League standings. Soon the Dodgers were seven games up on the defending-champion Cardinals, who lost ten of their first dozen games. Widely seen as a rubber stamp for Rickey, sure to disappear when Durocher returned the next season, Shotton stood up to the boss when he had to. Rickey wanted to send Lavagetto to the minors, but Shotton liked the creaky veteran as a late-inning pinch hitter and said no.

Cookie wanted to play. "Instead I'm nailed to the bench," he griped to his wife. Finally, in the ninth game of the season, Shotton sent him up to pinch-hit. Cookie was thirty-four, gray hair at his temples, crow's-feet at the corners of his eyes. His right shoulder, the one Rickey's pitching machine had smacked the year before, throbbed all the time. He couldn't play third base because his humpbacked throws took forever to get to first, but the shoulder didn't hamper his swing much. In that first pinch-hitting appearance, he homered to help lead the Dodgers to a 9–8 victory over the Giants. Mama Lavagetto's boy finished April one-for-one with a batting average of a thousand and a slugging percentage of a perfect four thousand, not that anyone noticed, any more than anyone but a few swooning bobby-soxers noted Al Gionfriddo's arrival in a trade three days later.

Gionfriddo noticed that Jackie Robinson waited for all his team-mates to shower before he went in to clean up. "Jackie, what are you waiting for?" the little outfielder said. "I'm not accepted any more than you, but we're on this team. So let's go together."

Soon the '47 Dodgers made their first trip to Chicago. The Cubs took a vote: Should they take the field against a team with Robinson on it? *No.* The Cardinals threatened a boycott in St. Louis. National League president Ford Frick conferred with Commissioner Chandler and responded to the threat. "If you do this," Frick warned the Cardinal players, "you will be suspended from the league. I do not care if half the league strikes. I don't care if it wrecks the National League for five years. This is the United States of America, and one citizen has as much right to play as another."

The Cardinals and Cubs backed down. So did the Phillies, who stood in the dugout aiming bats at Robinson as if the bats were rifles. They spat at him and made monkey sounds. Keeping his vow to Rickey, Robinson pretended not to hear. At last Stanky, the second sacker who had said, "I don't like you," had heard enough. Charging the Phillies, he shouted, "Pick on somebody who can answer back!"

In Cincinnati, a tipster told police that somebody was going to shoot Jackie Robinson. Agents from the Federal Bureau of Investigation spent two days patrolling roofs near Crosley Field, watching for snipers. Other G-men watched for snipers in St. Louis, where Robinson stayed with a black family while the rest of the team checked into a whites-only hotel.

On the field, Robinson plunged into a slump that dropped his average to .227. Some sportswriters called for an end to Rickey's "great experiment." All the while, Shotton was keeping a log of Robinson's at-bats—hits and outs as well as how hard each ball was struck. Robinson was oh-for-twenty when he showed Jackie the log, pointing to the hard-hit outs and saying they were base hits in his book. Robinson stayed in the lineup, and his line drives started falling in.

How cool a customer was Barney Shotton? All season he sat in the manager's office at Ebbets Field, where Durocher's photos of Durocher decorated the walls. Shotton never changed the pictures. Any worries he had he kept to himself. After tough losses he told his team, "There's always tomorrow." According to catcher Bobby Bragan, "It was just impossible to dislike Burt Shotton." A few of Bragan's teammates disagreed. Calling themselves Durocher men, they saw teetotaler Burt as a drab replacement. But most of the Dodgers agreed with Robinson, who said, "If you can't play for Shotton, you can't play for anyone."

Around this time Shotton developed a nerve condition that affected his right hand. He had trouble signing autographs and keeping notes on his scorecard. Doctors kept referring him to specialists until he quit keeping doctors' appointments and taught himself to write with his left hand.

On April 27, a pale and shrunken Babe Ruth trudged to a stand of microphones behind the plate at Yankee Stadium. He waited, nodding thanks, while a standing-room crowd filled the House That Ruth Built with the last ovation he would hear. "You know how bad my voice sounds," Ruth said in an amplified whisper. He was fifty-two, stricken with throat cancer. "Well, it feels just as bad." Sounding as if he had sand in his throat, he praised the game he loved. In baseball, he said, "You've got to start way down at the bottom when you're six or seven years old. You can't wait until you're fifteen or sixteen. You've got to let it grow up with you. And if you're successful, if you try hard enough, you're bound to come out on top." He closed simply: "I'm glad I've had the opportunity to thank everybody. Thank you."

He stayed long enough to shake a few hands. Bill Bevens got in line. Bevens had grown up idolizing Ruth, dreaming of seeing the Babe swat tape-measure homers here at Yankee Stadium, an unimaginable distance from Hubbard, Oregon. Clasping Ruth's bony hand twenty years later, he tried not to cry. Bevens always said he had three goals in life: to play for the New York Yankees, to meet Babe Ruth, and to pitch in the World Series. As of that day he was two out of three. "Ruth was in so much pain he could hardly talk," he told his wife.

By July the Yankees stood eight games ahead of Boston and Detroit. On July 19 Allie Reynolds beat the Tigers 2–1 to win his eleventh game against five losses, making MacPhail look prescient.

"There is an expectant feeling, an alert, confident feeling that comes over a ball club when it realizes that it can win it all," Barber wrote. "Bucky Harris was experienced, held the reins of discipline loosely, and was a good man to play for. And he certainly knew a star relief pitcher when he saw him."

Joe Page was a left-handed version of Firpo Marberry, the relief ace of Harris's 1924 Senators. Like Marberry, Page lacked a starter's stamina but could go all-out for an inning or two. A beetle-browed fastballer who mixed in an occasional spitball, Page spent late nights tomcatting with his road roomie DiMaggio, the league leader in one-night stands. Secretly shy and insecure, the Clipper liked carousing with extroverts like Page. He could sit quietly while Page did all the talking, working his way around to introductions: "This here is Joe . . . well, you know." Before long the great DiMag would take a dazzled girl's hand and lead her upstairs to his bed.

In August, Harris had the luxury of a twelve-game lead in the American League while struggling with an existential question: Larry Berra? A stocky twenty-two-year-old rookie catcher with a permanent five o'clock shadow, Lawrence Peter Berra was "the greenest green pea behind the plate anyone ever saw," in the words of Red Barber. But the kid could hit. Stepping in the bucket to smack an inside fastball, lunging at a pitch on the outside corner, he hit fastballs, curveballs, spitballs, *baseballs*. Bucky gave Berra forty-eight starts at catcher and twenty more in the outfield. The genial rookie looked clumsy but allowed only three passed balls behind the plate and made just one error in the outfield. Playing about half the time, he batted .280 with eleven homers and fifty-four RBIs. Soon the Associated Press carried a story that helped create Berra's legend. Harris told the kid to quit swinging at bad balls. "*Think* when you get up there. Make the pitcher get it over!" Berra nodded and said, "Okay, skip." His next time up, he took three called strikes and muttered, "How can you think and hit at the same time?"

With a healthy DiMaggio leading the way, the Yankees extended their lead. Snuffy Stirnweiss defined mediocrity on offense with a

.256 average, five homers, and five steals, but he teamed with Rizzuto to turn double plays like clockwork. Rookie hurler Spec Shea won fourteen games. Half a dozen Yanks enjoyed the season of their lives. The outlier was Bevens. Coming off his star-making sixteen-win season the year before, he won only seven games all season while losing thirteen. Bevens's 3.82 ERA was better than the league average; he kept the Yankees in the game again and again, only to end up as the losing pitcher. He had a word to describe his luck: he was snakebit.

Bevens lost his thirteenth game on the first of September. New York was still ten and a half games ahead of the second-place Red Sox. Harris's club coasted to the pennant, watching the National League standings to see who would be their victims in the World Series.

In Brooklyn that summer, Pete Reiser sprinted after a drive to center by the Pirates' Culley Rikard. There were no warning tracks then, and Reiser wouldn't have heeded a warning anyway. One of the best athletes the sport ever saw, he was the ultimate gamer, famous for sliding headfirst and running into outfield walls. While playing for an army team during the war, Reiser chased a fly ball into a thick hedge that served as the outfield fence, plowed through the hedge, and landed in a drainage ditch on the far side. He fell ten feet and separated his shoulder. Unable to throw right-handed, he switched gloves and played lefty until his right arm healed. In June of '47 he barreled skull-first into the concrete center field wall at Ebbets Field, then collapsed as if he'd been shot. Teammates ran to him. Right fielder Gene Hermanski was the first to arrive. Hermanski picked the baseball off the grass and stuck it in Reiser's glove. Umpire Bill Stewart, puffing to the scene a moment later, called the batter out, as a stretcher crew carried the unconscious Reiser to the clubhouse. A priest was called to administer last rites, but by then the patient was sitting up, lighting a cigarette to celebrate Brooklyn's 9–4 victory. Reiser spent ten days in the hospital, recovering from a fractured skull. Within a month he was back in the outfield, helping spark the Dodgers to thirteen wins in a row, but he had trouble tracking fly balls. Pistol Pete was diminished, finished as an everyday player at the age of twenty-eight.

Jack Pierce, Cookie Lavagetto's superfan, kept filling balloons and yelling, "Hey lookie lookie, here comes Cookie" while his hero waited for pinch-hitting opportunities. One day the plate umpire told Lavagetto to calm the man down. "He's making too much noise!" Cookie didn't know about that, but he walked over to Pierce and asked him to knock it off.

After the game he ran into Pierce, who had waited an hour to apologize. Weeping, he said he was sorry. And that got Cookie's back up. "Listen here," he told his number-one fan. "I'm apologizing to you for listening to that umpire. Make all the noise you want!" Pierce was back in his seat behind the enemy dugout the next day, filling balloons and singing his ditty about Cookie.

In August, the Cardinals' Enos Slaughter went after Robinson on a play at first base. The rest of the world had grown accustomed to Robinson's dashing presence on the field, but not the Cardinals. Robinson's foot was next to the base, touching the bag, the way it was supposed to be. Slaughter made a point of missing the base and spiking the first baseman. Country Slaughter had been scouted and signed years earlier by Wanzer Rickey, Branch's brother, who received a bonus of a shotgun and two hound dogs. Slaughter had been the hero of the 1946 World Series, racing home from first base on a single to score the Series-winning run. A less ornery man might have considered his ties to the Rickeys while running to first. Not Slaughter, who drove his cleats into Robinson's heel, just missing his Achilles tendon. Had he slashed the tendon, Robinson's career might have ended that day. As it was, the play left Robinson with a seven-inch gash and a bum heel to match DiMaggio's.

A month later the surging Cardinals trimmed Brooklyn's lead to four and a half games going into a do-or-die series in St. Louis. In one of Barber's pet phrases, tensions were higher than an angry cat's back. In the second inning of the first game, Cardinals catcher Joe

Garagiola grounded into a double play. He spiked Robinson at first, going for the Achilles just as Slaughter had done in August. In later years Garagiola would make a television career as a genial sportscaster and *Today Show* cohost known for his warmth and humor, but in 1947 he was known as one of the game's ardent racists. He and Robinson traded insults as players spilled from both dugouts. Plate umpire Beans Reardon preempted a brawl by warning Robinson and Garagiola, "One more word and you're out of the game!"

With peace restored, Robinson came to bat in the fifth inning. There is no record of what catcher Garagiola muttered through his mask, but there is a record of what happened next. Robinson launched a two-run homer. In the eighth, pinch hitter Cookie Lavagetto singled with the bases loaded to win the game, 4–3. The Dodgers never looked back.

Two weeks later the Dodgers clinched the pennant, and half a million fans lined the streets of Brooklyn for a ticker tape parade. The *Sporting News* named Jackie Robinson baseball's Rookie of the Year. Newspapers carried dozens of photos of Jackie and Rachel and a few of another celebrity couple, Leo Durocher and Laraine Day. Durocher told reporters that he couldn't wait to see his team go up against the Yankees in the World Series. "I'm looking forward to managing the Dodgers again in 1948," he said. That sent reporters scurrying to Shotton.

Burt, did you hear what Leo said?

You won the pennant! Aren't you safe for next year?

What's Rickey telling you?

Shotton shrugged, sipping a Coca-Cola. He said he hadn't spoken to Rick about 1948. He had a World Series to think about.

In the hoopla leading up to the Series, the New York Telephone Company announced that it would give updates on the score of each game every fifteen seconds to those calling the number MEridian 7-1212. Bookies made the Yankees 11-5 favorites. "The Yankees should win in five games," wrote Rud Rennie of the *Herald Tribune*. "With luck and good pitching, they may win in four straight and get it over with." After all, the Bronx Bombers had led the American League in batting average, runs, hits, and homers as well as earned run average. Bettors who took the underdogs hoped Brooklyn had the moxie to surprise the Yanks, a club the *Times* described as "a smoothly purring baseball machine." Shotton's Dodgers had led the National League in only two major categories, walks and stolen bases.

One item in the *Times* went almost unnoticed: SERIES TO BE TELEVISED—2 SPONSORS PAY $65,000. The story noted that Ford and Gillette would share the cost of airing the first televised World Series in New York and a few other cities along the East Coast. The Brooklyn-based Liebmann's Brewery had offered $100,000 for the rights, but Commissioner Chandler took less money from the carmaker and the razor company. It would be wrong, the commissioner announced, for televised baseball "to be sponsored by the producer of an alcoholic beverage."

TWO

Seven Games

CHAPTER 8

Sheer Hysteria

They came from the five boroughs and beyond, by car, subway, bus, streetcar, and on foot, streaming toward the stone arches of Yankee Stadium. Seventy-three thousand, three hundred sixty-five of them, the biggest crowd in World Series history. Many of the men wore fedoras, jackets, and ties. Women dressed as if they were going to a Broadway show. Seven thousand fans had paid four dollars apiece for standing-room tickets. Another twenty thousand watched from nearby rooftops. "Sheer hysteria," Yanks announcer Mel Allen called the run-up to the 1947 World Series.

The sky was clear with a light breeze, the stadium decorated in red, white, and blue bunting, flags, and ribbons. Fans pointed out VIPs in their box seats: former president Herbert Hoover; New York governor Thomas Dewey; Secretary of State George Marshall; the governors of Connecticut, New Jersey, Pennsylvania, and Rhode Island; Commissioner Happy Chandler; league presidents Ford Frick and Will Harridge; and an all-time All-Star lineup featuring Babe Ruth, Ty Cobb, and a spry, eighty-year-old Cy Young, who'd won a pair of games in the inaugural World Series of 1903.

The managers shook hands and smiled for photographers. Bucky Harris was dressed in Yankee pinstripes, Burt Shotton in a dress shirt, bow tie, and a silk Dodgers warm-up jacket. They couldn't help noticing a front-row spectator who might replace either of them next year. Leo Durocher, sporting a $175 suit made by Frank Sinatra's tailor, sat with Laraine Day and their Hollywood pal Danny Kaye. Durocher waved as if he were running for mayor, his cuff links glinting while some in the crowd cheered and some booed. He still commanded the spotlight, but it was Shotton and Harris who would call the shots on the field. "The two managers were handed jobs they didn't want and didn't expect," Red Barber wrote in that week's *New York Times* Sunday magazine. "Each inherited a troubled and tangled ball club. Neither drew public nor professional approval when he was named. Yet, here they are, on top of the heap."

Reporters asked Harris how winning the American League pennant of 1947 stacked up against the titles of his boy wonder years. "That was so long ago I can't remember," he joked. "But after twenty-two years it's a great feeling to lead another winner." After posing with Shotton, he retreated to the home team's spacious, wood-paneled clubhouse. There was no time to lose. Harris patted a few players on the back on his way to the manager's office, where a taller, older man stood waiting.

"Hello, Bucky," Ty Cobb said.

At sixty, Tyrus Raymond Cobb was fleshy, ruddy, and nearly bald. He looked more like a kindly uncle than the spikes-first hellion he'd been in his heyday, yet those who knew him swore the Georgia Peach was as sour-tempered as ever. "They were all against me," he told biographer Al Stump, "but I beat the bastards and left them in the ditch." Bucky Harris hadn't forgotten calling Cobb an old man and threatening to plunk a throw off his forehead in 1920. Shaking hands, he hoped Cobb wasn't carrying a grudge.

Cobb said, "You and I went at it pretty good in our playing days."

"Yes, we did."

"Well, I heard it's a little tough for you now, looking after your kids while you try to win the World Series. I'd be delighted to take them to dinner some night, just to give you a break."

Harris wouldn't have been more surprised if Cobb offered to suit up and play center. Had the old man heard about Bucky's troubled marriage? Bucky and Betty tried to keep their private life private, but baseball people gossiped as much as anybody else. "Thank you, Ty," he said. And though he never took Cobb up on the offer, he never forgot it. As Harris told his children, the most surprising thing about people is how they keep surprising you.

Turning from Cobb, the Yankee manager glanced toward the private dressing area set aside for Joe DiMaggio. Harris had admired the Yankee Clipper long before he became his manager. In 1939 he told Washington reporters that the twenty-four-year-old DiMaggio was a better all-around player than Ruth, Cobb, or Lou Gehrig. In the outfield, "He materializes out of thin air. I don't care where the ball is hit, he's there. At the plate, my Washington pitchers have one order: Throw the ball low and outside to him. And after that, say a prayer." A man apart, the great DiMaggio, now thirty-two, was called simply Himself by teammates who weren't close enough to call him Dago. He could be vain, petty, greedy, neurotically jealous of his rival Ted Williams and even lesser teammates like Tommy Henrich. Still he was heroic in his way. After two heel surgeries in less than a year, he played hurt every day. He grieved if he went four-for-four and the team lost. Harris managed him by leaving him alone. The Yankees were proud to be his followers.

In the visitors' clubhouse, Arthur Daley of the *Times* found Jackie Robinson sitting by his locker. The Rookie of the Year nodded when Daley asked about the pressure of being the first Negro in a World Series, moments from taking the field in front of the biggest Series crowd ever. Robinson thought that was funny. "Gosh," he said, "it can't be any more nerve-wracking than that St. Louis series."

Cookie Lavagetto reached into his locker for his jersey, feeling the itch even before he pulled the thing on. His scratchy uniform wasn't Cookie's only worry. Thinking back to the punchless .100 he'd hit in the 1941 Series, he was determined to contribute this time if he got a chance. Of course that depended on how Shotton used his bench. Coach Clyde Sukeforth praised Lavagetto as a useful pinch hitter—he'd get no argument from Shotton there—as well as the headiest man on the club, "a guy who never missed a sign in his life." Not that anyone took Cookie for an egghead. Rather than fret about his role on the club, he'd find a newspaper, light up a cigarette, and flip to his favorite comic strip, *Dick Tracy*.

Al Gionfriddo sat a few feet from Lavagetto, rubbing up his glove. A short-fingered relic the size of an oven mitt, Al's glove had a pocket no bigger than a baseball. But it felt like a second skin on his hand. He had no idea if he'd get to use it in the Series. He was hoping for a pinch-hit appearance, maybe an inning or two in the field, but Shotton might never call on him. In fact, he wasn't sure the manager knew his name. Teammates called him Al Gi (pronounced *Gee*) or just "runt" or "squirt"; in the rare instances when Shotton wanted him to pinch hit, he'd ask for "the little Italian."

Metropolitan Opera soprano Helen Jepson trilled "The Star-Spangled Banner," accompanied by Guy Lombardo and His Royal Canadians. Many fans stayed standing after the anthem to applaud a haggard Babe Ruth. The fifty-two-year-old Ruth took a drag off his cigar and gave the crowd a wave, acknowledging his last Yankee Stadium ovation as if it hurt to wave. His camel's-hair coat looked two sizes too big. He would be dead within a year.

Few in the crowd noticed a trio of television cameras suspended from the upper deck in wire-mesh cages. The cameras beamed live images to viewers in New York, Philadelphia, Washington, DC, and Schenectady (home of General Electric, which owned RCA and NBC). Television's reach would soon expand from its East Coast roots, but radio was still king in a year when U.S. factories produced a record 178,000 TV sets—and twenty million radios. Television sets cost anywhere from $225, or about $2,400 today, and up to ten times as much for the grandest models. The 1947 DuMont Teleset, with its mahogany console and cathode-ray screen, weighed more than a refrigerator. The vast majority of TV sets were in bars and restaurants; hardly anyone had one at home. One tavern installed a set at one end of the bar for Dodger fans, another at the far end for Yankee fans. Viewers crowded near the sets to squint at the tiny figures on their toaster-size screens.

Proponents of the new medium called this televised Series baseball's first "electric October," as if radio were smoke signals. Bob Stanton, longtime host of radio's *Cavalcade of Sports*, still saw his TV gig as a demotion. He figured he'd be lucky to reach 100,000 viewers while radio announcers Mel Allen and Red Barber reached millions.

It was still September as the first Electric October began. "Here's Eddie Stanky," Stanton announced at one thirty p.m. on September 30, 1947, as the Dodgers' leadoff man stepped in against the Yankees' rookie starter, Frank "Spec" Shea. On television screens, batter and pitcher appeared as ghostly figures about an inch tall— when they appeared at all. Harry Coyle, who directed the telecast for NBC, recalled that the early innings were marred by technical glitches. "The people watching probably saw the 'Please Stand By' sign on their screens as much as the game," he said.

Shea had won fourteen games against five losses. He owed his success to a fastball that touched ninety miles an hour and a sharp slider. He owed his nickname to the freckles that specked his cheeks when he was a boy. Harris risked second-guessing by choosing the rookie to open the Series instead of the nineteen-game winner Allie Reynolds, but the manager had his doubts about Reynolds's courage. "I'm not sure he can handle the heat," he admitted privately.

Shea went into his rocking-horse motion. Stanky flied out, and the world leaned in to watch Jackie Robinson come to bat.

Burt Shotton's name seldom comes up when people recall Robinson and baseball's "great experiment." Shotton was a supporting player, but a crucial one. A newspaper cartoon of the time shows a hobo—a Brooklyn bum—clinging to Burt as he steers a rusty bicycle over a tightrope while Rickey points the way forward. It was Shotton, not Rickey, who dealt with Robinson, Dixie Walker, and the rest of the Dodgers every day. It was Shotton, not Rickey, who saw Robinson more as a ballplayer than as a symbol of the Dodgers' organizational genius, who nursed the proud, worried Jackie through his early-season slump and never treated him as anything less than his most talented player. And when some of his teammates carped about Shotton, calling him aloof, out of touch, his boss's puppet, Robinson defended him. "I sure do like playing for that man," he said.

Robinson stepped into the batter's box.

In the Yankees dugout, Bucky Harris could recall a few black Senators fans in the 1920s who used to save the price of a ticket by climbing a tree outside Griffith Stadium in the segregated District of Columbia. As Harris wrote in his memoir, *Playing the Game*, one day a batter knocked one all the way to the tree, where "one of the dusky crew caught the ball" on the fly. Senators coach Nick Altrock shouted to the man, "Now let's see how you can throw!" The man in the tree called back, "No, suh! Les' see how you kin climb, Mistuh Nick." Jackie Robinson would have been about five years old at the time. Now here he was, waving his bat over the plate, leading his team against Harris's club in a city where millions wanted his autograph.

Robinson may have had a word or two for catcher Larry Berra. Berra had been telling reporters that his Newark Bears had faced Jackie's Montreal Royals in the minors the previous season. "He never stole a base on me then," he said, "and I don't expect him to steal on me in the Series," Berra said.

Shea walked Robinson, who promptly took off for second. Berra's throw was in the dirt. Robinson's aggressiveness got him in trouble an out later, when Shea speared a comebacker and trapped him between second and third, but he kept the rundown going until the batter, Pete Reiser, took second base. Reiser, still fighting headaches and dizzy spells after fracturing his skull in June, scored on Dixie Walker's single to give the Dodgers a 1–0 lead.

In the bottom of the first, Snuffy Stirnweiss led off for the Yankees. The stocky second baseman hoped he didn't look as nervous as he felt. He already had a 1943 World Series ring in a jewelry box at home, a keepsake he cherished almost as much as his wedding band and favorite rosary. It had a ten-carat diamond in a silver mounting shaped like a baseball diamond, but Snuffy never felt he had earned it, having batted only once in the Yanks' five-game victory over the St. Louis Cardinals. Now, in his first appearance in what he considered his first real World Series, Stirnweiss grounded out to Stanky at second. The Dodgers' lanky starter, Ralph Branca, proceeded to mow down the first dozen Yankee batters, fanning five including Stirnweiss and Berra in the top of the fourth.

A twenty-one-year-old with twenty-one victories in his first full season in Brooklyn, Branca had grown up a Yankees fan in Mount Vernon, just north of the Bronx. With a motion that was all knees and elbows, he resembled Ichabod Crane of nearby Sleepy Hollow, and he dared fate by wearing number 13. Branca stayed perfect until DiMaggio banged a fifth-inning shot between short and third. Pee Wee Reese snared the ball but the Clipper, sailing down the first-base line despite his tender heel, beat the throw. Branca visibly sagged. He walked George McQuinn without throwing a strike. His next pitch, a high and tight fastball, plunked Billy Johnson on the wrist. That brought up Johnny Lindell, the Yanks' brawny left fielder, with the bases full. Shotton leaned out of the Dodger dugout to wave his left fielder, Gene Hermanski, back and toward the line. A pitch later, Lindell pulled a double into the left-field corner. DiMaggio and McQuinn scored to put New York ahead 2–1. Branca looked up at an angry sun. He walked Phil Rizzuto to reload the bases, bringing pitcher Spec Shea to bat. Five Yankees in a row had reached base before you could say Jack Robinson.

Shea had settled down since the first inning, holding Brooklyn to a single and a walk. The book, baseball's invisible collection of unwritten rules, called for Harris to let him bat, particularly in a home game. But Bucky went against the book. He went for broke. In Red Barber's view, "The biscuits are on the table. A bases-loaded opportunity with nobody out might not happen again." Harris sent backup infielder Bobby Brown to pinch-hit for Shea.

Brown may have been the best-educated ballplayer of his time. An honor student at Stanford who spent off-seasons at Tulane Medical School, he roomed with Berra on road trips. One night Berra, reading a comic book, saw his roomie close a medical text and asked him, "How'd yours turn out?" But Brown's IQ mattered less to Harris than his .300 average and sharp eye.

Brown choked up on the bat. He watched Branca's first pitch miss the plate by a foot. The next was no closer, and now it was Shotton's turn to defy the book. Turning to coach Clyde Sukeforth, he said, "Go get him, Sukey. He's aiming the ball." (Shotton, wearing street clothes, was not permitted onto the field, so he relied on Sukeforth to handle pitching changes and discussions with umpires.) With the count 2-0, Sukeforth took the ball from the shell-shocked Branca, who left the mound ten minutes after taking a perfect game into the fifth inning. He would criticize Shotton's decision for the rest of his life.

Reliever Hank Behrman replaced Branca. A long-faced journeyman with a 6.25 ERA, Behrman had gone from Brooklyn to Pittsburgh in the Gionfriddo trade that spring, but after he gave up twenty-six runs in twenty-five innings, the Pirates sent him back. He finished walking Brown to force in another run.

Snuffy Stirnweiss smacked a grounder to Robinson at first. Jackie threw home to nail Lindell at the plate. One out, bases still loaded, Tommy Henrich coming up.

"Old Reliable" Henrich was famous for coming through in the clutch. He'd hustled to first when strike three eluded Mickey Owen in a key play of the '41 Series. A sandy-haired outfielder with a dimpled chin, Henrich had batted .346 with one hundred RBIs for the Cleveland Indians' top farm team in 1936, but he wasn't invited to spring training the next year. He thought the Indians were trying to hide him from the rest of the league, so he wrote to Commissioner Landis protesting his treatment. To everyone's surprise, Landis agreed with him. "This young man has been wronged," Landis said, declaring him one of the game's first free agents. Henrich entertained a dozen offers, but, like so many boys of the Ruth-Gehrig era, he was a Yankees fan. When he told the Yanks that another club was bidding twenty-five thousand dollars, they matched the offer. Called to the majors in 1937, he lugged his suitcase into the New Yorker Hotel on Thirty-Fourth Street. "A bellhop took my bag and sneered, 'So you're the new Yankee outfielder. How can you break in with DiMaggio? Have you seen him hit?'" The rookie knew all about DiMaggio, who was two years younger than he was.

"No, but he hasn't seen me, either. I plan to impress him," he told the bellhop.

He was talking through his hat. Henrich spent the night praying he wouldn't embarrass himself the next day. He went on to bat .320 as a rookie, often batting third in front of DiMaggio. "If we were ahead ten to one, he was just average," Bobby Brown said. "If we were behind ten to one, same thing. But in a big game he was terrific." DiMaggio called Henrich the smartest player in the game. He was thirty-four now, his sore knees putting the Old in Old Reliable. Still, he'd batted .287 in the regular season, leading the club with ninety-eight RBIs to Himself's ninety-seven. By modern metrics, he had a Wins-Above-Replacement (WAR) score of 4.6 that year, meaning that the Yankees won between four and five more games with Henrich than they would have won without him. (DiMaggio's WAR was 4.8. Snuffy Stirnweiss had an impressive 3.4 thanks to his defense, a team-high eighty-nine walks, and 102 runs scored. Pitcher Bill Bevens's WAR was 0.2. On the Brooklyn side, Cookie Lavagetto had a 0.4 WAR that season, while Al Gionfriddo's was −0.1, meaning that the Dodgers would have been slightly better off with a replacement from the minors.)

Stepping in against Behrman, Henrich lashed a single to left. His nickname rang out of the broadcast booths, box seats, and grandstand: Old Reliable! Rizzuto and Brown scored to boost the Yankees' lead to 5–1.

Harris went to his top reliever, Joe Page, in the top of the sixth. A former Pennsylvania coal miner like his manager, Page was a hard-drinking, high-living lefty, a middling starter who blossomed when

Bucky turned him into a late-inning reliever, the new Firpo Marberry. He gave up a run in the sixth, trimming the Yankees' lead to 5–2. To lead off the seventh, Shotton called on pinch hitter Cookie Lavagetto, who popped out to Stirnweiss at second. Pee Wee Reese singled and stole second. When Page's wild pitch got past Berra, Pee Wee took third and kept coming as Berra stumbled chasing the ball—scoring from second on a wild pitch. It was 5–3, and now Page was the man on a tightrope.

Nobody ever knew exactly what to expect from Joe Page. Tall and shifty-eyed, he mixed a ninety-plus fastball with an illegal spitball he liked to use on two-strike counts. Page had practically bluffed his way onto the Yankees roster that spring. After a nine-win season in 1946, he demanded a raise from club president Larry MacPhail. MacPhail came back with a dare. He said, "Joe, sign this contract and I'll make you a deal: I'll go to Bucky on payday, the first and fifteenth of each month. If he says, 'Page is my boy,' I will hand you twenty-five hundred-dollar bills." His offer appealed to the riverboat gambler in Page, who signed. They toasted their pact with a drink. As sportswriter John Lardner wrote, "Joe had a lot of stuff. He drank a lot of stuff. He was a switch drinker. He could lift a glass with either hand." MacPhail, true to his word, asked Harris about Page's status every two weeks all season. There were eleven paydays between April and October. Eight times, Bucky said, "Page is my boy." Eight times MacPhail handed twenty-five crisp hundreds to a smiling Joe Page, who won fourteen games, saved seventeen, and finished forty-four that season. Bill James believes that Page, not Marberry—Bucky's first bullpen ace, twenty-three years before—was the first truly modern closer. According to James, "Harris made Page a reliever. This event, more than any other one thing, brought about the general acceptance of the concept of full-time relievers as a positive asset to a team."

Bucky, who didn't mind a drink himself, liked to share a postgame whiskey with the writers. After Page closed out a Yankees win he'd raise a glass to toast the reliever, saying, "Gentlemen, Joe Page."

In the eighth, DiMaggio launched a drive to left-center that Carl

Furillo tracked down well over 400 feet from the plate. That ball would be a home run in all thirty of today's ballparks. It was one of innumerable homers DiMaggio lost to a home park where the distance to the left-center-field wall was 457 feet. (In today's Yankee Stadium it's 399.) Bill James has shown that DiMaggio lost more homers to his home park than any other player in the game's history. But the Yankee Clipper didn't react. He didn't curse or throw his bat or his cap. He put his head down, turned toward the dugout, and took a seat on the bench.

With the score still 5–3, Page walked Furillo to lead off the ninth. Bruce Edwards flied out to Henrich in right. That brought Lavagetto to the plate. With Furillo at first, Cookie represented the tying run.

Page struck him out.

Reese, the Dodgers' last chance, hit a bouncer to the mound, and Page flipped the ball to first to end the game. The Yankees had held serve, winning at home to take a 1-0 lead in the World Series.

Shotton sipped a postgame cola in the visitors' cramped, quiet clubhouse. "We lost. What is there to say?" he said. Robinson sounded a defiant note. "I wish Berra was catching in the National League," he said. "I'd steal sixty bases." Lavagetto stripped off his itchy jersey. Now one-for-twelve in two World Series, Cookie had a postseason batting average of .083. Gionfriddo, unnoticed, dressed in the street clothes he may as well have stayed in. He hoped the Dodgers could stay in the Series long enough for him to get a pinch-hit appearance, maybe an inning or two in the outfield.

In the Yankee clubhouse, a smiling Harris greeted reporters by lifting a dram of whiskey. "Gentlemen," he said. "Joe Page."

CHAPTER 9

A Horrendous Afternoon

On the morning of the second game, New Yorkers read the first reviews of baseball as television programming. The game was "difficult to capture on the tele-screen," the *Times*' R. W. Stewart wrote. "Yet despite the limitations of the scene reproduced by the electronic cameras, those in the tele-bleachers were getting a more intimate view of the game than those actually in the ballpark." Stewart praised NBC's Bob Stanton and called the tele-experiment a qualified success. "Stanton did not intrude. Television's coverage of its first World Series is a credit to those, both telecasters and sponsors, interested in its furtherance." The DuMont Network would take over TV coverage for Game Two, with game-show host Bill Slater (a great-uncle of the actor Christian Slater) at the microphone.

Snuffy Stirnweiss took a copy of the *Times* and a copy of the *Jersey Journal* to work. Like several Yankees and many of the Dodgers, Stirnweiss took public transportation to the ballpark. That morning he kissed wife Jayne good-bye and took a Jersey Central commuter train from Red Bank to Jersey City, where he bought the papers. He rode a ferry across the Hudson to Manhattan and took the subway to 161st Street in the Bronx, where the second baseman joined other early arrivals walking to Yankee Stadium. In some ways every home game felt like a homecoming for Stirnweiss. He'd grown up a couple of miles from the stadium, walked a police beat with his father on these streets. But his father got busted from the force and died in disgrace. The family's good name depended on him now. When New Yorkers heard the name Stirnweiss, they thought of a husky infielder with a good glove and not much of a bat. He brooded about his reputation as a wartime fill-in, and his oh-for-four in the first game did nothing to lift his spirits. Snuffy had a lot to prove.

While starting pitchers Allie Reynolds and Vic Lombardi warmed up, Bucky Harris told reporters he wouldn't hesitate to use Joe Page again, even after Page's four-inning save yesterday. "I may use Page every game," he said. But Reynolds would get the start.

The "big fuckin' Injun" DiMaggio couldn't hit had made Yankee boss MacPhail look brilliant for trading for him the previous fall. Reynolds had won nineteen games in his first season in New York. The broad-shouldered right-hander was three-sixteenths Muscogee; naturally his nickname was Chief. "He was glad to be Indian, but it wasn't powwows and war paint with him," his daughter, Bobbye Ferguson, says today. "It was about making your family and your people proud." Reynolds prided himself on a stoicism he saw as part of his heritage. His manager, a talker, thought the big Injun lacked spirit.

Allie Reynolds hailed from a part of Oklahoma that he said was so flat you could see Texas from the pitcher's mound. Married at eighteen, a father at twenty-one, he built up his arms by swinging a sledgehammer in an oilfield. In 1939 an Indian scout spotted him—a Cleveland Indian scout. The legendary Hugh Alexander, an outfielder who turned to scouting after an oilfield buzz saw sliced off his left hand, signed Reynolds for Cleveland. The muscular rookie joined Lou Boudreau's big-league Indians in 1943. Within a week the club's third-base coach, Burt Shotton, told Boudreau that the kid was going to be a star. Reynolds went 11-12 that season while leading the American League in strikeouts. Dealt to New York three years later for Joe

Gordon—the trade that made room for Snuffy Stirnweiss at second—Reynolds won nineteen and lost eight for the '47 Yankees, with four shutouts and seventeen complete games.

Vic Lombardi, Brooklyn's Game Two starter, was a little lefty from California. Like his teammates Lavagetto, Gionfriddo, Furillo, and Branca (plus five Yankees including DiMaggio and Phil Rizzuto), the twenty-four-year-old Lombardi was the son of an immigrant from Italy. He stood five foot seven on his tiptoes. Known in the papers as the "mite southpaw," "vest-pocket southpaw," "pipsqueak portsider," and other diminutives, he beat the uptown New York Giants nine times in a row in 1945 and '46 to earn a new moniker, "the little Giant-killer." A textbook crafty lefty, he mixed off-speed stuff with a fastball that topped out around eighty-five miles an hour. His regular-season record was only 12-11 but his 2.99 ERA was sixth in the league. Newer metrics suggest how efficient Lombardi could be. He ranked among the leaders in fewest hits per nine innings, fewest homers allowed, opponents' batting average, and Wins Above Replacement. His 3.2 WAR was a notch better than Jackie Robinson's 3.1.

Reynolds set down the Dodgers in the first. Stirnweiss chucked his glove under the Yankee bench and went to watch Lombardi finish his warm-ups. He had never faced him. Until regular-season interleague play began in 1997, batters faced pitchers in the other league only if they got traded from one league to the other or if their team made the World Series. Stirnweiss was nervous as usual before the game, his stomach in knots, but he was a good bet to get on base today. His batting average went up against left-handed starters and his slash at the ball was among the Yanks' best-balanced swings—a good approach to a pitcher who tried to keep hitters off-balance.

Stirnweiss swung at the first pitch he saw. The ball shot past second baseman Stanky for a single. The first postseason hit of Snuffy's career brought the home crowd to its feet. He hustled to third on Tommy Henrich's single, veering around second base like a halfback turning upfield. When Johnny Lindell banged into a round-the-horn double play, Snuffy scored the game's first run. The scoreboard under the clock in center field read BROOKLYN 0, YANKEES 1.

In the third inning, Pee Wee Reese walked and stole second. Reese advanced to third base when Eddie Stanky smacked a single up the middle. Stirnweiss ranged into short center field to knock the ball down, saving a run, but then Robinson blooped a two-out single to tie the game, 1–1.

Stirnweiss came up again in the bottom of that inning, with one out. This time he scalded a low liner to right-center. Center fielder Pete Reiser sprinted after it but could only kick the ball toward Dixie Walker in right. Snuffy cruised to third with a triple. He stood on the bag looking sober as a judge, the way a Yankee was supposed to look, but inside he was practically singing. Two straight hits in the World Series—the best ulcer cure ever.

Center fielder Reiser stared at the sunbaked turf at his feet. Was he shaking his head out of anger or trying to clear the cobwebs from his oft-cracked skull? Only he knew. An out later, Lindell belted a triple to center. Reiser gave chase, but he stumbled and fell. Stirnweiss trotted home to put the Yankees ahead 2–1.

Shotton sent Sukeforth to the mound to huddle with Lombardi. With Lindell at third and two outs, the Dodgers wanted nothing to do with the next batter, DiMaggio. They walked him intentionally, and Lombardi escaped by fanning George McQuinn. When Dixie Walker led off the fourth by reversing a Reynolds fastball, sending the ball on a high arc into a right-field grandstand jammed with dismayed Yankees fans, the score was 2–2. Walker shook hands with happy teammates when he reached the dugout—Robinson included. Dixie had made his peace with Jackie, though you weren't likely to see them showering at the same time.

Dodgers announcer Red Barber felt a premonition as afternoon shadows inched over the infield. Unlike Mel Allen, the bombastic voice of the Yankees, Barber entertained and enlightened listeners without rooting along with them. But he never claimed to be purely objective. After eight years in Brooklyn he knew the players' life stories, their wives' and children's names, and the burden they bore in going up against the Yankees in the Bronx. "The Stadium itself was a strong force," he recalled. "Visiting players had to be impressed by the threatening size of the place." Baseball's answer to the Colosseum in Rome, the game's only triple-tiered ballpark, Yankee Stadium held twice as many fans as cozy Ebbets Field. Late-afternoon sun shooting between its three decks blinded unwary outfielders. "Added to it all was the devilish wind factor," Barber went on. "The Yankees knew that the winds blew one direction up above, then the reverse on the playing area because the wind bounced back from the high construction of the stands."

Wind, sun, and fate would come into play in the innings ahead. In the bottom of the fourth, the Yankees' third baseman Billy Johnson stroked a long fly the *Times'* John Drebinger described as "sailing down the center of the fairway more than 400 feet away." With the fence in dead center a nearly unreachable 490 feet from home plate, Pete Reiser had plenty of room. He settled under the ball, lost it, turned sideways, fell. The ball bounced away as Johnson took third. Rizzuto, the next batter, lofted a pop-up. Left fielder Gene Hermanski lost the ball in the sun; it fell for a double. Lombardi escaped without further damage, but the Lilliputian lefty was straining as if he were pitching uphill. An inning later, Tommy Henrich led off with a long home run. Lindell followed with a double. Now Shotton sent Sukeforth to put Lombardi out of his misery. As Drebinger wrote, "Lombardi humanely was invited to depart."

Reliever Hal Gregg allowed a couple of runs while Reynolds, relying chiefly on his fastball, kept the Dodgers off the board in the middle innings. The Yanks led 6–2 going into the bottom of the seventh, when Shotton went to Hank Behrman for the second day in a row.

Branch Rickey, watching Behrman allow a single to George McQuinn, may have felt a pang of regret for ignoring his manager's entreaties. "Rick, I need pitching help," Shotton told Rickey again and again during the season, only to be sent away with a promise that all would be well. Beyond purchasing Dan Bankhead from Memphis of the Negro American League at the end of August and reacquiring Behrman from Pittsburgh, Rickey didn't add a single pitcher to the roster all season. And the Bankhead move was little more than a token of Rickey's esteem for his own experiment. The majors' first black pitcher, Bankhead threw just ten undistinguished relief innings in 1947 and would only pinch-run in the Series.

With none away in the seventh, Behrman wild-pitched McQuinn to second base. Billy Johnson lined one to center, a ball the befuddled Reiser played into a single and a two-base error. Yankee fans in the bleachers razzed the Dodger center fielder. A few laughed at him. An out later, Shotton called for an intentional pass to Larry Berra. With runners at first and third and Allie Reynolds up, Bucky Harris flashed the squeeze sign. Jackie Robinson charged in from first base to field Reynolds's bunt and throw to the plate—or so he thought.

"The agile Negro first-sacker, tearing in for a squeeze bunt, ran right over the ball without picking it up," Drebinger wrote. Another run scored.

Shotton turned wearily to his bench coach. "Go get him, Sukey."

As Sukeforth went out to pull Behrman, Shotton phoned the bullpen. He summoned a strapping young hurler with a fastball that buckled hitters' knees. Rex Barney, born twenty-two years before in an Omaha elevator, threw as hard as Bob Feller—close to one hundred miles an hour if not more. Unfortunately for anyone who crowded the plate against him, Rapid Rex never knew where his next pitch would end up. As an eighteen-year-old with the minor-league Durham Bulls, Barney fired his first professional pitch several feet over the batter's head, through a chicken-wire backstop, and off the noggin of a local newsman, who reported, "The lad has plenty of steam. He threw in the general direction of the plate."

With Brooklyn trailing by six, Barney unleashed a fastball to Snuffy Stirnweiss, who chopped it toward Robinson. Jackie fielded this one cleanly, but Barney forgot to cover first base. Snuffy got credit for a single, his third hit of the game. Barney's next pitch was wild. That brought another run home, and fans began making for the exits.

Allie Reynolds was coasting. In the ninth he allowed a run on a groundout. With the pitcher's spot coming up, Brooklyn needed a pinch hitter. Shotton had Carl Furillo and Cookie Lavagetto on the bench, but they both hit right-handed, so he called on the little Italian instead of the bigger ones.

Al Gionfriddo roomed with Furillo on the road. He knew that his roomie Skoonj, so called for his love of scungilli, could have a lousy at-bat or two or three without losing his spot in Shotton's lineup, but this might be Little Al's only chance. He saw that Reynolds wasn't throwing as hard in the ninth inning as earlier, when the big Indian's fastballs hit Berra's mitt with a firecracker *pop*. With a seven-run lead, he wanted to get the ball over and get the game over. Reynolds looked the runner back toward first, then served Gionfriddo a middling fastball that Al slapped to the opposite field—straight to third baseman Johnson. Al ran like hell but Johnson threw to second for a force play that ended the game. So much for Al's big chance.

The scoreboard read BROOKLYN 3, YANKEES 10. New York had taken a two-games-to-none lead in the Series. Bucky Harris thumped his players on the back as they clattered down the tunnel to their locker room. Facing a pack of reporters, he said the Dodgers "simply can't be as bad as they looked. They really had a tough day, didn't they?" Harris praised Allie Reynolds with the usual postgame words—*tough, clutch*—without retracting the doubts he'd confided to his favored reporters the day before. Reynolds had won with a big lead, sure, but how would he perform in a tight game? Bucky still wasn't convinced today's winner was up to that sort of test.

The Yankee players toasted Reynolds with beer and plenty of jokes about Injuns and firewater. The pride of the Creek Nation laughed, but he was quietly sick of hearing war whoops when he pitched and reading that he was on the warpath. He wanted to be a Yankee plain and simple.

The saddest guy in the Yankees' happy clubhouse was Larry Berra. The Yanks' catcher was oh-for-seven at the plate, and the Dodgers had stolen three bases on him. Connie Mack, the ancient manager of the Philadelphia Athletics, told reporters that Berra's performance was "the worst World Series catching I ever saw." Berra was starting to be known as Yogi, a nickname he owed to a newsreel his boyhood pals had seen of a Hindu snake charmer who waddled around like their short-legged buddy. Even his parents called him Yogi after that, and the name was slowly catching on. *New York Sun* columnist W. C. Heinz, who helped popularize the nickname, had befriended the rookie catcher. When Berra grumbled about his crummy performance in the first two games, Heinz told him to forget it. "You guys won, and you'll have a better day tomorrow," he said.

"I dunno," Berra responded. "I ain't very smart."

Heinz recalled an off day when he invited Berra to watch a game with him. Yogi had said he didn't like to watch ballgames. "It makes me nervous," the young catcher said. But he'd surprised the writer with cogent comments on the action.

"You have a fine baseball brain," Heinz said now.

"I dunno if you're right," Berra said.

Bucky Harris had already decided to bench him.

Vic Lombardi took his time getting dressed in the visitors' gloomy clubhouse after Game Two. He wasn't sure he'd get another start. The Series would have to go five or six games for him to get the ball again, and Shotton was making no promises about his starting rotation.

Ten yards away, Pete Reiser hurried out of the shower. Reiser couldn't wait to dress and get out of the Bronx. His headaches and bouts of double vision were bad enough; now he was wracked with guilt for hurting the ball club with his sloppy play in the outfield.

Shotton deflected attention from Brooklyn's goats. "There's always tomorrow," he said. Yes, Lombardi had struggled and Reiser looked lost in the outfield. Yes, the Series looked like a mismatch so far. Yes, Brooklyn's pitching looked awful. Yes, even Robinson fouled up from time to time. The enemy had dented the scoreboard fifteen times in two games without so much as an RBI from DiMaggio. Still, Shotton said things were looking up: "The boys got some bad baseball out of their systems. Tomorrow will be different. We'll be at home." When reporters pressed him for details—*Will you change the lineup? Who's pitching tomorrow?*—Shotton gave them a line that was unlikely to inspire confidence in Brooklyn. "You certainly can quote me that we'll be on the field," he said, "and that we will have a pitcher."

Bookies bumped the odds on the Yankees to 6-1. Columnist Red Smith filed a story headed FINIS FOR THE DODGERS while the *Brooklyn Eagle* ran a defiant headline: WE AREN'T AFRAID.

The *Times* pronounced the Dodgers victims of a "horrendous afternoon of misadventures, which included a bruising attack by the Bronx Bombers and an assortment of ghastly misplays on their own part." Using a term dating back to their days as the Brooklyn Robins under Wilbert Robinson, the paper reported that "Burt Shotton's Flatbush Flock took a terrible drubbing from Bucky Harris's Yankees."

The sun was setting when Harris left Yankee Stadium. That evening, he and Betty celebrated their twenty-first wedding anniversary. It was a brief, melancholy celebration. A sip of wine but no toasts to their future. Betty had never accepted her husband's long absences on road trips or his constant focus on his teams. Bucky hated making excuses for his job and coming home to find her drunk. They had agreed to wait for Dick, their second son, to finish high school before they divorced.

In the morning, workers finished hanging flags, streamers, and red, white, and blue bunting at Ebbets Field in Brooklyn. Game Three was do-or-die for the Bums. Win today and they'd be back in the Series with two more home games ahead. Lose and they would fall behind three games to none. No team had ever come from three games behind to win a World Series.

Speedy St. Louis Browns outfielder Burt Shotton in 1916. [LIBRARY OF CONGRESS]

Stanley "Bucky" Harris, President Calvin Coolidge, and Walter Johnson (left to right) in 1924, Washington's championship season. [LIBRARY OF CONGRESS]

Harry "Cookie" Lavagetto was a young Brooklyn Dodgers star—and a dutiful son. [COURTESY OF THE LAVAGETTO FAMILY]

Al Gionfriddo on May 3, 1947, the day the Pittsburgh Pirates traded him to Brooklyn. [ASSOCIATED PRESS]

Floyd "Bill" Bevens, a young fireballer from Hubbard, Oregon, intimidated hitters.
[COURTESY OF THE BEVENS FAMILY]

Before he joined the New York Yankees, George "Snuffy" Stirnweiss was a football star at the University of North Carolina. [COURTESY OF THE STIRNWEISS FAMILY]

Branch Rickey (kneeling at left) never tired of teaching his innovative techniques.

Shotton, Rickey, and Jackie Robinson changed the Brooklyn Dodgers'
fortunes.

Stirnweiss won a batting title in 1945, while many players served in World War II, and he worried that the "real" Yankees doubted his abilities. [GETTY IMAGES]

Rickey (in white cap at left) experimented with an electric strike zone while Robinson tended the machine, Shotton (in checked shirt) watched, and Pee Wee Reese waited for a pitch. [GETTY IMAGES]

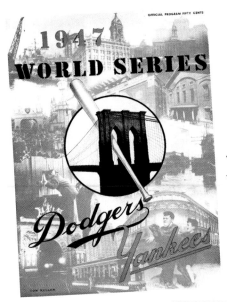

The 1947 World Series program would become a collector's item.
[COURTESY OF THE LAVAGETTO FAMILY]

Suspended manager Leo Durocher and his third wife, the Hollywood actress Laraine Day, upstaged Brooklyn skipper Shotton at the '47 Series.
[NATIONAL BASEBALL HALL OF FAME LIBRARY]

Harris and Shotton shook hands before Game One.
[ASSOCIATED PRESS]

Robinson sent Yankees shortstop Phil Rizzuto flying while Stirnweiss looked on.

Bevens shut his eyes releasing a pitch during Game Four. [GETTY IMAGES]

With the game and Bevens's no-hitter on the line, Lavagetto lined a fastball to right field. [GETTY IMAGES]

Cookie and Shotton
celebrated the
Miracle of Flatbush.
[ASSOCIATED PRESS]

Bevens and DiMaggio trudged to the clubhouse after Game Four.
[ASSOCIATED PRESS]

Cookie with the winning runs he drove in: Gionfriddo (left) and Eddie Miksis (right) in the Dodgers' happy clubhouse [COURTESY OF THE LAVAGETTO FAMILY]

Before Game Five, the hero posed with a photo of his wife, Mary, and their new baby, Michael. [ASSOCIATED PRESS]

The Yanks' rookie catcher wasn't known as Yogi yet. [COURTESY OF THE LAVAGETTO FAMILY]

Joe Page, known for extinguishing late-inning blazes, sported a gift from a Bronx fire station. [NATIONAL BASEBALL HALL OF FAME LIBRARY]

A rare photo of
Gionfriddo's grab—
would DiMaggio's shot
have cleared the fence?
[NATIONAL BASEBALL HALL
OF FAME LIBRARY]

A diagram of the
players' and umpires'
positions as Al went
back for the ball.
[NATIONAL BASEBALL HALL
OF FAME LIBRARY]

DiMaggio famously kicked the infield dirt, expressing emotion for once.
[GETTY IMAGES]

Joe D, Joe Page, and Yankees boss Larry MacPhail in the champions' clubhouse.
[GETTY IMAGES]

In later years, Bevens played along with photographers who asked him to pose with the guy who broke up his no-hitter. [ASSOCIATED PRESS]

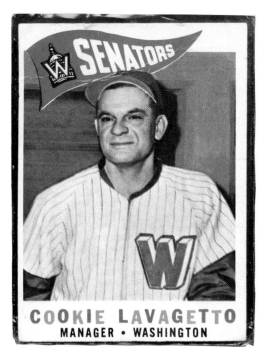

After years as a coach, Cookie managed the Washington Senators from 1957 to 1960. When the team moved to Minnesota in 1961, he became the Twins' first manager.
[COURTESY OF THE LAVAGETTO FAMILY]

Jayne and Snuffy Stirnweiss with four of their six children at home in New Jersey. [COURTESY OF THE STIRNWEISS FAMILY]

The Newark Bay train crash of September 1958.
[PHOTO: ASSOCIATED PRESS; TICKET: COURTESY OF THE STIRNWEISS FAMILY]

Late in life, the stars of '47 played golf. A mellowing Bevens met a deer friend at an Oregon course. [COURTESY OF THE BEVENS FAMILY]

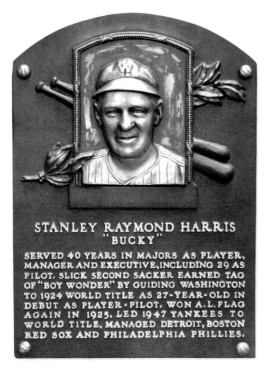

STANLEY RAYMOND HARRIS
"BUCKY"

SERVED 40 YEARS IN MAJORS AS PLAYER, MANAGER AND EXECUTIVE, INCLUDING 29 AS PILOT. SLICK SECOND SACKER EARNED TAG OF "BOY WONDER" BY GUIDING WASHINGTON TO 1924 WORLD TITLE AS 27-YEAR-OLD IN DEBUT AS PLAYER-PILOT. WON A.L. FLAG AGAIN IN 1925. LED 1947 YANKEES TO WORLD TITLE. MANAGED DETROIT, BOSTON RED SOX AND PHILADELPHIA PHILLIES.

As seventy-eight-year-old Bucky Harris listened on a special phone line, he was inducted into baseball's Hall of Fame in 1975.
[NATIONAL BASEBALL HALL OF FAME LIBRARY]

The Flatbush faithful flocked to their cramped little ballyard on foot, by subway, and aboard trolley cars running under webs of electric lines. Teenage boys in pleated pants and T-shirts jumped onto trolleys to ride for free until the conductor kicked them off. Some ran the rest of the way, threading through jammed streets to the rowdiest holy place in the borough of churches.

CHAPTER 10

Bums' Rush

"A community of three million people, proud, hurt, jealous," Branch Rickey called Brooklyn. The most populous, bumptious borough was the one his Dodgers belonged to and vice versa. "One could not live in Brooklyn and not catch its spirit of devotion to its baseball club, such as no other city in America equaled."

The seventeenth-century Dutch settlement of Breuckelen, named for a town in the Netherlands, was mostly farmland for two centuries. In 1776 it became the site of a major battle of the American Revolution. With his outgunned Continental Army routed by redcoats, George Washington retreated. His troops slipped across the East River through dense fog, perhaps grumbling, "Wait till next year," and won the flag in '83. By the 1940s, the underdog borough's population nearly matched Chicago's. More family-oriented and less highfalutin than "the City," meaning Manhattan, mid-century Brooklyn was a stew pot brimming with flavors and accents. Flatbush was largely Irish, Bushwick mostly German, Brooklyn Heights WASPy, Borough Park Jewish, Carroll Gardens Italian. Polish was spoken in Greenpoint, while you'd hear Norwegian and Finnish in Bay Ridge. Many black families were moving into Bedford-Stuyvesant, alarming neighbors who mistrusted any Negro who wasn't named Jackie Robinson. The whole borough teemed with tight-knit first- and second-generation families. As one Dodger fan said, "My brother visited a friend out on Long Island. It's terrible there—they have to sleep in their own room."

The *Brooklyn Eagle* proudly proclaimed, "Brooklyn *is* America." War movies featured wiseguys named Smitty or Izzy who said *dese* and *dose* and loved Dem Bums, the Dodgers, who thrilled fans all summer before breaking their hearts every fall. *World-Telegram* cartoonist Willard Mullin immortalized the Brooklyn Bum as an unshaven optimist in a dented fedora and moth-eaten suit, chewing a stubby cheroot and dreaming of a Series title. When the Dodgers surprised the National League in the summer of '47, a league-record 1,807,526 customers flocked to the park *Collier's* magazine called "the outdoor psychopathic ward that is Ebbets Field."

Charles Hercules Ebbets had built his baseball palace on land he bought cheap in a corner of Flatbush known as Pigtown. He began by plowing under the local dump, where feral pigs rooted through acres of trash. When Ebbets opened the park in 1913 his club was called the Superbas, a nod to a vaudeville hit of the day. A year later they became the Robins under manager Wilbert Robinson, who would soon get flattened by the aerial grapefruit that gave the Grapefruit League its name. The team was renamed the Dodgers, short for trolley dodgers, after the beloved Uncle Robbie got fired in 1931. Civic life in Brooklyn revolved around the ballyard at the corner of McKeever Place and Sullivan Place.

Fans lined up for $2.50 seats at a dozen gilded ticket windows. They entered through a wide rotunda of Italian marble. The floors were etched with red stitches like those on a baseball. A chandelier hung from the ceiling, its twelve round lamps painted to look like baseballs. Inside, ushers wore red jackets, blue slacks, and red caps. A colossal Schaefer Beer sign over the scoreboard signaled the official scorer's ruling on close calls: the *h* in *Schaefer* lit up if the scorer ruled a base hit, the first *e* lit up for an error. The club's tradition of letting patrons pour onto the diamond after games was no favor to the groundskeepers; fans regularly flattened Pete Reiser's turf in center on their way through the exit gates in the outfield wall.

Every day at game time, organist Gladys Goodding played the national anthem and "Follow the Dodgers." Teenage fans danced on the Dodger dugout between innings while the Sym-Phony Band, an off-key quintet, tootled "Take Me Out to the Ball Game" on a bass drum, snare drum, cymbals, and trumpets. If the umpires made a call that went the visitors' way, the Sym-Phony struck up "Three Blind Mice." They'd play a few bars of "Hey lookie lookie, here comes Cookie" as Lavagetto fan Jack Pierce filled his COOKIE balloons and released them over the stands.

Hilda Chester, a matronly widow in a flower-print dress, marched through the grandstands waving a frying pan, yelling at players and umps in booming Brooklynese. "Ya bum ya! Youse gotta lotta noive." She led fans in snake dances during rallies, pausing to hector the opposition. "Noive like a toothache ya got!" After Hilda had a heart attack and doctors said she shouldn't yell so much, she took to ringing a pair of cowbells because the game needed, well, more cowbell.

Burt Shotton began the morning of Thursday, October 2, with his usual coffee, toast, and scrambled eggs. Burt and Mary, his doting and doted-on bride of thirty-seven years, shared a suite at the Hotel St. George, near Rickey's office in Brooklyn Heights. A thirty-story limestone pile occupying a city block, the St. George boasted America's biggest saltwater swimming pool and the Grand Colorama Ballroom, the country's largest banquet hall. Its lobby bar would be the scene of Luca Brasi's murder in *The Godfather*. Upstairs, the Shottons' windows looked out over the rooftops of what the newspapers called "the baseball-mad borough." Shotton skimmed the papers that morning, avoiding the sports pages. Nothing good in there today.

After breakfast, he drove to Ebbets Field. The gates opened at nine. Several thousand one-dollar bleacher seats sold out in no time. The manager usually arrived around ten thirty for afternoon games, half an hour before the players were due. With World Series ceremonies moving everything forward, Shotton arrived early that day, but the blocks around Ebbets Field were already jammed. He ambled through the rotunda practically unnoticed, a grandfatherly fellow with a hint of amusement in his eye, as if his transit from semiretired scout to World Series manager were a private joke.

Like many of the Dodgers, Cookie Lavagetto took a taxi to the ballpark. Al Gionfriddo rode the subway like the workingman he was. Twelve miles away, the Yankees piled into a bus in their stadium's vast parking lot. Two motorcycle cops escorted the bus south through Manhattan, across the Brooklyn Bridge to bedlam. A reporter termed the next half hour "the wildest ride ever experienced by a Yankee." By Bucky Harris's estimate, the trip from the bridge to Ebbets Field featured "twenty narrow escapes" and plenty of eggs splattering the bus's windows.

In the cramped, dimly lit Dodger clubhouse, the showers leaked and players sat on three-legged wooden stools—all except Pee Wee Reese, who rode a swivel chair like Rickey's. Reese and the others liked to razz the manager about his colorful shirts and bow ties: "Ol' Barney's got a bad 'un on today!" Shotton would smile and say they looked like shit themselves.

With few pitching options, he entrusted the crucial third game to left-hander Joe Hatten. A rubber-armed Iowan, Hatten had gone 17-8 that year. He relied on a high-eighties fastball plus a curve that bit straight down when he was right and hung like a full moon when he wasn't. Two of his victories had come in a late-season doubleheader against Cincinnati, when he pitched a complete game in the opener and won the nightcap with five and two-thirds innings of shutout relief. But he preferred pitching home games. "Every day was a thrill in Brooklyn," Hatten said. He would face the Yankees' much-traveled Bobo Newsom. The lumbering, talkative Newsom had reached the majors with the 1929 Dodgers and pitched for thirteen big-league teams, winning 205 times and losing 213 times. At one time or another "Old Bobo" had led his league in innings, complete games, losses, walks, and earned runs allowed. Bucky Harris loved his work ethic. Newsom was with Harris's 1935 Senators when a third-inning line drive shattered his left kneecap. When Bucky went to the mound to take him out of the game, Bobo said, "You kidding me? I said it was broke, I didn't say I was dead." He finished the game.

Pregame festivities included an unscheduled salute to Leo Durocher. The Sym-Phony serenaded Durocher with a clanging "For He's a Jolly Good Fellow." Leo beamed and shot his cuffs. Laraine Day applauded. Shotton kept his eye on the field. He had no time to worry about the Dodgers' once and future manager.

Snuffy Stirnweiss opened the game with a single. Now batting .444 in the Series' early going, he was erased when Henrich rapped into a double play. Johnny Lindell grounded out to end the Yankees' first.

Harris had Sherm Lollar catching Newsom. At twenty-two, Lollar was the same age as Berra, but Bucky considered him a superior catcher and cooler customer. The manager had bucked Yogi up before the Series. "You're my kid," he said. He'd praised him in the press, too, saying, "Yogi's going to catch every game for me." At the same time, Bucky joined reporters who laughed at Berra's long arms and beetle-browed aspect, calling him the ape. *The ape can knock that ball out of sight!* But today he wanted to keep Jackie Robinson and Pee Wee Reese from stealing more bases on Berra. Nothing personal, he told Yogi. A skipper has the right to change course. "I want Lollar in there today." So Yogi sat and watched, feeling like a flop.

In the home first, with a standing-room crowd of more than thirty-three thousand in full howl, Robinson singled and stole second base. Lollar's low throw to Rizzuto skipped away as Robinson scrambled to his feet. Jackie took a step toward third. But Stirnweiss, backing up second base, was already grabbing the ball and flipping it to Rizzuto. Jackie dived back to the bag. Out! The play was typical Stirnweiss, a heady move by a supporting player. He doesn't appear in the play as it was telecast and filmed for newsreels—in the visual record, Rizzuto takes a throw from offscreen and applies the tag.

With two out, Newsom walked Pete Reiser. Shotton wanted his Dodgers to be the aggressors; he flashed the steal sign. Reiser took off for second. The play was close, but fate wasn't through with Reiser. The ump called him out and he twisted his ankle on the slide. The star-crossed outfielder limped off with what the Dodgers would call a bad sprain. In fact, his ankle was broken.

With one out in the second, Newsom walked Brooklyn's Gene Hermanski. Bruce Edwards doubled, Reese singled, Hatten singled. According to Red Barber, "The din was beyond belief." In the *Times'* account "the crowd, though less than half the size of either of the two great Stadium gatherings, appeared to make twice as much noise as ever had been heard in the Bronx." Eddie Stanky doubled home a pair of runs. "From here on it was hitting, pitching, running, arguments," Barber recalled, "a slam-bang battle."

With two out, Vic Raschi relieved Newsom. A fastballer from Massachusetts known as the Springfield Rifle, Raschi gave up a single to Robinson. Carl Furillo, batting for Reiser, doubled. By the time the Dodgers finished spinning around the bases the score was Brooklyn 6, New York 0. The jubilant little ballpark was jumping. After a third-inning pitch in the dirt, plate umpire Eddie Rommel picked up the baseball. He was inspecting it for damage when a shout came from the seats: "The ball's all right, ya bum ya!"

DiMaggio and company clawed their way back. With two out in the third, Joe D and Lindell singled in a run apiece. Stirnweiss singled home a fourth-inning run to cut Brooklyn's lead to three. Then the Dodgers struck back with two of their own. It was 9–4 Brooklyn when DiMaggio came up in the fifth. Lindell took a lead off first. DiMaggio timed Hatten's first pitch, striding from his wide stance to launch a drive to left-center. "Joe swings," said CBS TV announcer Bob Edge, "and starts one on a trip to Mars!" His two-run homer might have been a double at Yankee Stadium. In Brooklyn it reached the second deck to trim the Dodger lead to three runs once again.

Hatten was running out of gas. Shotton dispatched Sukeforth to the mound and called for Ralph Branca. The starter and loser of Game One, Branca had made only seven relief appearances all season. Shotton would defend the move by calling him "the best arm I had." The gaunt Branca allowed a sixth-inning run to make the score 9–7. With two out he walked the bases loaded but escaped the inning on a pop-up. The crowd heaved a collective sigh of relief.

Trailing by two, Bucky Harris went to his bullpen ace. He thought his team could score at least two more runs. If Joe Page could hold the Dodgers, the Yankees might quiet the mob and sweep the Series tomorrow.

Jaunty Joe Page owed his role on the club to his manager's long fuse. Back in May, Harris brought DiMaggio's barhopping wingman out of the bullpen after Spec Shea loaded the bases. Page had been nothing much till then. "A starting pitcher who couldn't finish and couldn't win," Barber called him. "But Harris knew he had something, and decided to try him as a relief man." Thinking Page might be a latter-day Firpo Marberry, Bucky watched with pleasure as he wiggled out of the jam. "The Yankees won that game and in discovering Page's relief ability did much toward winning their pennant then and there."

Page retired the Dodgers in the bottom of the sixth. In the visitors' dugout, Harris pointed to Berra. "Get ready. You're hitting for Lollar." Berra had spent the afternoon feeling alone and unloved at the end of the bench. Facing Branca with one away in the seventh, he clubbed a home run over the Schaefer Beer sign atop the scoreboard, the first pinch-hit homer in World Series history.

Shotton stood on the top step of the home dugout in his satin Dodgers jacket, rubbing the stubble on his cheek. With Brooklyn's lead pared to a single run, he sent Sukeforth to the mound again. Sukey took the ball from Branca as Hugh Casey emerged from the bullpen.

The thirty-three-year-old Casey was a Brooklyn character to match just about anyone this side of Branch Rickey. He'd been discovered by Wilbert Robinson, Uncle Robbie himself. In the early '30s, Robinson went on a hunting-and-drinking expedition in Georgia, mainly drinking, when he spotted an overgrown schoolboy flinging stones at whiskey bottles lined up on a fence. Robinson signed him to pitch for the minor-league Atlanta Crackers. After a brief stint with the 1935 Cubs, Casey knocked around the minors for four more seasons before returning to the big leagues. A tall righthander with an ornery streak, he won fifteen games for Brooklyn in 1939. Three years later, during spring training in Havana, he and a couple of teammates went skeet shooting with Ernest Hemingway. The famous novelist invited the players to his house for drinks. Late that night he challenged Casey to a boxing match. The pitcher was putting on his gloves when the author sucker punched him. Casey crashed into a tray full of tumblers and bottles. Then he got back to his feet. As the Dodgers' Billy Herman recalled, "Without saying a word, Casey started hitting him. Really belting him. Casey belted him across some furniture, and there was another crash as Hemingway took a lamp and table down with him. Hemingway was getting angry. He'd no sooner get up than Hugh would knock him down again. Finally, he made a feint with his left hand and kicked Casey in the balls."

Beating up Ernest Hemingway cemented Casey's standing with his teammates, but he didn't make his name with the public until Durocher began using him as a reliever. In 1946 he earned eleven victories and finished a league-leading twenty-seven games with a 1.99 ERA. Known for dousing late-inning rallies, "Fireman Casey" posed for photos in a fire helmet. He opened Hugh Casey's Steak and Chop House and became Brooklyn's favorite saloonkeeper. "Mr. Casey pours a mean drink," the *World-Telegram* reported, "and serves an enticing mess of corn beef and cabbage in his bar and grill." The beer-bellied proprietor bought drinks for the house when Brooklyn clinched the 1947 National League pennant in September. Dodger players and their wives partied past midnight, forming a conga line that spilled out the door onto Flatbush Avenue.

The Ebbets Field fans watching Casey warm up a month later couldn't help recalling his pitch to the Yanks' Tommy Henrich six Octobers ago. That moisturized breaking ball got by catcher Mickey Owen for the passed ball that extinguished Brooklyn's chances in the 1941 Series. The faithful breathed easier when the first Yankee he faced, Page, grounded to short. Then Casey struck out Snuffy Stirnweiss to end the inning. Game Three was now a thoroughly modern bout between the game's best relievers.

Page gave up a double by Spider Jorgensen in the bottom of the seventh. With two out, Jackie Robinson whacked a shot to deep center. DiMaggio, gliding to the ball with his thoroughbred strides, hauled it in to retire the side.

Tommy Henrich led off the eighth. Still leading 9–8, remembering 1941, Casey walked him. Lindell singled to bring DiMaggio up with nobody out. Henrich, the tying run, took a walking lead off second base. Lindell, the lead run, led off first. This was a nightmare in the making for Casey, Shotton, Hilda Chester, the Sym-Phony Band, and everyone else who was pulling for Brooklyn. With the game in the balance, DiMaggio spanked a grounder to second baseman Stanky, who tagged Lindell on the base path. Or did he? Lindell, Harris, and the Yankees would swear he'd missed the tag. But with no replay, second-base umpire Bill McGowan's upraised thumb was all that mattered. Stanky's throw to first beat DiMaggio to complete a double play. McQuinn grounded out to Jackie Robinson to end the inning.

Page retired the Dodgers in the eighth.

In the ninth, with every fan standing and Howling Hilda clanging her bell, Casey got two quick outs on a grounder to first and a fly ball to Dixie Walker. Yogi Berra plodded to the plate. Representing the tying run, Berra smacked a shot up the middle. Casey stabbed at the ball but it bounced off his glove—toward second baseman Stanky, who gobbled it up and threw to Robinson to end the game. Fireman

Casey walked off the mound with his head down. Teammates mobbed him, hugged him, smacked him on the butt and back, and knocked his hat off.

"Hugh Casey and the Dodgers—the toast of Flatbush!" Bob Edge told his tele-viewers.

Ralph Branca greeted his teammates in the clubhouse: "Three to go! Three more to go!" Mild-mannered Burt Shotton grabbed a reporter and shouted, "I feel a lot better than I did yesterday!" Pee Wee Reese hugged Robinson, Dixie Walker, and anyone else who got near him. Casey reported to the trainer's room for a rubdown from assistant trainer John Griffin. "My arm aches all over, every inch of it, but I'll be all right tomorrow," Casey announced as photographers snapped pictures of him and the hobbled Reiser, who lay on the trainer's table with heating pads on his ankle.

Newsmen hunted up superlatives for a Series that had just become a lot more interesting. Game Three was "the most exciting staging" of the "best-of-seven traveling circus." A record 300,665 fans had dialed the special New York Telephone Company number for inning-by-inning updates. To Rickey's delight, ticket sales had added $161,625 to the club's coffers in a single day. Bookies dropped the odds against his team from 6-to-1 to 16-to-5.

"A lowly worm turned in Flatbush yesterday," read John Drebinger's front-page account in the next morning's *Times*, "and in the process kicked up such a terrific uproar that it is unlikely the 33,098 who witnessed the spectacle ever will forget it. Certain it is, no World Series encounter in recent years has produced more slambang thrills."

And he ain't seen nothing yet.

CHAPTER 11

The Twenty-Seventh Out

Larry and Dan Bevens shushed each other on Friday, October 3. They didn't want to wake their father on a day when he was pitching. Like most hurlers, Bill Bevens had a game-day routine. He liked to wake early and linger over breakfast, listening to the radio. He'd shave and shower at home, then drive to the ballpark, leaving about ten thirty in the morning for afternoon home games that started three hours later. But Game Four would be in Brooklyn, so he'd have to start an hour earlier. That meant he had to get up at eight, and his boys knew better than to bug him till then.

"Hush up," nine-year-old Larry told his little brother. They were peeking through the bedroom door at their dad's slumbering form.

"*You* hush up," said five-year-old Dan.

When he woke on the day of the biggest start he'd ever make, Bevens squeezed his right biceps. It felt okay. So far, so good.

The Bevenses rented a three-bedroom flat in Hudson View Gardens at the northwest tip of Manhattan, within earshot of traffic on the George Washington Bridge. Picking at his breakfast, Bev told himself there was nothing to feel sick about. His stomach always roiled before a start. What mattered was, his arm felt strong. After weeks of pains that ranged from a razor digging into his elbow to something more like a toothache in his shoulder, he felt like he could throw a saltshaker through a brick wall.

He shaved, showered, put on a dress shirt and blazer. He kissed Millie good-bye. "See you after," he told her. Waving to the boys, he climbed into a roomy DeSoto Deluxe, on loan for free because he and Rizzuto and several other players had posed for publicity photos at the assembly line: *The Yanks Can't Wait for the 1947 DeSoto!*

Millie and the boys had tickets to Game Four. Millie would be there with the other wives and special guests, but Bill had given their sons' tickets to Al Lightner, a sportswriter friend from Oregon, and Lightner's wife. Larry and Dan didn't mind because they were going to spend the day with a friend whose family had a television.

Bevens drove to the Bronx. He parked the DeSoto in the players' lot at Yankee Stadium and boarded the team bus with Allie Reynolds, his best friend on the club. As the bus rolled south, Bevens thought about the Dodger lineup: Eddie Stanky, Pee Wee Reese, Jackie Robinson, and the rest. His buddy Reynolds had made short work of Brooklyn's hitters in Game Two, but Allie had the good fortune of starting a home game. The stadium was more forgiving than Brooklyn's little bandbox. One hurler said pitching at Ebbets Field was like pitching in a phone booth. Still, Bevens felt ready. Let the Dodgers do the worrying.

Bucky Harris had surprised pundits and fans by making Bevens part of his Series rotation. When Harris announced his four starters at a postseason banquet—"Shea, Reynolds, Newsom, and Bevens"—reporters wondered aloud about the last entry. Bucky said, "Yeah, Bevens. He may pitch the best game of anybody."

In the moments before the game, Bevens joined Dodgers starter Harry Taylor behind the plate to shake hands for the cameras. The fresh-faced Taylor was all smiles. Bevens looked like he was sucking a lemon. The rituals of public relations annoyed him. Why pretend to be friends when he hoped Taylor would fall apart and give up ten runs in the top of the first? Bevens was glad when the formalities were over and he could warm up.

Tommy Henrich asked Joe Page to make himself useful. Henrich wanted to practice catching caroms off the right-field wall. Page was surely nursing a hangover because he was (a) awake and (b) not drinking yet. But he dragged himself to short right field and smacked fungoes over Henrich's head—off the Burma-Shave and Gem Razor signs in right-center; off a billboard advertising Danny Kaye's new movie, *The Secret Life of Walter Mitty*; and off haberdasher Abe Stark's HIT SIGN, WIN SUIT ad under the scoreboard—while Old Reliable got a feel for the angles.

Pete Reiser tried taking batting practice with the Dodger regulars but soon gave up. Reiser limped to the clubhouse, where trainer Doc Wendler examined his broken ankle. "You might as well put on your street clothes," Wendler said. "You can't play."

Reiser said, "Tape it up."

Upstairs, Branch Rickey watched with glee as the stands and aisles filled with Dodger fans. Yesterday's sellout crowd of 33,098 was being surpassed as hundreds more fans bought standing-room tickets. If the Dodgers won today, the World Series would be deadlocked. They'd be two victories from their first Series title. Wait tell next year? Fuhggettabout it, next year was here.

Leading off for the Yankees, Snuffy Stirnweiss drilled Taylor's first pitch for a single to left. Henrich followed with a single. Yogi Berra, back in the lineup, smacked a bullet to first baseman Robinson. Jackie tossed the ball to shortstop Reese to start a double play—and Pee Wee dropped the ball! The *e* in the Schaefer Beer sign lit up. All three runners were safe. The bases were jammed with nobody out as DiMaggio strode to the batter's box.

Hilda's bell was no help to Harry Taylor. He walked DiMaggio to force in a run. Shotton dispatched Sukeforth to take the ball from Taylor, who departed after only eleven pitches. Hal Gregg came in to replace him.

Gregg hailed from Orange County, California, where he'd won

schoolboy bets by "picking" oranges from fifty or sixty paces—firing an orange to knock another off a branch. He reached the majors during the war, facing the cheese champions of wartime lineups. His middling fastballs looked like melons even to them. He won nine games for the 1944 Dodgers, lost sixteen, and led the National League in earned runs allowed, walks, and wild pitches. He'd been worse yet in '47: four wins and five losses with an ugly 5.87 ERA. Shotton used him because he had few options. At least Gregg threw hard.

With the bases full and nobody out, the Yanks' George McQuinn lifted a pop-up to Reese. Billy Johnson then banged into a double play and just like that the inning was over. Brooklyn escaped the first trailing by the lone run Stirnweiss scored.

Bevens walked Eddie Stanky in the bottom of the inning. Stanky danced off first base. Everyone from Flatbush to Timbuktu knew the Dodgers planned to run on Yogi Berra. Bevens flung a sinker to Reese, who ripped it past him into short center field, a sure hit—until Stirnweiss smothered the ball and came up throwing. His peg to first nipped Reese. Like Snuffy himself, the moment would play a little-noticed role in the drama to come.

After a scoreless second, DiMaggio walked with two out in the third. McQuinn dribbled a swinging bunt in front of the plate, and when catcher Bruce Edwards threw the ball away, Joltin' Joe channeled Country Slaughter: he tried to score all the way from first. Dixie Walker charged in from right field, snapped up the ball, and threw home. His throw beat DiMaggio by a country mile—a cherce play that earned Walker a standing ovation from the Ebbets Field crowd. DiMag retrieved his glove and trotted out to his position in center. Expressionless as ever, he was irked. It wasn't like him to get thrown out from here to Canarsie. It looked mortal. And in fact—not that he'd say it—the fault was third-base coach Charlie Dressen's, not his. DiMaggio had glanced toward Dressen as he rounded second base, the way a runner's supposed to, and spotted the coach windmilling his arms, *Go go go!* So he went. Still the fans in the bleachers were calling *him* a dummy. DiMaggio did what he always did: he seethed and went about his business.

In the third, Pete Reiser came out of the tunnel and took a seat in the home dugout. He wasn't sure he could hit on a taped-up broken ankle, but his presence gave Shotton one more option off the bench. Moments later, Robinson lofted a fly ball over third base. Yankee left fielder Johnny Lindell raced in to make a sprawling, tumbling catch. Maybe this was the snakebit Bevens's lucky day. A fourth-inning RBI double by Lindell put New York ahead 2–0. In the last of the fourth, DiMaggio raced deep into center field to haul in Gene Hermanski's blast, preserving the shutout. He twisted his ankle but stayed in the game.

A few miles away in Manhattan, nine-year-old Larry Bevens and his five-year-old brother found something else to watch. "We switched channels to a sci-fi show," Larry remembered seventy years later. Bev's sons could see baseball anytime, but not spaceships.

Brooklyn finally scored in the fifth. Two walks, a bunt, and a fielder's-choice groundout brought home a run without a base hit. A pair of Sym-Phony musicians tap-danced atop the Yankee dugout.

Still leading 2–1, Bevens retired the Dodgers in the sixth and seventh with darting sinkers and curves. "His ball was moving like crazy," Berra recalled. Bevens had walked eight and uncorked a wild pitch, but he'd held Brooklyn hitless through seven innings. "That's when I started thinking about a no-hitter," he said later. "The Dodgers did, too." Nobody had ever thrown a World Series no-hitter. "Every ball they hit, they'd yell from the bench, 'There it goes! There goes your no-hitter!'"

In the eighth, Jackie Robinson grounded out to third. Dixie Walker hit a shot up the middle; Bevens gloved it and flipped to first. Four outs to go.

Snuffy Stirnweiss came to the mound. "Don't worry, Bev. Just make 'em hit the ball," he said.

The batter was Gene Hermanski, whose fourth-inning bomb had sent DiMaggio to the center field wall. Now he stroked one deep to right—a wallop that sent Henrich to the base of the scoreboard, where he jumped for the ball. As *New York Herald Tribune* columnist Red Smith saw the play, "Henrich backed against the board and leaped either four or fourteen feet into the air. He stayed aloft so long he looked like an empty uniform hanging in its locker. When he came down he had the ball." Bevens mopped his brow with the back of his glove. Eight innings in the books, still no hits for the Dodgers.

In the top of the ninth, Stirnweiss singled to lift his Series average to .412. When the Yanks filled the bases with one out, Shotton brought in Fireman Hugh Casey. Tommy Henrich pounded Casey's first pitch back where it came from. Casey stabbed it and threw home to start a double play that kept the score at 2–1. The Dodgers were still in the game.

"Bevens, a strong, silent man from Oregon, held the bats of Brooklyn's Bums more silent than a tomb," one newsman wrote. But the pitcher had felt an ominous ache since the middle innings. He had thrown 120 pitches without surrendering a hit. Now every pitch hurt, and the Dodgers were dead-set on making him throw as many as they could. "Wait him out," Shotton told his hitters. "He's wild. He's tired." According to Red Barber, "Shotton had his hitters taking, taking, taking—making Bevens pitch, pitch pitch."

Bevens not only pitched, he threw harder. After forty wins and thirty-six losses over four big-league campaigns, after leading the club in losses two years in a row, here stood farm boy Floyd Clifford Bevens on the brink of forever, three outs from the first no-hitter in World Series history. He was wild. He was tired. His stomach was full of caterpillars. But he'd be damned if he'd let up before his arm fell off.

Brooklyn catcher Bruce Edwards led off the last of the ninth. Ebbets Field was quiet for once. "Tension silence," Barber called it. "It didn't last long."

Edwards brought the crowd to life, walloping a towering drive to left. Lindell backpedaled until he ran out of room. Then he leaped. Thirty-three thousand fans groaned as he came down with the ball.

Jake Pitler, coaching first base for the Dodgers, flung his cap to the ground in disbelief.

Bevens then walked Carl Furillo. His ninth free pass of the afternoon tied a record for most walks allowed in a World Series game—a footnote to the ongoing no-hitter.

Now Shotton made a mistake. He left Furillo in the game to run the bases. As any Brooklyn schoolboy could tell you, Furillo was to baserunning what Leo Durocher was to modesty. The problem wasn't that he was snail-slow—Skoonj had average wheels. He was no dummy in civilian life, but somehow he was born with the baserunning brain of a mollusk. During the regular season he'd been called out seven times for missing bases, an unofficial world record. Fortunately for the Dodgers, he managed not to wander off first base before Spider Jorgensen hit a pop-up to first baseman George McQuinn.

McQuinn squeezed the ball for the second out. The Yanks were an out away from taking a 3-1 lead in the Series. Bevens was an out away from a feat the sport would never forget.

Shotton belatedly replaced Furillo, sending Al Gionfriddo to run for Skoonj. No harm done. With Fireman Casey due to bat with two out, the manager looked down the Dodger bench for a pinch hitter. He saw Cookie Lavagetto, utility man Eddie Miksis, backup catcher Gil Hodges . . . and Pete Reiser.

Shotton didn't think much of Reiser. Pistol Pete had been a shell of his former self since cracking his skull in June. And he was a Durocher man. As Shotton well knew, Reiser and Ralph Branca fed unflattering quotes about him to the *Daily News*' Dick Young, portraying Shotton as Branch Rickey's flunky. Young mocked the pennant-winning skipper as "K.O.B.S.," short for Kindly Old Burt Shotton. Some managers would have buried a guy like Reiser at the end of the bench. Not Shotton, who might refer to Reiser and Branca in private as a couple of shits, but would pinch-hit the devil himself if he thought Lucifer could get on base.

He stared at Reiser. "Ain't you going to volunteer?"

It was a sharp move by old Barney. Reiser, sitting there with mummy bandages on his ankle, could decline. He could say, "I'm hurt." Doc Wendler would agree. But that wouldn't be Reiser, and Shotton knew it.

Reiser said, "I'm ready."

The decibel level at Ebbets Field went off the scale as he hobbled to the plate. The Mutual Radio broadcast team had hung a microphone from the upper deck to catch crowd noise, the better to give listeners a sense of being at the game. At this point the fans' roar rose until the crowd-noise mic drowned out the announcers. An engineer switched it off. Barber, Mel Allen, and CBS TV's Bob Edge still had to shout over a din like no other they'd heard at a ballgame.

Gionfriddo took a three-step lead off first base. Bevens, fighting his control, ran the count to Reiser to two balls and a strike. He was rubbing up the ball when Shotton took a do-or-die gamble: he flashed Little Al the steal sign.

Kindly bold Burt Shotton was taking his team's fate in his creased hands. By sending the runner, he risked ridicule and worse. If Gionfriddo gets thrown out, Bevens's no-hitter is complete and Brooklyn's buried in the Series, down three games to one. If Gionfriddo gets thrown out, a Series game ends on the worst baserunning blunder since Babe Ruth got caught stealing with two down in the ninth to end the 1926 Series. Ruth was the goat that October, but if Yogi Berra throws Gionfriddo out, it won't be the Flea wearing goat horns, it'll be Shotton.

Head down, baggy uniform flapping, Gionfriddo was halfway to second when Berra received Bevens's fastball. Yogi sprang from his crouch and gunned a near-perfect peg to Rizzuto at second. The throw was a little high, just over belt level, drifting a bit toward first base. Gionfriddo made a headfirst dive for the bag. Rizzuto snapped the ball from the air and swiped at the runner's foot. In time? Second-base umpire Babe Pinelli stuck out his arms: *Safe!* Rizzuto jumped like he'd stepped on the third rail—*Whaddya mean safe?* The Scooter waved at the sky, but there was no help from the heavens. Maybe his tag caught the runner's heel, maybe not. History is in the details:

Pinelli's call was final. Gionfriddo was safe. The Dodgers had sneaked the tying run into scoring position.

The pitch Gionfriddo stole on was called a ball. Now it was Bucky Harris's turn to risk everything. With a 3-1 count to Reiser, he held up four fingers.

Conventional wisdom says a manager never puts the potential winning run on base. "Harris violated all ten commandments of the dugout by ordering Bevens to walk Reiser," Red Smith wrote. But with a 2–1 lead and first base open, Harris wasn't going to let a power hitter beat him. He knew Reiser was the last left-handed batter on the Dodgers' bench, a fellow who might plant his still-healthy right ankle and send a game-winning homer over the Burma-Shave billboard. By going against the book, risking months and maybe years of second-guessing, Bucky was a forerunner of modern managers who use advanced metrics to back up daring decisions. But all he had was experience and intuition.

Yogi Berra stood up, his mitt hand extended. Bevens lobbed ball four. His only intentional pass of the day broke the Series record for walks in a game, but nobody would remember the walks if he got one more out. With Gionfriddo at second and Reiser limping to first, Bill Bevens was still twenty-six twenty-sevenths of the way to the first no-hitter in World Series history.

This time Shotton made the right substitution immediately: he sent speedy Eddie Miksis to pinch-run for Reiser. Now the players were in their places for the final act: Gionfriddo leading off second and Miksis leading off first; second baseman Stirnweiss pounding his glove; DiMaggio watching calmly from center field; Bevens breathing hard on the mound; and Eddie Stanky waving a bat on his way to the plate.

Stanky may have been Brooklyn's last hope, but with the tying run at second he was a solid hope. A slap hitter with a penchant for getting on base, the hard-nosed Philadelphian had twice led the National League in walks, once in on-base percentage. His .252 regular-season average was a disappointment, but in June he'd broken up a no-hitter by the Reds' Ewell Blackwell. On this day he'd already reached base twice in three trips. So why was the Brat cursing and pounding his bat on the ground? Because Shotton was calling him back to the dugout. In the third all-in managerial gambit of the inning, Shotton sent Cookie Lavagetto to bat for the Brat.

The move left reporters and most of the Dodgers scratching their heads. Stanky had been their leadoff man all year while Cookie warmed the bench. He and Cookie both batted right-handed, so there was no platoon advantage in play. Stanky had made 680 trips to the plate and Shotton had pinch-hit for him once. Once! He had rapped 141 hits and scored 97 runs to Cookie's 18 hits and 6 runs. Even Lavagetto wondered what the manager was thinking. "He had to tell me twice he wanted me to go up and hit," Cookie recalled.

Shotton never explained his reasoning. There was no explaining except to say that he was less methodical than Bucky Harris. Less analytical, but no less convinced that he knew how to win the game. He was playing a hunch.

Jackie Robinson and the other Dodgers crowded the top step of their dugout to see how it turned out.

⚾

In a bungalow on Fifty-Second Street in Oakland, Mary Lavagetto turned up the radio. Cookie's wife had been nursing their first child, Michael, when she dozed off. Cookie hadn't met the baby yet. With the World Series coming up and Oakland a four-day train ride from Brooklyn, there wasn't time. Mary had been listening to the Mutual Radio broadcast, hoping her Harry might get an at-bat. She woke just in time to hear Red Barber's voice: "Lavagetto, batting for Stanky." Mary sat up straight. She began saying Hail Marys under her breath.

In Flatbush, Cookie swung two Louisville Sluggers on his way to the plate, tossing one away so that the other would feel lighter. Bevens, his jersey dark with sweat, peered in for a sign from Yogi Berra. He went into his stretch, shooting a glance toward Gionfriddo at second.

Cookie had never faced Bill Bevens. He knew the guy threw hard, but that was about it. He was hoping to see a fastball out over the plate. Cookie's bum shoulder and stale reflexes made it almost impossible for him to put solid contact on hard stuff inside. His plan was the same as for any other at-bat: fight off anything on his hands, jump at a curve or a fastball outside. In the *Times*' story, "The swarthy-complexioned veteran swung viciously through the first pitch."

And came up empty. Bevens was one strike closer to a no-hitter. He had thrown 136 pitches so far. He'd throw 136 more if that's what it took, but 137 would get the job done if the next one was good enough.

Berra called for another fastball.

Bevens nodded.

Berra would claim that the scouting report on Lavagetto—a thin one, given Cookie's marginal role—called for pitching him high and outside. But that was wrong. The rookie catcher may have been covering his ass, or his pitcher's. Maybe he misremembered. As Yogi himself might have put it, "I can't remember how much I forgot." In fact, Harris sent third-base coach Dressen to the mound to remind Bevens and Berra: *Bust this guy with fastballs on his hands.* Their scouting report was correct. Cookie could track and smack a curveball the way he used to swat flies in his father's wine room, and he could still catch up with a fastball if you let him extend his arms, but he had a hole in his swing the size of a mailbox. "I couldn't get around on a fastball inside," he admitted later. That's why the Yankees had their outfielders—Lindell in left, DiMaggio in center, Henrich in right—shaded toward left field. They figured Cookie would pull Bevens's inside pitch if he happened to hit it.

Bevens stretched and fired, his jaw straining, eyes clamped shut with effort as he released the pitch. He was aiming inside, but his fastball sailed high and away.

Cookie could take it for ball one, but he wasn't thinking of working the count. Heart pumping a mile a minute, eyes tracking the pitch while a corner of his head said a Hail Mary, he swung. This time he connected. In newsreels his bat makes a sound like a finger snap as the ball takes off toward the right-field fence.

With two out, Gionfriddo and Miksis took off at top speed. Thirty-three thousand fans, thousands more watching TV, and millions leaning toward their radios waited for the last out as Henrich chased the ball to the right-field wall. At first Bevens thought it was just a long fly ball, "but it kept carrying. I was numb for a second, watching the ball. You start to say things you probably shouldn't."

Henrich had a decision to make. He could play the carom, maybe keep the man on first from scoring, or he could go for the catch—save the game and Bevens's no-hitter. He went for the catch.

The ball carried over him. Bevens's shoulders slumped as Cookie's liner hit the wall, bounced off Henrich's chest, and fell at his feet. Gionfriddo raced around third to tie the score. A moment later, Miksis slid home to win the game. Red Barber called the sound that followed "the biggest explosion of noise in the history of Brooklyn."

The Dodgers mobbed Lavagetto. Fans poured from the stands to join the celebration. In the broadcast booth, Barber reverted to his Mississippi roots: "Well, I'll be a suck-egg mule!"

His teammates carried Cookie down the tunnel to their clubhouse. "After five mad minutes of mayhem," the *Daily News* reported, "a disheveled Italian-American guy was dumped in front of his locker, tears in his eyes and a mile-wide grin on his usually impassive face."

Jackie Robinson deadpanned, "We had 'em all the way."

Pee Wee Reese feigned sympathy for Bevens. "I was sorry for the guy," he hollered. "It broke my heart square in two when I saw those runs crossing the plate!"

Cookie stripped off his itchy jersey. Doused in beer, he fought his way through reporters and teammates to clasp Shotton's hand. "I want to tell you how much I appreciate the chance you gave me!" he said.

Shotton led his pinch hitter to a rotary telephone in the manager's office. Reporters crowded around as Cookie dialed his home number. He yelled, "Mary! Did you hear what happened, honey?"

"I did!" she said. "I'm so proud of you!"

Cookie laughed. "These darned Brooklyn fans ripped my clothes to pieces! They've ruined my uniform! How's our baby?"

"We're both so proud!"

"Mister Shotton told me to talk all I wanted. He said this phone bill would be on the club!"

Branch Rickey spent ten minutes collecting his thoughts before he spoke to reporters. "Speed won it," he said, congratulating himself for acquiring base-stealer Gionfriddo. Rickey praised Hugh Casey, who had thrown a single pitch, the double-play ball to Henrich in the top of the ninth, to become the winning pitcher. Six years after losing back-to-back games in the '41 Series, Casey had just won two Series games in twenty-four hours.

"The unhappiest man in Brooklyn is sitting in the far end of the press box," Red Smith wrote for the *Herald Tribune*. "The 'v' on his typewriter is broken. He can't write *Lavagetto* or *Bevens*."

A few seats from Smith on press row, the *Times*' Arthur Daley wrote, "A demented Hollywood scenarist in the final stages of delirium tremens wouldn't have dared produce a script as utterly fantastic as the stark drama unfolded before the eyes of the Flatbush faithful at Ebbets Field. As one stunned and incredulous press-box tenant remarked, 'Don't bother writing about it, because no one will believe you anyway.'" Daley then turned his gaze to the losing pitcher. "Floyd (Bill) Bevens has been rebuffed so often by Lady Luck during his major league career that it looked like a mismatch from the start. But the old gal waited until the ninth inning to play on him the shabbiest trick of all. The strapping right-hander from Oregon was just about to step into the Hall of Fame when the prankish Miss slyly stuck out her foot and tripped him."

Photographers caught an indelible image: Bevens leaving the field with his head down, DiMaggio a step behind.

Once the Yankees had all passed through the tunnel to the clubhouse, Bucky Harris locked the door. Reporters waited twenty minutes while the visitors absorbed their sudden defeat. According to the *Daily News*' Dick Young, "Bevens buried his face in his hands, fought back the bigger tears that a strong man can't release." But Young saw no such thing. He wasn't there.

When Bucky opened his clubhouse, he deflected questions about Bevens's last pitch. "This was a rough one to lose," he said. "I expect you boys will question my judgment in ordering that pass to Reiser in the ninth, putting the winning run on. Well, I'd do it again tomorrow. I'm not going to let him whack one over the fence. I suppose it was against baseball legend to order that pass, but the second guess is always the best one, and I get only one."

While Bucky fielded questions, the losing pitcher escaped into a city abuzz with talk of the Miracle of Flatbush.

Bevens met Millie and their friends the Lightners at a tavern on the Upper West Side. There was a television over the bar. The owner and a profitable crowd had watched the game, pulling for Bevens to throw a no-hitter. Now the place was nearly empty. When the pitcher himself showed up, the owner did a double take.

"Aren't you . . . ?"

Bevens nodded. "Yeah."

The barkeep shooed a couple of drinkers out the door. "Closing for a private party," he said. With the bar to themselves, the Bevenses and Lightners settled in. Bevens described how he'd felt watching Lavagetto's double hit the wall: like a guy who'd just dropped ten stories in an elevator. "My heart and brains and everything went right down to my spikes." Before long, though, they were laughing about old times in Oregon. This was good medicine for Bev, who needed some. His arm hurt so much that he couldn't imagine pitching anytime soon.

CHAPTER 12

First and Second Guesses

The diocese of Flatbush practically canonized Cookie Lavagetto after Game Four. A *Brooklyn Eagle* headline read NOW WE'RE COOKING. Another promised MORE MIRACLES TODAY. Hy Turkin of the *Daily News* dubbed Cookie the Emperor of Brooklyn. "There was talk of changing the name of Ebbets Field to the Cookie Jar," he wrote. "Gladys Goodding, organist at the park, made 'Lookie Lookie, Here Comes Cookie' the theme song of the day." Goodding also proved she knew the hero's given name with a bouncy rendition of "I'm Just Wild About Harry."

Branch Rickey cast a beatific gaze from his upstairs office, watching a Saturday crowd fill the ballpark to capacity and beyond. The Dodgers were about to shatter their attendance record for the third day in a row, with more than a thousand standing-room fans crowding through the turnstiles. The *Mirror* reported that the Bums "will have to refund over $3,000,000 for ticket orders they couldn't fill."

Lavagetto got out of a cab within shouting distance of the players' entrance. Still it took him a few minutes to work his way through all the Cookie-lovers on his way to the door, and then through ranks of reporters and photographers to get to his locker. For one day he knew how it felt to be DiMaggio. But DiMaggio never handed out cigars to the boys on press row. That's what Cookie did to celebrate the birth of the baby everyone was asking him about. Somebody handed him a photo of his wife in the hospital with baby Michael. A couple of writers figured it made a better story if the baby had been born yesterday, within minutes of the game-breaking double, rather than two weeks ago. Cookie went along. Why not? He said yeah, the timing was amazing. He led a press parade to the dugout, where he knelt by the bat rack and posed with the photo of Mary and baby Michael, grinning like a lottery winner. The deputy mayor of Oakland, in town for the Series, presented him with a watch in honor of yesterday's timely hit.

Cookie knocked three batting-practice pitches over the left-field wall to the tune of "Hey, Lookie Lookie," flashing his lopsided grin between swings. Al Gionfriddo, whose stolen base gave Cookie a chance to win Game Four, went unnoticed until a reporter tracked him down. The newsman pointed out that Gionfriddo had swiped only two bags all season. Al said, "So what? I was safe on the big one."

Larry MacPhail blamed the previous day's defeat on his club's pitcher and catcher. Agreeing with Rickey for the moment, he said, "The game was lost because of Gionfriddo's steal. Bevens didn't hold him close enough, and Berra made a high throw."

Berra felt lousy enough already. He'd spent a long night thinking back on the ninth-inning throw that could have ended the game. The papers said manager Harris was sure to bench him. If not, according to the *Times*, "Yogi Berra will have to take out burglary insurance. The Brooks have stolen five bases on him in only three games."

Everybody knew who Harris would send to the mound today. Spec Shea, the winning pitcher in Game One, was ready to go after his usual three days' rest. The sturdy rookie came from Naugatuck, Connecticut, a town whose factories churned out Keds sneakers and Mounds candy bars. Nicknamed the Naugatuck Nugget, he'd seen action as an army air corpsman a few days after D-day. He was lugging cans of gasoline up the beach at Normandy when a German sniper's bullet struck a can and set his clothes afire. After months in a burn unit, Shea came home mostly unscarred but differently freckled. He wasn't the type to fret about World Series pressure.

He had paid close attention to Bevens's outing. Before Game Five, Shea told the veteran, "Bev, I'm going to get 'em back for you." If so, it would be with a different catcher. Harris was indeed benching Berra as well as Game Three catcher Sherm Lollar in favor of the slow, injury-prone Aaron Robinson.

Shotton played his pitching choice close to the vest, as usual. His secrecy left Harris no choice but to prepare two lineup cards, one to face a right-handed starter and one for a lefty. Whether Shotton was undecided or just wanted to keep the Yankees guessing was anyone's guess. He enjoyed putting the press and even his own team on edge. While never the strategist Harris was, Brooklyn's manager could be canny about playing the angles. More of a hunch player than Harris, Shotton may have felt more confident than ever after his ninth-inning moves paid off in Game Four.

He had two likely candidates to start Game Five: Ralph Branca, starter and loser in the first game but still a twenty-one-game winner; and Game Two loser Vic Lombardi, a twelve-game winner with a 2.99 earned run average. That morning Shotton ambled into the clubhouse and hung up his topcoat. He peered at the players through his gold-rimmed granny glasses. Less than two hours to game time and they still didn't know who would make the start.

Shotton walked past Branca, so it looked like Ralph wasn't getting the call. Must be Lombardi. But it wasn't—Shotton passed Lombardi and made his way to Rex Barney. Five-game winner Rex Barney with his 4.75 ERA. "You're starting," he told Barney.

The others were surprised but not *that* surprised. As one writer noted, "They had shaken their heads at Shotton's moves all year." Ninety minutes later, the Dodgers jogged onto their home field for the last time in 1947. The name of today's pitcher came as a surprise to fans and even to public-address announcer Tex Rickards, who announced the lineups from a folding chair at the end of the home dugout. Known for the occasional malaprop—he once asked patrons who had hung their coats from a front-row railing, *"Will the fans sitting down the foul lines please remove their clothes?"*—Rickards tapped his microphone and announced the home nine without a hitch: *"Number twelve, Eddie Stanky, second base. Number one, Pee Wee Reese, shortstop. Number forty-two, Jackie Robinson, first base . . . ,"* all the way to *"Number twenty-six, Rex Barney, the pitcher."*

A good-natured Nebraskan, Barney always swore he loved Brooklyn even more than Omaha. "The Dodgers, Ebbets Field, and baseball was the greatest triple play God ever executed," he said. "If a player didn't fall in love with Ebbets Field, there had to be something wrong with him." Scatter-armed Rex had to hope the crowd would love him back after today.

Organist Goodding played the jolly intro to "Follow the Dodgers" as the team finished its warm-ups. The fans stood and sang about the boys of Brooklyn, their beloved underdogs, dem bums, who deserved a hooray as they took the field against the Yanks.

⚾

Rex Barney and Spec Shea were ready. Shea wanted to avenge Bevens's loss and give the Yankees a three-games-to-two advantage. Barney wanted to keep his fastballs near the strike zone and do the same for Brooklyn. They squared off on a day of sharp turns and managerial gambles.

⚾

Snuffy Stirnweiss drew a walk to open the game. After Henrich doubled, Barney walked Lindell to bring up DiMaggio with none out and the bases full. The kid was already fighting his control.

Shotton turned to Clyde Sukeforth. "Sukey, go talk to him."

Sukeforth trotted to the mound. "Nothing to worry about," he told Barney. "Just strike this bum out and get the next one to hit into a double play."

Barney got two quick strikes on DiMaggio, who would tell friends that Barney's heater was quicker than Feller's. The next fastball came in on his hands. DiMaggio swung through it for strike three. George McQuinn tapped a one-hopper to the mound for the second out. And then Barney fanned Billy Johnson to get out of the inning.

In the second, Dixie Walker ripped a liner over second. Stirnweiss leaped, reached for the sky, and snagged the ball in the webbing of his glove—another highlight for the defensive star of the Series so far. Spec Shea proceeded to mow down eight of the next nine Dodgers to take a shutout into the fifth. He also drove in the game's first run, yanking Barney's fastball to left for a single that made the score Naugatuck Nugget 1, Rapid Rex 0.

In the fifth, Barney faced DiMaggio for the third time. After striking out in the first and grounding into a rally-killing double play in the third, Joltin' Joe must have been frustrated. He timed a Barney fastball, connecting with a bang that was audible a block away. The ball traced a long arc to the upper deck, landing near the spot where his Game Three homer had come down. DiMaggio rounded the bases poker-faced as ever.

A batter later, Barney walked Johnson without throwing a strike. "He's wild as a hungry chicken hawk," Red Barber told Mutual Radio listeners. The Brooklyn starter had allowed only two runs on two hits but had already walked nine, threatening Bevens's day-old Series record for walks—and it was only the fifth inning. Barber said the Dodgers were "in the pickle vat again."

Shotton said, "Go get him, Sukey."

He brought in Joe Hatten, the curveballer who had lost Game Three in scattershot fashion. Fittingly enough in this screwball of a Series, Hatten proved untouchable for an inning and a third.

Hatten's spot in the batting order came around in the sixth, and Shotton sent Al Gionfriddo to bat for him. Another hunch. With left-handed Pete Reiser and Arky Vaughan available, plus Lavagetto and Gil Hodges from the right side, he chose Little Al, a .175 hitter.

It worked. Gionfriddo drew a walk. An out later, Reese worked a full-count walk of his own. A minute after that, Robinson whipped his bat at a fastball and shot it up the middle. "Jackie Robinson whistled a single over the button of Shea's cap," said Barber. "Gionfriddo scores and it's Yankees 2, Dodgers 1." Reese tested center fielder DiMaggio's arm, beating Joe's throw to third base as Robinson cruised into second.

That left a choice for Bucky Harris. Shea looked wobbly. The Dodgers had Reese, the potential tying run, on third and Robinson leading off second, twitching his shoulders, ready to run. Coming to bat was cleanup man Dixie Walker, the number-one cherce of thirty-three thousand fanatical fans.

Shea rubbed up the ball. Would Harris send him to the showers? Not yet. Bucky subscribed to the old saying, Sometimes the best move is no move.

Walker popped out to third. Had the Yankees dodged a bullet? Not yet. With two out, Gene Hermanski leaned into a slider from Shea and lined it to center. Reese and Robinson took off, but DiMaggio glided into the ball's path and gloved it for the third out.

Still nursing a one-run lead, Shea walked Bruce Edwards to lead off the seventh. At this point the book says bunt. Brooklyn needed to get Edwards into scoring position. But the batter, Carl Furillo, was a free swinger, less than adept at dropping bunts. This time Shotton went by the book. He flashed the bunt sign. Furillo tried, but fouled off two weak attempts. With two strikes he swung away and lifted a lazy fly to DiMaggio. An out later, craggy old Arky Vaughan stroked a pinch-hit double, sending Edwards to third. With two out and runners at second and third, Shotton sent Reiser up to hit for Eddie Stanky. Poor Stanky, yanked at a key spot for the second day in a row, stalked to the bench, looking like he could chew bullets.

Shotton's move made no tactical sense. With first base open, he should have expected the Yankees to walk Reiser. A day after Bucky Harris defended his intentional pass to Pistol Pete—"I'd do it again tomorrow"—he did it again today. By using Reiser now, Shotton had lost the pinch hitter the Yankees feared most.

With the bases full, Reese worked the count full as well. Shea fired a borderline pitch. Pee Wee gave it a long look and started toward first while Edwards trotted home. Just then, umpire Bill McGowan waved his thumb. *Stee-rike!* Instead of a 2–2 tie, New York still led 2–1.

In the eighth, still trailing by the margin of DiMaggio's fifth-inning homer, Shotton turned to his fireman. Hugh Casey, making his fourth relief appearance in five Series games, welcomed the chance.

Casey planned to give the Yankees the Hemingway treatment: punch them out. With a runner at third and two out, he struck out Snuffy Stirnweiss.

Shea answered with a one-two-three eighth of his own.

Tommy Henrich led off the top of the ninth against Casey. The Fireman blinked his ice-blue eyes, looking in for a sign. *Fastball.* Henrich fought it off, sending a bouncer to second—Eddie Stanky's position. But Shotton had pinch-hit for Stanky, and backup infielder Eddie Miksis booted the ball. One on, none out. When Lindell tried to bunt the runner over, Casey made matters worse by buzzing him under the chin. The ball nicked Lindell on the arm. Two on, none out, DiMaggio coming up, Dodger fans holding their breath.

Joe D planted his front foot and swung for the bleachers but hit the top half of Casey's fastball. Reese scooped up the resulting grounder and started a double play. DiMaggio's line on the day: strike-out, two double plays, homer. But Casey wasn't out of the woods yet. Henrich had advanced to third on the play. Just as in 1941, Old Reliable kept finding his way into key Series moments. When Casey bounced a breaking ball that skipped past the catcher, Henrich broke for the plate. Casey charged off the mound as Bruce Edwards ran the ball down, spun, and threw. Pitcher, runner, and baseball converged at the plate, with umpire McGowan circling sideways for a better look.

Henrich came barreling down the third-base line. Casey blocked the plate and Henrich crashed into him, trying to knock the ball loose.

Catch, tag, thumb. McGowan cried, *"Yer out!"*

The score was still New York 2, Brooklyn 1. Casey gave Henrich a tap with his glove to say, *Good close play.*

Bucky Harris had Joe Page warming up as Shea pitched the last of the ninth. Edwards led off with a single, and Shotton sent pitcher Vic Lombardi to run for the slow-footed catcher. Passed over as the Dodgers' starter, Lombardi had a chance to tie the game on the bases.

Harris stood in the dugout in his Yankee pinstripes, trim and tense. Shotton stood in the Dodger dugout in his jacket and bow tie. Shotton had Carl Furillo coming up next. Furillo again! The situation—man on first, nobody out, home team down by a run— demanded a bunt to get the runner to second. Skoonj couldn't bunt, but Shotton let him try again.

This time he bunted a ten-hopper toward the pitcher. Shea speared it and threw to first while Lombardi carried the tying run to second base.

Spider Jorgensen socked a fly to right that took off like Cookie's famous double, but this one didn't carry. Henrich grabbed it near the *Walter Mitty* sign. Two away now, the Yankees an out from a 2–1 victory, the Dodgers a single from tying the score. Just like yesterday.

Shotton chose Cookie Lavagetto to bat for Casey. Of course. Once again Enrico Atillio Lavagetto would be the Dodgers' last hope. Again Cookie swung two bats on his way to the plate. Gladys Goodding played "Hey, Lookie Lookie" while the crowd stood and cheered.

Harris left Spec Shea in the game. He was asking for a thousand second guesses. Twenty-four hours after Lavagetto had spoiled Bevens's no-hitter, Bucky risked letting him beat Shea while Page waited in the bullpen. Hadn't he said he'd use Page every game if he needed him?

It was a close call, Bucky said later. He stuck with Shea because the Yankees thought they knew how to pitch Lavagetto.

They knew he couldn't get around an inside fastball. Bevens had missed his spot, that's all. Shea may have thrown eight and two-thirds innings under constant pressure, but Harris thought he had enough left to get Cookie.

Millions listened on Mutual Radio. Al Gionfriddo was one of them. The moment found him on a wooden stool in the clubhouse, listening to the game. After pinch-running in the sixth, Gionfriddo had been taken out of the game. Later he went to stow his glove in his locker and got transfixed by the radio broadcast. He wasn't alone—several sportswriters milled around, waiting to gather postgame quotes. In those days reporters were allowed in the clubhouse even while games were under way. They all heard Mel Allen's voice calling the game. "*Here's Lavagetto,*" Allen said.

"Write down a home run," Gionfriddo told the writers. They asked if he was serious. Al said hell yes. "Cookie's gonna hit one, mark my words."

Cookie ran the count to two and one. Then he took a slider just off the plate. Now Shea had to throw him a strike. If he walked the winning run to first, Harris was sure to bring Page in. If Shea wanted to finish the game, he had to retire Lavagetto.

Cookie guessed slider. "They want me to hit the ball on the ground," he thought. So he leaned toward the plate, looking for a breaking ball.

Shea delivered it. A mid-eighties slider, down and away, just as Cookie expected. He strode into it, swinging hard.

"I got my pitch," he said later, "and fouled it off."

Now the count was full. Shea threw a curve this time. A high, slow one. A mistake. Page would have zipped a fastball under Lavagetto's creaky wrists, not a blooper like this. Cookie swung even harder this time but mistimed his cut. He swung right through the pitch, falling back on his heels as McGowan waved his thumb. "Yer out!"

Shea danced what the *Times* called "a jig of joy" on the mound as the Yankees ran to mob him.

DiMaggio wrapped his arms around Shea and planted a smooch on his cheek. "You pitched a helluva game!" the Yankee Clipper told him.

Manager Harris shook hands all around. He said he was looking forward to a good night's sleep. "Going down to the last pitch is too much wear and tear on the nerves," he said.

Cookie tore off his jersey. A few hours ago he was Emperor of Brooklyn. Now the usually sunny veteran frowned at the floor. He told reporters he was a dummy who shoulda laid off Shea's full-count curve. "You're a hero one day, a bum the next," he said. "The toast of the world one afternoon, forgotten the next."

Stanky sat nearby, steaming. The Brat blamed Furillo for failing to bunt in the seventh. If Skoonj got that bunt down, "We'd still be playing, tied at two all." The writers took that quote to the manager's office, where Shotton shot it down. "If Furillo bunted Edwards over, how do you know Vaughan would have gotten the same pitch from Shea that he got when he doubled?" Every ballgame was a forest of branching possibilities; he wasn't going to revisit every decision tree. He had Game Six to think about.

"So who's starting for you?" somebody asked. "Branca?"

"You can be sure we'll have someone on the mound," Shotton said. "Everybody will know who he is when he starts warming up."

Custodians swept the stands for the last time before Ebbets Field shut down for the year. The biggest crowd in Brooklyn's baseball history dispersed, thousands of them filing out through the center field gates. A few headed straight for the Bronx.

At seven that evening, fans began lining up at 161st Street and

River Avenue, the bleacher gate at Yankee Stadium. First in line was Joseph Smith, a twenty-three-year-old Dodger fan with blankets under his arm. He would sleep on the concrete that night and claim his four-dollar ticket in the morning. Smith told a reporter that the Dodgers were a lock to win Game Six and force a deciding game on Monday. No doubt about it—especially if they got some pitching tomorrow. Brooklyn needed a starting pitcher to go at least five innings, a job none of them had been up to in the first five games. Preferably a starting pitcher who wouldn't walk so many. As every skipper from Burt Shotton to Wilbert Robinson to Connie Mack could tell you, walks aged managers but weren't always fatal.

"They don't always murder you," Shotton told the *Times*' Arthur Daley. "We had a game with St. Louis when Howie Pollet allowed ten hits, gave nine walks and still won, 3 to 1." Still, Daley noted the belief that there was "nothing more pestiferous" than walks. He recounted an old tale about George Stallings, the manager of the "Miracle Braves" of 1914. Years later, Gentleman George fell into a coma. According to Daley, "Learned doctors gathered around him. 'I can't understand it,' said one. 'There seems to be nothing wrong with him. What is it that's killing him?' Thereupon Stallings sat up straight on the bed and said, 'Bases on balls.' Then he relapsed into a coma and died."

CHAPTER 13

The Robbery

Joe DiMaggio swung and the ball took off like a bullet. With
two out in the sixth, the Dodgers were clinging to a three-run lead.
Substitute outfielder Al Gionfriddo put his head down and took off
after it. He got a quick jump on the ball but it looked a mile off, climbing toward the left-field bleachers while tens of thousands of Yankees fans cheered it on its way.

DiMaggio's blast marked another decision point in a World Series
fat with them. The *Times* would call Game Six one of the most extraordinary ever played—right up there with Games Four and Five. A
homer off DiMaggio's long, heavy Louisville Slugger would tie another
nail-biter that had reporters racking their noggins for adjectives they
hadn't used yesterday and the day before that.

Gionfriddo was fast but there were limits. He couldn't hurdle the
gate to the Yankee bullpen, where the ball was headed, to grab it
before it started bouncing around in there. All he could do was turn
his back to the plate and run.

Earlier that day, bleacher fan Joseph Smith and 74,064 others filled the arena Red Barber described as "vast, menacing, flag-draped, triple-decked Yankee Stadium." The throng broke the all-time attendance record the Game One crowd had set. Brooklyn fans endured a barrage of Bronx cheers from the Yankee faithful. Some carried copies of the *Brooklyn Eagle* with its reassuring headlines CALM YOURSELVES! and WE'LL TIE IT UP AGAIN. Not far from Smith sat a thirteen-year-old from Yonkers, David Halberstam, who would grow up to write several of the century's most important books. "It was October 5, 1947, and I was in the Yankee Stadium bleachers," he remembered. Young Halberstam's ticket cost only $4; the average ticket price was $5.31.

Shotton made the first move on this sunny Sunday, selecting left-hander Vic Lombardi over Ralph Branca to make his second start of the Series. Branca, the team's ace, was getting tired of being jerked around. The manager's choice made no sense to him or to most of the Dodgers, but Lombardi made old Burt look prescient by sailing through the first two innings.

In the third, back-to-back doubles by Jackie Robinson and Dixie Walker helped give Brooklyn a 4–0 lead, chasing Allie Reynolds to the showers. Then the empire struck back. Catcher Sherm Lollar, starting again while Yogi Berra cooled his heels on the bench, doubled. Lombardi wild-pitched him to third. Third baseman Spider Jorgensen then booted Snuffy Stirnweiss's grounder, and Lollar scored the Yanks' first run. Shotton did his damnedest to look calm while squeezing the life out of a rolled-up scorecard. Errors gave him indigestion. Handing a club like the Yankees an extra out was asking for trouble. Sure enough, the next five batters went single, single, single, single, single. Lombardi allowed the first three and got a quick hook for it. In came tall, gaunt Branca, looking as jolly as an undertaker. He gave up the next two singles and the score was 4–4.

Maybe Brooklyn was bound to lose. Dodger fans didn't want to think so, but they had no evidence to the contrary. Many belonged to the Society for the Prevention of Disparaging Remarks about Brooklyn, whose half a million members included newsmen Damon Runyon and Walter Winchell, *A Tree Grows in Brooklyn* author Betty Smith, and President Truman. They believed that if anybody was going to lip off about the bumbling Bums, it ought to be them. Some told an old joke about a Dodger fan who left a game early. His buddy yelled, "Where ya going? The Bums got three men on base," and the first fan said, "Oh yeah? Which base?" Others told the true story of the time the beloved Wilbert Robinson benched the future Hall of Famer Max Carey to play a rookie, Oscar Roettger. When writers asked Uncle Robbie how to spell Roettger's name, he sputtered and finally said, "Oh hell, let Carey play!"

The fourth inning brought more plot twists. After an RBI single during the Yankees' third-inning rally, outfielder Johnny Lindell told Bucky Harris he couldn't go on. "Bucky, I'm hurting." Only the two of them knew Lindell was playing with a broken rib. He'd cracked it trying to break up a double play the day before. He couldn't breathe without wincing. Harris sent Berra to replace him in the outfield.

An inning later, Branca allowed another pair of singles. Berra followed with a shot over first base to put New York ahead 5–4. The Bronx Bombers had nibbled their way out of a four-run hole with a double, an error, and eight singles.

With a lead to protect, Harris had his closer warm up. It was only the fifth inning, but Joe Page was rested. Why wait, when every out was a nail in the coffin Bucky was measuring for kindly old Burt?

And so Page came in to face the dangerous Dixie Walker, with one out in the fifth. Walker struck out. A pop-up ended the inning. With Page on the mound and shadows creeping over the diamond, Harris allowed himself to think an hour ahead. He had the right team, the right pitcher, a one-run lead—a clear path to a second World Series title, his first since he was Washington's wonder boy in 1924. Sadder but wiser now, his marriage in tatters, Bucky could write his name in the game's history and send everyone home for the winter by beating Brooklyn today.

Branca retired the Yankees in the last of the fifth.

In the sixth, the Dodgers changed the script again. Bruce Edwards singled. Furillo doubled. Edwards wheeled toward third, chugging past a sight that would strike today's fans as odd if not comic: a pair of gloves lying in short left field. Dodgers shortstop Reese and center fielder Furillo still followed the age-old practice of leaving their gloves on the field while their team batted, a custom that lasted until it was banned in 1953. Corner defenders—the third baseman, first baseman, left fielder, and right fielder—would drop their gloves in foul territory as they jogged off the field, but the shortstop, second baseman, and center fielder usually left their gloves in the grass just beyond the infield at the end of an inning, then retrieved them when they took the field again. There is no record of a player tripping over a glove or a batted ball bouncing off one, but it must have happened now and then. The Yanks' Phil Rizzuto, who was phobic about insects, was an exception: Rizzuto took his glove to the dugout after opponents started sneaking bugs into it.

With runners at second and third, Shotton called on his best pinch hitter. Cookie Lavagetto reached for a couple of bats to swing on his way to the plate. "Dramatic stuff," Barber called it.

Cookie knew what to expect from Joe Page. He swung late on a fastball. Strike one. Opened his stance a half inch to get around a little quicker—missed another fastball. Strike two. He called time, rubbed dirt on his hands. Stalling, probably mumbling a Hail Mary. He fouled off the next pitch and was grateful when Page called for a new baseball. Page might be stalling a little now, gathering himself for the strikeout he wanted, but the new ball was a little whiter than the other one, a little easier to pick up as it flew through the shadows to the plate.

Page stretched and delivered. Cookie reached out and sent a fly ball to right field, almost the same trajectory as his double off Bevens. This one didn't carry as far, but it got the tying run home. Edwards tagged up and scored from third. New York 5, Brooklyn 5.

Pinch hitter Bobby Bragan doubled in another run, and Shotton sent in Dan Bankhead to run for Bragan. Bankhead promptly took third on a single by Stanky. The untouchable Page had now faced five batters in the sixth, allowing two singles, two doubles, and Lavagetto's sacrifice fly. "Sometimes your pitcher wakes up on the wrong side of the bed," Harris said later. He patted Page on the back and brought in Bobo Newsom, who entered with the bases loaded, as they often seemed to be in this Series.

Pee Wee Reese greeted Newsom with a two-run single. Bobo retired Robinson and Walker, but the damage was done. Brooklyn 8, New York 5.

In the bottom of the inning, Shotton kept Lavagetto in the game to play third base. He wanted Cookie's bat in the lineup. He sent left-hander Joe Hatten to the mound for Brooklyn and dispatched Al Gionfriddo to play left field. With a three-run lead, he wanted defense out there. As Gionfriddo recalled, "I'm sitting on the bench enjoying the ballgame when I heard Shotton call, 'Gi.' Shotton never could remember my name. He used to say, 'What's that little Italian's name?'"

Pinch hitter Allie Clark led off the home sixth with a liner to short. One out. Stirnweiss, stomach churning, worked the count until he walked. Henrich pulled one down the left-field line, home-run distance. Old Reliable! But it went foul. Then he hit a pop-up for the second out. Berra spanked a single, and the Yankees had a threat in the works: Stirnweiss at second, Yogi at first, DiMaggio genuflecting in the on-deck circle with his bat on his shoulder. He stood and walked to the batter's box without a wasted motion, *sprezzatura* in the flesh.

DiMaggio scared third basemen. They played him deep, three or four steps behind the bag, partly out of self-defense because he weaponized line drives. His single in the third inning had practically decapitated Spider Jorgensen, who fell backward, stabbing at the ball, but couldn't catch it. Now Cookie, in for Jorgensen, took a step back. With two on and two out, DiMaggio represented the tying run. If he lined one to third, Cookie could save the inning by catching it or save a run by knocking it down.

In left field, Gionfriddo squinted in toward the Dodger dugout. "The shadows of the stands were covering the infield, but I was in bright sunlight," he recalled. He saw Shotton and Sukeforth pointing toward the left-field line. "They're waving me toward the line to play DiMaggio to pull. I thought I was playing awfully shallow."

"With two men on and two men out, Joe DiMaggio hit a tremendous drive," David Halberstam would recall. "A huge roar went up."

Gionfriddo closed the gap. The ball was headed for the bullpen in left-center, near a sign on the outfield fence that read 415 FT. "As I was running, I looked over my shoulder, saw the ball, then put my head down and kept running. I looked over my shoulder again, got a glimpse of the ball and then jumped."

Television viewers saw DiMaggio's shot leave the screen. Millions more heard Red Barber's call on Mutual Radio. Barber and Mel Allen switched off in each Series game, with one calling the first four and a half innings and the other the rest. By accident—a coin flip before the Series—Barber got the late innings of Games Four and Six, two of the best ever played. Like any good announcer, he kept his eye on the outfielder rather than the baseball at the key moment of the sixth game.

"*Back goes Gionfriddo, back back back back back back . . .*" said Barber, repeating the word six times as Little Al peeked over his shoulder, nearing the waist-high bullpen gate at top speed, his cap flying off as he stuck out his glove.

"*He makes a one-handed catch against the bullpen! Oh, DOC-TOR!*"

"I twisted a little bit to take the shock of hitting the fence with my ass instead of my stomach," Al recalled. "If that ball would have flown into the bullpen, it would have tied the score eight to eight." After realizing he had caught the ball, he held up his glove to show the world the white dot in the webbing. First baseman Jackie Robinson threw his arms up with joy. For a moment, Robinson and DiMaggio were in the same frame on TV. DiMaggio had been cruising into his home-run trot when Gionfriddo came down with the ball. Now his reaction shocked fans almost as much as the catch. In what amounted to a tantrum for the Yankee Clipper, DiMaggio kicked a clump of infield dirt between first and second.

Furillo, coming over from center, retrieved Al's cap. They jogged homeward together, Furillo thumping his roomie on the back.

Al knew he'd made an important play. Just how good a catch it was has been a subject for debate. Barber called it a "remarkable catch, one of the all-time great ones in baseball history." Fans, including the young David Halberstam, agreed. So did veteran reporters from the *Times, Eagle, News, Mirror,* and dozens of other papers. But writers who came later had their doubts.

"He had almost overrun it," wrote Jonathan Eig in his 2007 book on Jackie Robinson, *Opening Day.* Eig said Al got lucky on "a stumbling, bumbling play." Richard Ben Cramer waxed louder in his 2000 DiMaggio biography, which found "Al Gionfriddo dancing a spirited tarantella—unsure where to run, which way to turn, how to get under the ball. Joe was digging for second base, when Gionfriddo, in an act of God, stumbled under the ball, stuck his glove over the wire fence, and—*Cazzo! Figlio di putana!*—stole the home run away."

How great a catch was it? Almost everyone on the scene that day swore that it kept the ball from flying into the bullpen for a home run, but nobody knows for sure. There is no video of the whole play, only the swing as DiMaggio connects and looks up, watching it go, and Al's last few steps and snow-cone catch, followed by Joe's famous kick of the infield dirt.

It's clear that Al's speed was all that kept him in the big leagues. He was a .175 hitter who could run, that's all. When Shotton and Sukeforth waved him toward the line just before the play, they made his run a little longer. He covered about fifty yards in the time it took Barber to describe the chase, a distance Al described as "a long drive in a Buick."

Bucky Harris called the play "a miracle." DiMaggio called it the best play anybody ever made on him. Taking his position in center field the next inning, the *Times* reported, "DiMaggio was walking inconsolably in circles, doubtless wondering whether he could believe his senses."

Baseball fans like to say that the guy who makes a spectacular defensive play always comes up to lead off the next inning. This is a fallacy, a trick of human memory. We tend to remember unusual, striking moments and forget all the times when the hero didn't come up next.

Leading off for the Dodgers in the seventh: Gionfriddo. "I had to go up and hit!" he recalled. He grounded out to third.

Hatten walked a tightrope in the bottom of the frame, loading the bases, but Stirnweiss flied out to Furillo in center to end the threat. Game Six went to the ninth inning with the fans hooting, whistling, stamping their feet until it felt like a subway train was running circles under the stands. Brooklyn 8, New York 5.

Billy Johnson led off the last of the ninth with a single. Shotton had Hugh Casey ready in the bullpen, but this time old Burt chose to play the percentages. He let the left-handed Hatten pitch to lefty-hitting George McQuinn.

Hatten walked McQuinn.

"Go get him, Sukey."

Sukeforth went out to tell Hatten he was done. Casey started toward the mound. This would be Casey's fifth appearance of the Series, and the Yanks hadn't scored on him yet. As Barber recalled, the stone-faced reliever walked from the bullpen to the mound "with a sureness of purpose that said he was not coming to his execution, but to execute others, and with his own right hand." Sukeforth handed him the baseball and left without a word.

After finishing his warm-ups, Casey checked the runners: Johnson leading off second base, McQuinn at first.

Phil Rizzuto stroked a fly ball to center. Furillo gathered it in. One out. Aaron Robinson kept the Yankees alive with a single to left. Gionfriddo scooped up the ball and fired it to the infield as third-base coach Dressen held the runner—no need to risk an out at the plate with the Yanks down by three. Again they had the bases full, with pinch hitter Lonnie Frey coming up. The crowd noise went up a notch.

Frey shot a grounder to the right side. Jackie Robinson nabbed it and threw to Reese for an out as Johnson scored from third to make the score 8–6. Two out now with runners at first and third, Snuffy Stirnweiss coming to bat.

Snuffy's insides were boiling, but that was nothing new. Milk didn't help, Pepto-Bismol didn't help. Hits helped. He had seven hits in the Series to go with his highlight-reel defense, but he was oh-for-four today and hitless in his last seven at-bats. What would it take to prove that he wasn't just a cheese champion and the son of a crooked cop? For Snuffy the answer was simple. The answer was more. More hits, more plays in the field, more wins—and then maybe people would think of him as a real Yankee and hear the name Stirnweiss the right way.

Casey dealt him a fastball. Snuffy topped it to the first-base side. He ran for his life, but Casey pounced, flipped the ball to Robinson at first, and the Dodgers jumped for joy.

Jackie Robinson, Dixie Walker, and Pee Wee Reese spent half an hour posing for pictures and toasting Gionfriddo in the Dodgers' happy clubhouse. Reese kissed Little Al until he ran out of pucker and said, "Hey, somebody else kiss the little guy for a while!"

Bucky Harris held court in the Yankees' quiet clubhouse. "You can't beat those catches they're making," he said. Asked to forecast Game Seven, he said, "Somebody is going to win."

The writers crowded DiMaggio, who was in no mood for questions about Gionfriddo's catch. "I guess I've hit a few harder in my career," he said, "but I can't remember when." Joe Williams of the *World-Telegram* took it on himself to answer for the Clipper. "Some anonymous character on the Brooklyn team leaped clear out of the park," Williams wrote, "to take a home run from the only real big-league ballplayer in the series."

Larry MacPhail was less diplomatic. After stewing for several minutes, the Yanks' president burst into the locker room and announced that whatsizname Gionfriddo was the luckiest man on the face of the earth. "He's liable to drop one right in his hands tomorrow," MacPhail said. "He won't even *play* tomorrow." With that he stormed into the trainer's room. Aiming a finger at Johnny Lindell, he called Lindell a disgrace to the team. "You're not doing the ball club any good!"

Lindell, sitting by trainer Eddie Froelich's desk, begged to differ. While Froelich applied a heating pad to Spec Shea's arm, Lindell said, "I'm sorry, sir. I disagree with you. The only reason I played is because I want us to win." After two singles today he was batting .500 for the Series. He was doing his best, he said, but "my side hurt when I swung at the plate as well as when I breathed." He said he'd gone for X-rays that proved his rib was broken.

MacPhail challenged him. "Have you the X-ray negatives?"

Lindell said no. "I didn't bring them to the park."

MacPhail stormed out of the losers' clubhouse. "But for this verbal explosion," the *Times* reported, "the clubhouse was quiet as a morgue."

Bookies adjusted the odds. With Bill Bevens and Hal Gregg listed as probable starters in the seventh game, the Yankees were 8½-to-5 favorites. If Bevens made the start, he would do it on two days' rest after having thrown 137 pitches on Friday.

Al Gionfriddo spent the night celebrating. The managers patted a few players' backs and returned to their apartments to think about tomorrow's lineups and matchups. Cookie took a cab back to Brooklyn. Snuffy rode the ferry to Jersey City and caught a train home to Red Bank, kicking himself all the way for making the last out of Game Six.

Bevens drove home to West 186th Street. He kissed Millie and collapsed on the couch. He didn't need the evening papers to tell him he was expected to start Game Seven for the Yankees. Bucky Harris had told him he would, "if you're up to it." Bev just nodded. He hadn't told Harris, Froelich, or anyone else that his arm was killing him. He didn't know if he'd be able to throw his best fastball tomorrow, or a slower sore-arm version that might make him the goat of the year. But it wasn't as if he had a choice. Suppose he won the game—that's a big-league contract next year for sure.

"I gotta pitch," he told his wife.

Millie put their sons to bed. After that she sat next to her husband for hours, massaging his right arm, trying to rub out the pain.

CHAPTER 14

Battle of the Bronx

Monday, October 6, brought perfect weather for a ballgame. The autumn sun warmed a shirtsleeves crowd of more than 70,000 that lifted the total World Series attendance to a record 389,763. Joe Williams of the *World-Telegram*, tapping out his column in the Yankee Stadium press box, wondered, "Doesn't anyone in this town ever go to work?" Like just about everyone else, Williams was still talking about Gionfriddo's grab the day before. He called it "the greatest catch since the FBI caught Dillinger."

A town that had barely noticed Al Gionfriddo now hailed a hero the *Brooklyn Eagle* described as "not much larger than a matchbox." The *Times* compared Al to a Munchkin, a fast one who could run "like a striped ape." The *Herald Tribune* ran a front-page picture of THE CATCH THAT SAVED THE DODGERS. That photo went out over the AP and UP wires to newspapers all over the country.

"Al Gionfriddo works as a fireman during the off season," Arthur Daley wrote in a *Times* column headed THE IMPOSSIBLE IS STILL HAPPENING. "In his spare time he makes miraculous catches at crucial moments in the World Series. This Gionfriddo chap came to the

Dodgers as a sop in the Higbe deal, dozed away most of the summer in the shade of the bench and then finally got into the ballgame because Burt Shotton was running out of outfielders. If he doesn't watch out, he'll soon be enshrined in the Flatbush holy of holies along with Cookie Lavagetto." Daley's paper generally focused so thoroughly on the Yanks that Brooklynites considered it Yankees propaganda, but that day's *Times* paid special tribute to the Bums, "who are more uniquely American than any other sports team we can think of."

Gionfriddo was smiling when he met the team bus in the morning, a little buzzed after yesterday's excitement and the toasts he drank last night, the first of countless free drinks he'd enjoy in years to come. The opposite of hungover, he was ready to go if Shotton put him in the lineup.

Hunch-player Shotton added a pair of spiffy two-tone shoes to his usual ensemble. Old Burt announced the lineup in his tinny voice: Stanky at second, Reese at short, Robinson at first base, Walker in right, Hermanski in left. . . . So Al would be on the bench again. Batting ninth and pitching was Hal Gregg, who had the least-imposing credentials in Game Seven history. In fact, Gregg took the mound with the fewest regular-season wins (four) and highest ERA (5.87) of any pitcher ever to start a World Series game.

The Bombers had a surprise starter of their own. The papers all listed Bill Bevens as New York's Game Seven pitcher, but Bucky Harris didn't like the look on Bev's face. When he asked Bevens how he felt, the pitcher shrugged, not wanting to say his arm felt half dead. That would make him look like a coward. At the same time, he couldn't say, "Tip-top, skip." What if he started and gave up eight runs? Everyone would blame him, the club might cut him at contract time, and that could end his career. So he shrugged and said he wanted the ball.

"You may get it," Bucky said—but not as the starting pitcher. Part of a manager's job is to read the signals his players give him as reliably as they read the signs he flashes from the dugout. Bevens couldn't admit he was a bad risk, but they both knew it.

Harris considered bypassing his starters. He could send closer Joe Page to the mound in the top of the first. That would surprise the Dodgers! He'd spent half the night considering such a move and would have tried it if Page hadn't given up four runs yesterday.

The Yankees gathered around Bucky before the deciding game. There was no pep talk. "I'm giving Spec Shea the start," he told them. With Johnny Lindell nursing his cracked rib, Tommy Henrich and Yogi Berra would flank DiMaggio in the outfield, "and we'll get Spec some runs." After his complete-game victory in Game Five, Shea would be working with one day's rest.

Bucky thought his club was better than Shotton's, but Brooklyn had survived six games on spit and miracles. "They're lucky we didn't beat them four straight," he told Daley, "and now it wouldn't surprise me if we got licked."

Gionfriddo signed autographs and posed for pictures before the game as Dodger fans whistled and cheered in the Stadium crowd. Branch Rickey stood nearby, reminding reporters that he had acquired Gionfriddo as a throw-in when he shipped Kirby Higbe to Pittsburgh. "I always liked that boy!" he crowed.

The Dodgers needled the mighty Yanks during batting practice, razzing Allie Reynolds with Indian war whoops. Lavagetto picked on fretful Snuffy Stirnweiss, using Snuffy's stuffy-sounding given name: "Hey, *George*, we're still here, *George*. We're comin' after you!" DiMaggio stepped into the cage to sarcastic applause from Brooklyn's Rex Barney. "Lookit this guy, I bet he's talking to himself," Barney yelled. "He hits every ball like a shot and we take his hits away!"

When a photographer asked DiMaggio to sign a photo of Gionfriddo's grab, Joe D turned away. "Ask the other guy," he said. "He made the catch."

At one thirty, soprano Lucy Monroe sang the season's final national anthem. Bill Slater greeted thousands of DuMont Television viewers. Red Barber said, "Hello, friends," to millions of radio listeners. Spec Shea finished his warm-ups. The Yankees threw the ball around the horn and the last game of 1947 began.

Shea had allowed the Dodgers only two runs in fourteen innings thus far, but how strong could he be less than forty-eight hours after throwing a complete game? The Dodgers planned to swing early and knock his block off.

Eddie Stanky opened hostilities with a single. The next batter was Pee Wee Reese. Shotton flashed the hit-and-run sign to third-base coach Ray Blades, who relayed it to Reese, who almost always took the first pitch. Was Shotton overmanaging? Reese swung through strike one as Stanky took off for second. Catcher Aaron Robinson gunned the ball to Stirnweiss, who tagged Stanky for an easy out.

Reese walked. Jackie Robinson scorched a liner to left for the second out. Dixie Walker drove a Shea fastball into the right-field seats—just foul. Five minutes into the game, Shea had given up a single, a line drive, and a long fly that could easily have been a two-run homer. At this point Shotton could have let the inning turn his way. He could let Walker take another rip. Instead he flashed the steal sign. Reese ran, and Aaron Robinson threw him out. The Dodgers had let Shea off the hook by running into two outs. Hunch-player Shotton was oh-for-two.

Hermanski smacked a second-inning shot down the right-field line. Yogi Berra, still an inexperienced outfielder, chased it into the corner. Yogi slipped as the ball bounded past him, and by the time he chased it down Hermanski had a triple. Bruce Edwards singled to put Brooklyn ahead 1–0. Carl Furillo followed with another single.

Bucky Harris called time. He'd decided that a quick hook was better than a quick four- or five-run deficit. He patted Shea on the butt and took the baseball. Would he turn to Joe Page in the second inning? It wouldn't have surprised Sukeforth and the other coaches, not the way Bucky had talked about starting Page today.

Instead he called for Bevens, who plodded toward the mound like a man on his way to the gallows. Bucky didn't know what to expect from Bevens and neither did Bevens, who hadn't dared throw hard in the bullpen. He had only so many bullets left. He flung eight warm-up pitches, none touching ninety miles an hour. Catcher Robinson shook his fist in the air—*Let's go.* Bevens nodded. He went into his stretch, shooting a glance toward the runner at second. Still only one out.

Spider Jorgensen pulled Bevens's fastball down the right-field line. Lucky for Bev it went foul. Still, it was a foul omen for the Yankees. Jorgensen, a lefty whose height was generously listed at five foot nine, had trouble hitting hard stuff on his hands. The fact that he'd pulled a fastball suggested that Bevens was throwing in the eighties rather than the ninety-plus he commanded when he was right. He reared back and tried to throw harder, but Spider pulled this one, too—a dart that bounced into the right-field seats for a ground-rule double. Hermanski trotted home with Brooklyn's second run. Dodgers in the dugout waved their caps. Still only one out, with runners at second and third. They had Bevens on the ropes. A hit would give Brooklyn a four-run lead.

Gregg tapped a roller to Rizzuto at short. To the Scooter's surprise, Furillo took off from third, trying to score another run. Rizzuto threw Skoonj out—another baserunning blunder by the Bums, who still led 2–0. Then Stanky hit a pop-up and Bevens was out of the inning.

Rizzuto's RBI single in the bottom of the inning cut Brooklyn's lead in half. After that, Bevens worked two scoreless frames to keep the Yankees close. Reaching back for all he had, he struck out Reese and Jackie Robinson in the third. With his arm hanging heavy between pitches, he poured fastballs and sinkers over the plate for two and two-thirds scoreless innings, reducing his World Series ERA to 2.38. By the time Bevens's slot in the batting order came around in the fourth, he was spent. Bucky Harris thanked him: "You kept us close." The other Yanks thumped Bev on the back while he worked his sore arm through the sleeve of a warm-up jacket, found a spot on the bench, and settled in to watch.

Bobby Brown, the egghead who roomed with Berra, was already late to fall-semester classes at Tulane Medical School. Brown poked a fourth-inning double to left, tying the game. Yogi's roomie was perfect in the Series with a walk, a single, and two doubles. His three pinch hits set a World Series record that still stands. Two batters later, Tommy Henrich lashed a single to put the Yanks up 3–2. With the bases loaded, Berra came to the plate with a chance to break the game open. Yogi smashed a dart over first base—a three-run double that Jackie Robinson turned into an out, spearing the ball to end the inning, keeping Brooklyn within a run.

The Yankees led 3–2. If they stayed ahead, hard-luck Bill Bevens stood to be the winning pitcher.

Harris had Joe Page and Allie Reynolds warming up. Both had pitched the day before, when Reynolds allowed three earned runs and Page got pasted for four runs.

Bucky asked coach Frank Crosetti to phone the bullpen. "How do they look?" Crosetti asked coach John Schulte. A moment later, Crosetti nodded and relayed Schulte's verdict: "Page hasn't got a thing, and the Indian is knocking the glove off his hand!"

Bucky knew who he wanted. This was the sort of moment he privately called "nut-crunching time," a time to lean on the men who'd brought you this far. According to Larry MacPhail, who had sneaked into the tunnel between the clubhouse and the dugout, this was "the most dramatic moment I had experienced in baseball. I held my breath as I waited to hear what Harris would do. Then Bucky turned around and saw me hiding" in the tunnel. "He grinned."

Harris called his order to Crosetti: "Give me Joe Page."

Page trudged to the mound and commenced throwing fastballs. "Aspirin tablets," MacPhail called them. Page set down the Dodgers in order in the fifth inning. When his catcher called for a slider or curve, Page shook him off. He retired the Dodgers in order in the sixth.

Rizzuto singled in the Yankees' sixth. He stole second and scored on a single by Allie Clark, a little-used pinch hitter—another Harris decision that worked—and the Yankees led 4–2.

Now Shotton played another hunch, sending utility man Eddie

Miksis to play left field. Why not Gionfriddo? It wasn't twenty-four hours since Al robbed Joe D with what was already one of the most celebrated plays in Series history. As Gionfriddo remembered, "None of us could understand Shotton's thinking. We had a lot of people sitting on the bench who could play the outfield. Here it was, the seventh game of the World Series, and he's playing a utility infielder in left!"

One of baseball's mysteries is how, at key moments, a baseball finds the weakest link on defense. In the last of the seventh, the Yankees' Billy Johnson skied a ball to deep left. Miksis misjudged it. Peering into the afternoon sun, seeing the ball carry over his head, he chased it toward the fence, turning right and then left. The ball fell twenty feet short of the spot where Gionfriddo had caught DiMaggio's blast. As Daley saw it, "If Burt Shotton had had his communication with the spirit world intact, he'd have had a bit of ectoplasm named Al Gionfriddo in there and the mighty mite would have caught that one in his back pocket." Johnson scored on a sacrifice fly to put New York ahead 5–2.

Page checked Brooklyn in the eighth, one-two-three. He had faced twelve Dodgers and retired them all. Harris let him bat in the bottom of the eighth. The day now belonged to Page and Hugh Casey, the ace relievers. After Page grounded out and Stirnweiss flied to Furillo, Tommy Henrich sent a fly ball to left. Miksis camped under this one, garnered a few Bronx cheers for catching it, and the last game went to the ninth inning.

Page had thrown twelve innings in the Series, appearing in four of the seven games. An hour ago he'd had nothin' in the pen. Now he'd pitched four perfect innings with the season and the Series in the balance.

After Dixie Walker grounded out to Stirnweiss, Miksis gained an ounce of redemption by looping a single in front of DiMaggio. Brooklyn fans sniffed a rally in the making. Another base runner would bring the tying run to the plate.

At 3:49 p.m., Bruce Edwards slapped Page's fastball to short. Rizzuto gloved the ball and flipped it to Stirnweiss, who planted his foot on second base and threw to first. "It's a double play," Mel Allen told millions of listeners, "and the World Series is over!" The Yankees had claimed their eleventh World Series title. The Dodgers, still seeking their first, would wait at least another year.

The Yankee players mobbed Page, hugged him, kissed him, rubbed his left arm. They lathered his hair with champagne while he told reporters, "They probably would have shot me if I lost!" Bucky Harris greeted his men as they poured into the dugout, pounding their pin-striped backs. Old Reliable Henrich had batted .323 with a Series-high ten hits, Rizzuto .308, Billy Johnson .269 with eight runs scored in the seven games. DiMaggio had clubbed two homers. Leadoff man Stirnweiss had seven hits and eight walks for a .429 on-base percentage, best among the regulars, proving his worth in the crucible of Series competition. Still, the manager saved his first toast for his finisher. In the clubhouse, lifting a glass of champagne instead of his usual whiskey, he repeated his favorite salutation: "Gentlemen, *Joe Page*." Nodding toward Page, he said, "What a way to win! What a pitcher when the chips are down. If this wasn't the greatest World Series, it will do until a better one comes along."

Word came from the press room that the official scorer had awarded Page the victory despite the fact that he'd entered the game with a one-run lead. Bevens, the putative pitcher of record, felt snake-bit again, but it was hard to quibble with the scorer's decision. The beer-bellied closer had smothered the Dodgers for five innings, facing fifteen batters and recording fifteen outs. Asked how he'd done it only a day after getting knocked for a loop in Game Six, Page said, "I had to do it for Joe." For DiMaggio.

The great DiMaggio sat on a stool in his private dressing area. Taped up like a mummy, the Clipper lit a postgame cigarette. He had led his team to victory. Again. He allowed himself a smile while the other Yankees, one after another, came over to shake his hand.

⚾

Branch Rickey bustled up to Burt Shotton on his way to the visitors' clubhouse. Wrapping an arm around his old friend's shoulder, Rickey said, "I am proud of you." Then he added, "You'll be asked about next season. When they ask, I'd rather you didn't answer those questions one way or another." The Machiavellian Mahatma had his mind on the Durocher question. He knew reporters would ask Shotton if he'd be back to manage the Dodgers in 1948. Or would he step aside when Leo returned from his suspension? If he had expected a vote of confidence from the boss, here was the opposite. Rickey was asking him to help keep Rickey's options open.

Shotton walked to the clubhouse with his head held high. By almost any accounting he had been outmanaged in the Series. Still he had come within a whisker of beating a Yankee club that was superior to his, shuffling a pitching staff so unreliable that no Dodger starter had lasted even five innings.

The Brooklyn clubhouse was so quiet, you could hear a jockstrap drop. Rickey spoke first, telling the Dodgers they had nothing to be ashamed of. "You were and are the best team in the National League, and you mustn't feel downhearted."

Then it was Shotton's turn. He echoed the boss's sentiments. What else was there to say? After a few minutes, they opened the clubhouse door to the press.

"I have no regrets," Shotton told the writers. No, he hadn't thought about next season one way or the other. No, he hadn't had time to congratulate the other manager. "I'd like to do that through you newspapermen. Tell him from me: When you get beaten by Bucky Harris, you have lost to a good guy and a good manager." Pressed for a comment on the Dodgers' near future, he said, "A better club beat us, but I'll tell you this: We'll beat the Yankees over the next ten years a whale of a lot more than they will beat us."

The Rookie of the Year sounded stoic. "We lost. We've got no alibis," Jackie Robinson said.

The Yanks' winning share of World Series receipts amounted to $5,830 per man, a sensational bonus for a young player like Berra, whose salary was $5,000. The Dodgers, whose losers' portion came to $4,081 per man, voted to give Leo Durocher a full share of their postseason bonus. Commissioner Chandler vetoed the idea, declaring that rewarding Leo for his sexual and other infractions was against the best interests of the game. Still, the vote was a slap at Shotton.

☻

The Yankees held an all-night victory party at the Biltmore Hotel atop Grand Central Terminal. Music, laughter, and champagne flowed through the Biltmore's chandeliered Cascades Ballroom. DiMaggio made a suitably stellar entrance, limping down marble stairs with a tall blonde on each arm. He signed a few autographs and sat at a front table. His dates wanted to dance to the swing band, which was fine with him. DiMaggio chatted with teammates while the blondes did the Lindy and the jitterbug with other partners. Everyone knew they would be going upstairs with the Clipper when he called it a night.

Snuffy Stirnweiss danced with his own shapely blonde, Jayne Stirnweiss, whose high heels made her several inches taller than her husband. Bucky Harris, estranged from his wife, arrived alone. "Congratulations were showered upon popular manager Harris, who, after 23 long years, is once more a world champion," the *Times* reported. "It will be remembered that back in 1924, 'boy manager' Bucky piloted the Washington Senators to the title." Harris was shaking hands and accepting praise for winning the best-ever Fall Classic when club president Larry MacPhail barreled into the room. Reporters hurried toward the ever-quotable executive.

"Stay away or get punched!" MacPhail barked.

Earlier, at the ballpark, he had burst into tears when Rizzuto and Stirnweiss turned the game-ending double play. Then he'd announced, "We won! I'm quitting! I can't take the pressure anymore."

He rushed downstairs and found Rickey in a cluster of fans, writers, and photographers. He stuck out his hand and said to the Dodger president, "You've got a fine team. I want to congratulate you." Rickey clasped MacPhail's hand, leaning close to say, "I'm shaking hands with you because all these people are watching, but I don't like you. Don't ever speak to me again." After that, MacPhail spent several hours with a bottle of scotch.

At the Biltmore, Sid Keener of the St. Louis *Star-Times* got a few quotes from the reeling executive. MacPhail called Rickey a "Bible-quoting, hypocritical, tightwad son of a bitch," and Commissioner Chandler a "goddamn hayseed." He said, "They think I'm a pop-off. Well, I gave New York another championship, didn't I?"

He wasn't done. Lurching through the room, he confronted farm director George Weiss and cursed him out. When Weiss talked back, MacPhail fired him on the spot. Weiss sat shocked while his wife broke down in tears. Next MacPhail took a seat beside John McDonald, a friend from his Brooklyn days, and blasted Rickey with every insult he could think of. When McDonald defended their old colleague, MacPhail said, "You Judas!" and socked him in the eye.

Co-owner Dan Topping stepped between them. MacPhail now turned his ire on his front-office partner. "Hey Topping," he said, "do you know what you are? A guy born with a silver spoon in your mouth who never made a dollar in your life."

Topping, younger and stronger than the fifty-seven-year-old club president, grabbed his arm. "Come here," he said, wrestling MacPhail through the nearest door. "I've heard enough from you." In a kitchen off the ballroom, Topping told MacPhail, "We've taken everything from you we're going to take. If you act up again, Larry, I'm going to knock your head off."

Topping went back to the ballroom alone. Half an hour later, MacPhail returned. He saw Joe Page and Page's wife, Kay, and lit into the Series hero.

"What were you, Joe, before I picked you up? A bum," he sneered.

"You and this broad here, you were nothing." Page stood up. According to the journalist Roger Kahn, "Topping was approaching with a murderous look. Mrs. Page burst into tears. MacPhail weaved away from the couple. Then this wondrous, bizarre, driven character staggered out of the room and out of the victory party and out of baseball."

Wednesday was warm with afternoon rain. Burt and Mary Shotton gathered up their belongings at the Hotel St. George, preparing to return to Florida, still unsure whether Burt or Durocher would manage the Dodgers in '48.

At a midday press conference in the Waldorf-Astoria, Dan Topping announced that he and his co-owner Del Webb had bought out Larry MacPhail's one-third interest in the club for $2 million. MacPhail was nowhere to be seen. Topping said MacPhail had suddenly offered to resign the night before. He and Webb hadn't expected such an offer, he said, "but so long as he asked for it, we decided to let him have it."

With that, Topping introduced the New York Yankees' new general manager: former farm director George Weiss. In the *Times*' report, "Weiss accepted congratulations with his usual modesty, and said he expected things to go along as usual. Bucky Harris was sure to remain as manager."

Weiss called Bucky his friend, and Bucky believed him.

Bill Bevens and Snuffy Stirnweiss cleaned out their Yankee Stadium lockers and drove home to Hudson View Gardens and Red Bank, respectively.

Al Gionfriddo took a train home to coal country in time for a parade in his honor that Sunday, Al Gionfriddo Day in Dysart, Pennsylvania.

Cookie Lavagetto headed west to reunite with his wife, Mary, and meet their new baby.

Bevens, Stirnweiss, Gionfriddo, and Lavagetto would be marked forever by the roles they played in the 1947 World Series. They were now stars of one sort or another, and that gave them a leg up on every other scuffler who was hoping to stay in the majors next year. As World Series heroes, all four thought their big-league jobs were safe.

One of them was right.

THREE

Six Futures

CHAPTER 15

The Year After Hell Broke Loose

There was a sawmill in Dysart, Pennsylvania, along with a train station, a general store, and a tavern that shared space with the post office. Eight hundred and fifty-one people lived in Dysart, but five thousand turned out for Al Gionfriddo Day on the Sunday after the World Series. The mayor's car crept through the throng to meet Little Al's train. A cheer went up when the guest of honor stepped onto the platform. Men and boys whistled and threw their hats in the air. Gionfriddo rode shotgun with the mayor on the way to the local diamond, reaching out to touch his fans' hands.

At the diamond, a band played "Take Me Out to the Ball Game." Proud parents Paulo and Rose Gionfriddo looked on while the city fathers presented a set of luggage to their son. Baggage was getting to be a theme of Al's career. First there was the suitcase he carried from Pittsburgh to New York, packed with the hundred thousand dollars that made him an afterthought in the Kirby Higbe trade, and now this brand-new set he could use if the Dodgers sent him packing.

Al played center field for a Dysart nine against the semipro Coalport Moose in an exhibition game, going three-for-four with three

RBIs in a 5–3 victory. Then he signed autographs for the Coalport players.

He and his wife, Arlene, hoped to spend the winter in Pittsburgh. When they couldn't find an affordable apartment there, they rented rooms in Cresson, near Dysart, where Al sold electrical supplies. He often gave speeches at dinners and smokers attended by baseball fans and businessmen. "There was no money in it, just talk," he recalled. "Everybody wanted me to talk about that catch on DiMaggio. I got tired of it. I appreciated their interest, but I was just a guy trying to hang on to a big-league job."

Bill Bevens turned thirty-one in mid-October, two and a half weeks after his one-hit loss in the Series. Sometimes he dreamed about the high-outside fastball he'd thrown Cookie Lavagetto, wishing it back into his hand. But he also remembered his performance in Game Seven. Page got the win but Bevens did his bit—two and two-thirds shutout innings with the world watching.

Back home in Oregon, he found a letter from the New York Yankees in his mailbox. The letter congratulated him for being one of twenty-seven Yankees to receive a full share of the champions' World Series bonus: $5,830.02. After deductions for federal and state taxes, his bonus came to $4,524.62, nearly half his annual salary.

"When I came home, people turned out at a breakfast for me," he said. "Governor [Earl] Snell was there. He took me aside and said, 'Bill, we're going to ask everybody for a donation so we can buy you a new car.' Three days later he died in an airplane crash." So much for the car. And Bevens's luck was about to get even worse. Later in October he accepted an invitation from an Elks Club in Oakland, California. The Elks paid his way south for an exhibition game starring the man who had almost thrown the first World Series no-hitter. "I wanted to impress them," he said later, "but I tried too hard, and pulled some shoulder muscles."

He went back to work at the Paulus Cannery in Salem. Described by the *Oregonian* as the state's "number-one sports citizen," Bevens was certainly its most prosperous cannery worker. Including his World Series share he made a little over fifteen thousand dollars that year, enough to pay off his mortgage. That made 1947 his best year despite his 7-13 regular season record, but it was hardly enough to set a man up for life. So Big Bill spent another off-season lifting cans onto the conveyor belt. Millie massaged his arm most nights, working her way from the elbow to the shoulder until the ache died down and he could sleep.

⚾

After the Series, Cookie Lavagetto drove cross-country to join Mary and their baby. Mary told him how scared she'd been when she went into labor two weeks early. They had tried for years to have children. After Mary miscarried twice, they prayed for another chance. Now here she was, a first-time mother at thirty-five, proud wife of a World Series hero. God must have wanted it this way, they thought—two miracles in two weeks!

Cookie figured his Game Four heroics would buy him another season in the majors. He'd gone one-for-seven in the Series, but what a one! Like Gionfriddo, he spent much of the off-season giving talks about his magic moment, but while Al got tired of giving his "I robbed Joe D" speech, Cookie enjoyed retelling his story at sports banquets, high school convocations, and Knights of Columbus meetings. Too busy with Mary and the baby to face Bevens in the Oakland Elks Club game, he worried almost as much about his own right arm and didn't dare test it that winter for fear of making it worse.

⚾

Snuffy Stirnweiss turned twenty-nine in late October. As a key cog in the Yankees' victory, he accompanied DiMaggio to some of the numerous banquets where Joe D described what he called "the best World Series ever," and became the Yankee Clipper's valuable ally. DiMaggio loathed giving speeches. Almost neurotically wary of anyone outside his circle of cronies, he'd stand up to accept some award or another and say a few words. After a minute of thank-yous and "How about that World Series?" he'd nod to Snuffy, who got a shorter round of applause and filled fifteen or twenty minutes talking about playing for the Yanks. At the end of his talk he'd describe a great play or game-winning homer by Joltin' Joe, who stood up again to nod and wave to the adoring crowd, and the evening was over.

Sometimes the two of them had a nightcap afterward. DiMaggio never thanked Snuffy, but he didn't have to. Even to Snuffy, a little time with Joe D was thanks enough.

DiMaggio and Jayne Stirnweiss got along, too. Fashion-model Jayne, who still appeared in the occasional department-store ad, flirted with Joe, who flirted back. But both of them knew she was devoted to her husband.

Sometimes DiMag babysat for them. "He was shy with grown-ups but playful with me," recalls Susan Stirnweiss, Jayne and Snuffy's daughter. "Joe used to pick me up and whisper in my ear, 'You know, George over there isn't really your father.' Then he'd whistle and touch my chin, and say, 'I am.'" It would be years before Susan told her mother what Joe had said.

A *Sporting News* reporter visiting the Stirnweiss home in New Jersey found Snuffy doing diaper duty. A sign out front read SNUFF'S ACRE. Snuffy posed for pictures, changing baby Edward's diaper. "I'm still resting from the World Series," he said. "That was about as thrilling a baseball competition as one could imagine. And too close for comfort!"

He joined several other Yankees on a barnstorming tour of Japan. Phil Rizzuto and Snuffy were settling into their hotel room when Rizzuto yelled from the bathroom: "What a place! The toilet's got a bowl to keep ice for your beer." The Scooter had discovered the bidet.

After the tour, Stirnweiss came home and spent weeks remodeling his house. The Bat House, his family called it after he lined his den with baseball bats. Long before anyone realized that a Babe Ruth bat or jersey might someday be worth millions, Snuffy gathered up

Ruth bats, Gehrig bats, DiMaggio bats, dozens more. A round bat was hard to mount on the wall of his den, so he sawed them in half length-wise, destroying any future value they had, and used them as wain-scoting. "Daddy's bat cave," his daughter calls the den lined with bat halves. "He'd have a drink and talk to his friends on the phone. I wondered if he was talking to Joe, and if Joe would tell him our secret."

In December, Branch Rickey announced that Leo Durocher would return to manage the Dodgers in 1948. Burt Shotton would serve as a minor-league instructor at Dodgertown, the organization's new train-ing facility in Vero Beach, Florida.

At a Kiwanis Club lunch in his honor, Shotton said he expected his new job would keep him busy, "but I don't expect it to interfere too much with my fishing." He returned to New York for a Baseball Writers Association dinner at Toots Shor's restaurant, where the writ-ers presented him a radio inscribed THE COMEBACK OF 1947. Rickey stood to thank his old friend for leading Brooklyn to a pennant and then stepping down so gracefully. When it was Shotton's turn to speak, he said he'd stick to listening to big-league games on the radio. "I'll never manage a ball club again, here or any other place."

Rickey, surprised, bounced back to his feet. "I'm sorry Barney said that. There is such a strong bond of friendship between us," he said. "I know he would come back to the Dodgers if I needed him."

Their friendship would be tested soon enough.

Rickey began his off-season work by shipping Dixie Walker to Pitts-burgh. The People's Cherce had signed his ticket out of Brooklyn with his anti-Robinson petition the previous spring. World Series hurlers Vic Lombardi and Hal Gregg went to the Pirates with Walker while right-handed pitcher (and reputed spitballer) Elwin "Preacher" Roe came to Brooklyn along with infielders Billy Cox and Gene Mauch. Roe would become a pillar of the Dodger rotation; Cox would be a

Dodger mainstay for the next six years; Mauch never hit but would manage in the big leagues for twenty-six years. Next, Rickey shipped Eddie Stanky to the Boston Braves so that Robinson could play second base, a move that also allowed Gil Hodges to switch from catcher to first base while another rookie, the Negro League star Roy Campanella, took over behind the plate.

Another of Rickey's plots bore fruit in 1948. A year earlier, amid the storm surrounding Robinson, he had quietly hired baseball's first full-time statistician. Alan Roth was a balding, epileptic Canadian who kept stats for the National Hockey League but preferred baseball. Roth had peppered the Dodgers with letters claiming that some batters hit left-handed pitchers better, some hit better when they were ahead or behind in the count, some almost always pulled the ball. Rickey finally hired him. Roth lugged satchels full of notebooks to Ebbets Field and began charting every pitch. The first of the quants who would revolutionize the game more than half a century later, he began as the well-paid (five thousand dollars a year) source of an occasional tip. Roth told Rickey that Dixie Walker was hitting more and more balls to the opposite field, a sign of declining skills that reinforced Rickey's desire to trade the People's Cherce. Like Jackie Robinson, Roth was what Rickey liked most of all: a weapon nobody else had.

Shrewd as he was, Rickey failed to anticipate the upheavals of 1948. The season started going to hell when Robinson, plumped by an off-season on the rubber-chicken circuit, reported to spring training twenty pounds overweight. Durocher had defended Jackie at the now-famous Mess Hall Meeting, but now Leo wanted to make sure everyone knew this was *his* team. He called Robinson "Fatty" and made Jackie take infield practice in a rubber suit so he could sweat off the extra pounds. "He was skinny for Shotton, fat for me," Leo griped.

Cookie Lavagetto had a bad feeling from the day he reported to Dodgertown in March 1948. He never liked the proud, preening Durocher, who had ripped him in 1940—the year Cookie played through a fever that left puddles of sweat at his feet. Durocher called him lazy, "a baby." Cookie keeled over in Cincinnati and was rushed to Christ Hospital, where doctors removed a ruptured appendix in time to save his life. The next day he posed in his hospital bed, smiling, urging his teammates to "start a winning streak." A year later, after Cookie joined the army, *Daily News* columnist Jimmy Powers wrote, "It would be a nice gesture on the part of the Dodgers to refund him the expense of his hospitalization for appendicitis, deducted from his salary last year."

Now Durocher was back in charge. Cookie didn't hit much at Dodgertown, and Durocher cut him. Rickey went along with the move. Five months after Cookie's game-winning double made him a national celebrity for a day, the Dodgers released him. He packed up his gear and began the long drive home from Vero Beach to Oakland.

Rickey assured Al Gionfriddo he'd have a spot on the roster. Arlene Gionfriddo set out to find a Brooklyn apartment, but rents were out of reach. Finally she placed a classified ad in the *Eagle*: "Dodger player desires three or four furnished rooms." Suddenly swamped with offers, the Gionfriddos chose a flat near Ebbets Field. "Little Al, a World Series hero, says it isn't so about a housing shortage in Brooklyn," the *Sun* reported. "He discovered a furnished four-room apartment in 24 hours flat."

Al went into April as the sixth or seventh man in what the *Times* called Brooklyn's "overstocked flychasing department." He knew he wouldn't play much, not with Hermanski, Furillo, Reiser, Arky Vaughan, and Don Lund ahead of him, not to mention twenty-one-year-old slugger Duke Snider, who might come up from the minors any day. Gionfriddo expected to serve as the last man at the end of the bench, repeating his role from '47. Then, two weeks before Opening Day, Durocher surprised him. "You're going to Montreal," the manager said. So much for the four-room flat in Flatbush.

Al was sixty days short of qualifying for his major-league pension. He blamed Rickey for lying to him and began nursing a grudge that would last for the rest of his life.

"In baseball, the feats of one season win no pennants in the next," wrote the *World-Telegram's* Dan Daniel. "Obviously, Gionfriddo got his chance. He couldn't make the varsity. Quite obviously, too, Cookie Lavagetto had no special function in the 1948 picture."

Cookie signed on with the Triple-A Oakland Oaks, playing third base and serving as an unofficial coach under manager Casey Stengel. He and the fifty-seven-year-old Stengel were a pair of odd ducks with crooked grins and quirky attitudes that made it easy to forget the brains under their caps. Cookie became a leader of Stengel's 1948 Oaks, a veteran outfit that won Oakland's first Pacific Coast League pennant in twenty-one years.

Bill Bevens's arm was killing him. Massages eased the pain, but his fastball looked like a changeup. General Manager George Weiss sent him to a specialist who turned out to be a quack. The man injected saltwater into the pitcher's biceps. When Bev pitched worse, Weiss demoted him to Newark. "It's just for now," he promised, "till you're back to your old self."

Bevens tried rest. He tried heat. He tried ice. The harder he tried to throw, the longer the ball took to get to the plate. He would make only one start for the 1948 Newark Bears. At least it was a good one—two runs in nine innings, with a Bev-like six bases on balls.

The Gionfriddos found an *appartement* in Montreal, where Al took out his frustrations on minor-league pitchers. To the astonishment of everyone, including his wife, the five-foot-six Flea batted .294 and led the minor-league Montreal Royals in home runs. His twenty-five round-trippers topped the seventeen smacked by his six-foot-five teammate Chuck Connors—who would go on to Hollywood fame as the star of TV's *The Rifleman*—and dwarfed Little Al's big-league total of two.

☻

Snuffy Stirnweiss made it through spring training without injury or outhouse encounters with bears, and once the season began he manned second base as a Yankee in good standing. He regressed as a hitter in 1948, hitting only .216 through the middle of August, but made up for that by "working wonders around second," in one sportswriter's words, "clicking off double plays with his partner, Scooter Rizzuto, like a mechanical man." So reliable was Stirnweiss that he went on to set major-league records for fielding percentage by a second baseman (.993) and fewest errors in a season (five). He and Rizzuto asked Harris to let them room together on the road, an arrangement that backfired on the Scooter when he discovered that Snuffy, with his nasal problems, snored like a locomotive.

Snuffy got his average over .250 in September but kept thinking Harris might pull him from the lineup. When the Yankees were at bat, he sat as far as possible from the manager. His teammates couldn't resist playing tricks on worrywart Snuff. During one game Yogi Berra said, "George, I've been asked to tell you that Bucky's gonna pinch-hit for you. You might as well leave the dugout." Stirnweiss looked stricken. He was plodding toward the tunnel to the clubhouse when Yogi and the others cracked up laughing.

Rizzuto told Berra to knock it off. Even if Snuffy was asking for a hard time, Yogi lacked the standing to give it to him, being only a second-year player. That was a job for a veteran like Rizzuto, who took a pair of scissors to Snuffy's best suit, lined his jockstrap with itching powder, and woke his roomie one night by roaring like a bear. They were pals for life.

☻

Bucky Harris left his veterans alone for the most part. Team-first guys like Rizzuto and Stirnweiss could look after themselves. DiMaggio, it went without saying, was above managing. He never gave less than his all, never threw to the wrong base or overran a base the way lesser men did. Bucky's job, as he saw it, was to let the veterans follow Joe D's lead while Bucky made substitutions and worked young players like Berra into the long victory march that was Yankees history.

The Yanks were expected to repeat as American League champions. *Baseball Digest* predicted that they'd win by a dozen games. Berra split his time at catcher and in the outfield again, batting over .300 while writers, fans, and bench jockeys mocked his looks. With his beetle brow and long arms, he reminded people of a gorilla. Yogi joined in the laughter, claiming to be the only catcher who got better-looking with his mask on. His manager, however, saw something special in him. "Don't think Berra's a dope," Harris told reporters. "He hasn't had much schooling, that's all. I'll make a prediction: Within a few years he'll be the most popular player on the Yankees. Henrich, Rizzuto and DiMaggio have fans who admire them, but I mean more than that. People are going to love this little guy because he's such a character."

Berra was grateful. "Bucky was always trying to build up my confidence," he recalled, "but even he called me The Ape. After batting practice he'd say, 'Did you see The Ape hit that ball today?'"

DiMaggio, Henrich, Rizzuto, and Berra led the 1948 Yankees into a tight pennant race, with the "Big Three" starting pitchers—Allie Reynolds, Vic Raschi, and Eddie Lopat—on their way to fifty-two combined wins. New York swept Connie Mack's Philadelphia Athletics in August to pass Philly in the standings. A month later, reliever Joe Page went five and a third innings to beat Ted Williams and a Red Sox club skippered by Joe McCarthy, Harris's predecessor with the Yankees. That was two blows by fifty-one-year-old Bucky against his illustrious elders (Mack was eighty-five; McCarthy, sixty). Page's victory put New York in a three-way tie with Boston and Cleveland with a week left in the season.

All season, Bucky pleaded with the front office: "I need more pitching." With his Big Three wearing down and Spec Shea 6–10 in

late August, Harris told George Weiss that his rotation needed rein-
forcements. A young right-hander named Bob Porterfield had been
tearing up the International League, but Weiss insisted that the kid,
who was already twenty-five, needed "more seasoning." Soon the
papers were running "Where's Porterfield?" articles. Weiss accused
Bucky of planting the stories with his friends in the press box. By the
time Porterfield came up, he had already thrown 178 minor-league
innings. He went 5-3 with a 4.50 ERA down the stretch for the Yankees, looking tired.

Bucky thought Weiss might be undermining him on purpose.
Reporters confided that the general manager had called him a lucky
stiff who barely managed his star-studded team. "Harris merely goes
along for the ride," he said. When the writers asked if Harris would
be back in 1949, Weiss said he didn't know.

Bucky asked the writers to drop the subject. "If I lose this pennant, I'll ask Weiss what's what. If he wants me back, okay. If not it
will be okay too. There will always be a job for me somewhere."

Porterfield beat Philadelphia on September 29 to keep the Yankees alive. But Lou Boudreau's Cleveland Indians—featuring pitchers Bob Lemon and Bob Feller, ex-Yankee Joe Gordon's thirty-two
homers, plus fourteen homers and a .301 average from Larry Doby,
the first black player in the American League—won five of seven
down the stretch to finish in a tie with the Red Sox, both teams
nosing out the Yanks. (In a one-game playoff at Fenway Park, the
Indians dispatched the Red Sox, too.) DiMaggio (.320, 39 homers,
155 RBIs) topped Williams (.369, 25, 127) in MVP voting, but they
came in second and third to player-manager Boudreau (.355, 18, 106),
Burt Shotton's former protégé. The Indians went on to win the World
Series, a feat they haven't matched since.

☯

Another of Bucky Harris's elders had a quiet off-season. Burt Shotton spent the winter and early spring in Florida, scouting Dodger prospects in the mornings, yanking bass and speckled perch from the

Kissimmee River most afternoons. Meanwhile, a thousand miles north, Jackie Robinson slumped as the new season opened. Robinson finally came alive in June and July, lifting his average over .300, but his hot streak didn't impress Leo Durocher, who doubted his commitment to the team. "Jackie played for Shotton, but he won't play for me," Durocher complained. Reporters took that quote to Robinson, who chose not to rise to the bait. All he said was, "I loved playing for Shotton."

The Dodgers had sunk to sixth place in July. Six months after bringing Durocher back from his yearlong suspension, Rickey looked foolish for having replaced steady old Burt with baseball's loosest cannon.

To Rickey's delight, an enemy rescued him. The New York Giants, Brooklyn's fiercest National League rival, were mired in fourth place when Giants owner Horace Stoneham asked to meet secretly with Rickey. Stoneham wanted to fire Mel Ott, the easygoing Giants manager who had inspired Durocher to say that nice guys finish last.

Stoneham wanted Rickey's permission to hire Burt Shotton as the Giants' manager. Rickey could scarcely believe his ears. Here was the answer to his problems—if he played his cards right. "You have my blessing," he said. "But let me ask you a question. Suppose I said you could have Shotton or Leo Durocher. Which man would you choose?"

Stoneham jumped at the chance to hire Durocher, saving Rickey the trouble of firing Leo, leaving him free to put Shotton back in charge for the season's second half. The Mahatma, having played the angles like Minnesota Fats, reached for the phone.

As manager of the pennant-winning Dodgers, Shotton had been entitled to manage the National League All-Star team in 1948. But Commissioner Chandler announced that the now-retired Shotton was ineligible and named Durocher the National League manager against Bucky Harris's American Leaguers at the All-Star Game in St. Louis. "Honorary manager" Shotton was invited to throw the ceremonial first pitch. "Burt Shotton, the forgotten man, cut loose with a pitch that was a trifle low and outside," the Times reported.

Harris piloted the American League to a 5–2 victory. Shotton left St. Louis for St. Paul, Minnesota, to look in on Brooklyn's farm club there. That night he received a message from Rickey: REPORT TO CINCINNATI BY 11 TOMORROW.

His plane to Ohio was late. By the time he arrived, the press knew more than he did. Without consulting him, Rickey had issued a six-word statement: "Durocher is out, Shotton is in."

"The visiting clubhouse at Crosley Field is an old clapboard building behind the stands," the *Sun*'s W. C. Heinz reported from Cincinnati. "The rain was coming down, and on the radio Guy Lombardo's band was playing a tune called 'Seems Like Old Times.'" Jackie Robinson and Hugh Casey played cards while Pee Wee Reese lay on the training table, getting a rubdown. "One of them looking out the window saw Shotton, walking around puddles in the macadam, wearing slacks and a yellow sports shirt and a sports jacket and a snap-brim straw hat, newspapermen on both sides of him. Shotton was smiling."

So were Robinson and Reese. Led by a happier double-play duo, the Dodgers won eight of their next nine to climb into second place. And just as he'd done with Robinson the year before, Shotton made a special project of helping a rookie who would one day make the Hall of Fame. When Duke Snider, called up from Montreal in August, slumped so badly that Rickey wanted him benched, Shotton said Snider would come around. But that's not what he told the press. Holding court in the clubhouse after a loss, he said, "I need to give Snider a rest. He's all worked up and can't hit a lick. A few days on the bench may straighten him out." Snider read the papers. He felt awful. But he was still in the lineup the next day. The grateful rookie socked a tape-measure home run and soon lifted his average from .197 to .244.

Shotton installed Snider in center field, moved Carl Furillo to right to play caroms off the Gem Blades sign, and brought up left-hander Carl Erskine from the minors. The Boys of Summer were gathering, with good old Burt entertaining the press. "First thing I do every day," he said, "is open my mail to see how I should have run the club yesterday."

After going 35–37 for Durocher, the Dodgers won 48 and lost only 33 for Shotton. Still, they fell short in September. Durocher's fifth-place Giants beat them three straight, giving Leo the satisfaction of knocking them out of the race. Brooklyn finished third behind the pennant-winning Boston Braves, led by their star pitchers Warren Spahn and Johnny Sain, with Stan Musial's Cardinals in second place. Still, Shotton and Harris were expected to skipper the Dodgers and Yankees the following year, with Durocher running the Giants. New York baseball would stage another bang-up show in 1949.

At a postseason banquet, the city's baseball writers named Harris their man of the year. "I never played for a smarter manager or a guttier guy," said Tommy Henrich. DiMaggio said, "If you can't play for Bucky, you don't belong in the major leagues." But there was talk that Harris might be on thin ice. George Weiss had his own drinking buddies, and Bucky wasn't one of them. The manager's press-box friends told him, off the record, that Weiss was saying that Harris had a drinking problem.

"I smelled a rat," Bucky said.

A few days after the season ended, he drove to Yankee Stadium to collect some paperwork. He wondered why his secretary looked at him funny as he went to his office. Then he saw why. His desk was no longer there. It had been moved to a common area where clerks and stenographers worked.

Bucky took in the scene. He went to his desk. He sat down, sharpened a pencil, and began making notes on scouting reports.

CHAPTER 16

Late Innings

On October 4, 1948, the day of the Cleveland-Boston playoff, Bucky Harris met with Yankees owner Dan Topping and general manager George Weiss. The meeting lasted less than twenty minutes. Bucky said the Yankees would win the pennant in 1949. He said he wanted to manage them.

The next morning a *Times* headline read HARRIS IS DROPPED AS MANAGER OF YANKEES. Describing the deposed manager as "undeniably popular with the players, press and public," the story attributed his firing to a rift between Harris and Weiss. Bucky had no comment other than to say he planned to attend the World Series, where, the *Times* noted, "he might have been managing if he had been favored with more luck and better pitching in 1948."

Two days later the Yankees announced that Casey Stengel, last seen managing Cookie Lavagetto and the minor-league Oakland Oaks, would replace Harris. It wasn't an obvious choice. In two stints as a major-league manager Stengel had lost 161 more games than he won. At a time when the game featured more and more black players, he called them jigaboos and jungle bunnies. Years later, when catcher Elston Howard became the first black Yankee, Stengel said, "When I finally get a nigger, I get the only one who can't run." Stengel's prime credential was his loyalty to Weiss, who told reporters that Bucky Harris had been "too damn easygoing," not to mention Bucky's supposed drinking problem, which Weiss was eager to mention in private conversations.

Some of the writers sided with Weiss. Others saw Harris's firing as a means of eliminating a potential rival to the general manager. They knew Harris enjoyed a drink or two or three, but none of them had ever seen him drunk. In fact, Bucky handled his liquor better than many a pickled member of the press corps, which isn't to say he never had one too many in the long nights ahead, thinking of the pennants and World Series he might have won if he had held on to his job.

With Harris out of work, reporters wondered whether Branch Rickey might hire him to run the Dodgers. Such a move would make the sort of headlines Rickey dreamed of. Suppose Bucky Harris came down from the Bronx and led Brooklyn to its first World Series title, perhaps by beating the Yankees—wouldn't that be a story?

"If they want me, I would love to have the job," Bucky said of a crosstown move.

Reading that quote in the papers ruined Burt Shotton's morning. Shotton told Rickey to make up his mind: "It's him or me, Rick."

BURT SHOTTON IS RETAINED BY RICKEY, the *Times* announced. According to the *Times'* John Rendel, "Shotton, the sedate gray 64-year-old veteran," had been given a one-year contract for 1949. "The announcement dispelled a rumor that the next manager of the Dodgers would be Bucky Harris, recently ousted manager of the Yankees." Shotton settled into a holiday season of preparations for his first full year at the helm in Brooklyn while Harris shifted his focus to other clubs. As the holidays approached he met with Washington Senators owner Clark Griffith, who seemed always to have visions of Manager Harris dancing in his head, and Detroit Tigers executive Spike Briggs. He also flirted with a socialite who would become his

second wife, a woman who had never met such a sports-minded fellow. They were leaving a cocktail party in Manhattan late one night
when Bucky asked her, "Who was that skinny kid we talked to?" She
thought Bucky Harris had to be the only American who didn't recog-
nize Frank Sinatra.

Just before Christmas, he surprised everyone by signing to manage the minor-league San Diego Padres of the Pacific Coast League.
He had his reasons: a salary that topped the pay of many big-league
skippers; a break from the New York baseball circus; a promise from
owner Bill Veeck that he might have a shot at managing the world-
champion Cleveland Indians, the Padres' parent club, in a year or
two. In January 1949 Bucky loaded his car and drove west through
thunderstorms, sleet, and a prairie blizzard. On arrival he said, "California looks mighty good." One Padres booster said that hiring Harris
was "the best thing that ever happened, baseballically thinking."

San Diego sportswriters peppered him with questions about the
Yankees. "That's something I'm trying to forget," he said. Pressed on
the subject, he gave the reporters a bitter quote: "I guess I was lucky
to win the pennant and World Series in 1947, and a poor manager
not to repeat in 1948."

He loved the weather in Southern California, liked the golf, and
was pleasantly surprised to have a roster featuring future major leaguers Al Rosen, Luke Easter, and Minnie Minoso. Still, he felt
marooned in San Diego, far from his family and friends. He often
phoned New York and Washington for news of the big-league game
that went on without him.

Al Gionfriddo played every day for the 1949 Montreal Royals, knowing he was out of luck. If his twenty-five homers and .294 average
the year before couldn't get him back to the majors, what would? He
fell off to .251 with nine homers in '49, establishing a norm for three
seasons with the Royals in which he pulled his weight, scoring more
than one hundred runs a year. His roommate, a left-handed pitcher

named Tom Lasorda, called Al one of the best teammates he ever had. They used to lean out hotel windows, dropping paper bags full of water on other players. Lasorda was headed for the majors—a stint in Brooklyn followed by twenty-one years as the manager of the Los Angeles Dodgers. Gionfriddo went the other way.

Soon after Al's thirtieth birthday, Brooklyn demoted him to the Fort Worth Cats of the Double-A Texas League. Still two months short of qualifying for his major-league pension, which would pay a few hundred dollars a month for life, he remembered Rickey's looking him in the eye and saying, "We'll see to it that you get that pension." But that was the last meeting he ever had with the Mahatma. He never made it back to Brooklyn and never got his pension.

Cookie Lavagetto felt cheated, too, but Cookie wasn't the type to hold grudges. He said he missed the big leagues but was glad to be home, living in his own house ten miles from Oakland, playing for the Oaks. Mary gave birth to a second son, Ernest, in 1948. They bought a low-slung ranch house with aluminum siding in the green hills of Orinda, where Cookie trimmed the bushes in front of their cement porch and two-car garage. He batted .290 for the 1949 Oaks, a club managed by his friend Charlie Dressen, who had coached third base for the Yankees until he got fired along with Bucky Harris.

With Cookie manning third base, looping his throws to first, Dressen's Oaks finished second to the Hollywood Stars but ahead of Harris's fourth-place Padres in the Pacific Coast League standings. Luke Easter hit .363 to win the batting title while a struggling pitcher, Bill Bevens, won a game and lost two for the Seattle Rainiers. But for Cookie, what stood out about that season was the second baseman he took under his wing.

Alfred Manuel Martin, known as Billy, came from the sandlots of Berkeley. An amateur boxer with an outsized nose and ears to match, he reached the Oaks in 1948 as a good-field, no-hit third base-man. The kid immediately complained about batting eighth in the order. Manager Casey Stengel told him, "Look at it like this. You're my second cleanup man." Stengel assigned Cookie to look after the new arrival.

Calm Cookie and the fiery twenty-year-old Martin made an unlikely pair of roommates. Martin got into fights on and off the field. "Billy," one teammate said, "is the only guy who can *hear* someone give him the finger." But Martin also listened when Lavagetto talked about the big leagues. Cookie put the kid through double-play drills—having Billy work on his pivot by hopping over a pillow on the floor of their hotel room—but mostly they discussed hitting. According to Cookie, hitting at the sport's highest levels had a lot to do with conquering fear. The fear of failure, of striking out and looking bad, that was part of it, but there was also plain physical fear. "You can't be scared," Cookie said. Major-league pitchers threw breaking balls that "spin so tight you think they'll hit you in the head, and then they go under your hands for a strike."

"Nothing scares me," Martin said.

Cookie said he was wrong. "You flinch. I've seen it." He described at-bats when Billy flinched. "It's natural. I was scared every day in the big leagues."

Martin took extra batting practice between games. Cookie pitched, slipping a few rubber balls into the bucket of baseballs he took to the mound. He threw the soft ones right at the kid's ear. In time, Martin learned to stand in against any inside pitch.

Cookie had less luck keeping Billy sober. This was due in part to Martin's mother, Jenny, who sometimes went bar-hopping with the Oaks and drank them under the table. Still Billy hit .286 with twelve homers and ninety-six RBIs for the Oaks at age twenty-one in 1949. When he was called up to the majors, his graying roomie gave him some parting advice: treat veterans with deference. For instance, Cookie said, a rookie never asks an established player to have dinner with him. He waits to be asked.

Billy Martin joined the Yankees in 1950. He made the All-Star team in 1956 and went on to manage New York to victory over

Lasorda's Dodgers in the 1977 World Series, the high point of a long, turbulent career he owed partly to Cookie Lavagetto.

Naturally, Martin had barely set foot in Yankee Stadium in 1950 when he strutted up to Joe DiMaggio. "Hey Joe," he said, "let's go eat tonight, you and me." The great DiMaggio, startled by the kid's brass and naïveté, said yes, and they became pals.

Bill Bevens couldn't lift his pitching arm above his shoulder. A *Sporting News* reporter found him back home in 1949, playing weekend games with middle-aged men. "Bevens, the former Yankee hurler who two years ago came within a pitch of tossing a no-hit game in the World Series, is now playing the outfield and first base for a local softball team in Oregon," he wrote. Bev couldn't pitch, but his sheer athletic talent still dumbfounded his softball teammates and opponents. Some of his home runs carried so far that nobody went looking for them.

Later that year his arm felt better. In a four-game stint with the Seattle Rainiers of the Pacific Coast League, pitching at Seattle's ominously named Sick's Stadium, the creaky thirty-two-year-old won a game and lost two. He struck out only three minor-league batters in twenty-three innings. What galled him was that his overall strength was undiminished. One day his sons' school bus broke down, so Big Bill put his shoulder to the bus and pushed it half a mile to the parking lot. He was as strong as ever, except for his arm.

With money getting tighter, Millie Bevens took a job in a grocery store. Bill put in an occasional shift driving a truck, and taking time off from throwing seemed to do him good. Working out for San Diego manager Del Baker in the spring of 1950, he popped the catcher's mitt.

"Bevens is throwing as if he never had a sore arm in his life," an *Oregonian* writer enthused. "The news of his comeback has spread over the entire region." Bev made thirty Coast League appearances that year, splitting his time between San Diego and Sacramento, but his comeback fizzled. In seventy-seven ugly innings he struck out sixteen batters and walked seventy-one. He won three, lost eight, and went home.

"We loved having him back," his son Dan recalls. "It was like being around a giant." Bev's sons still marvel at his feats of strength. During the winters he drove an eighteen-wheeler; the pay was pretty good and he liked the solitude of long nights on the road. "During breaks, the drivers used to sit around on the loading dock. They'd bet on who could squat and move the big scales they used to weigh freight," Dan Bevens remembers. "A couple of them impressed everybody with 500 pounds. Then somebody goes to 510! Dad would go up and match that, and then do 600 pounds, and top out at 750."

Bevens never asked for special treatment but never objected to it. After a day behind the meat counter at Erickson's Grocery, Millie came home to a living room that featured one of the first television sets in Hubbard. A TV dealer gave her the set because he was a fan of her husband. A barber in nearby Salem, where Bill got his hair cut, turned a corner of his shop into a shrine to his hero, with Bev's baseball cards and clippings mounted on the wall.

The barber, the TV dealer, the truckers, and the mayor all wanted to know: Was he finished? Or did he have another try in him? He was only thirty-three.

In the spring of 1951 he gave his sportswriter friend Al Lightner a scoop. "I am going to give it one more shot," he said. Bevens sucked up his pride and joined the Salem Senators, a club in the Class B Western International League, four levels down from the majors. Throwing free and easy for the first time in years, he pitched a career-high 263 innings, firing sinkers past overmatched bushers who'd never seen a big-league fastball vanish as they started their swings. Bevens won twenty games with a 3.08 ERA, earning a spring-training audition with the Cincinnati Reds in 1952.

"They offered a six-thousand-dollar contract if he made the team," Dan Bevens says. "He knew it was his last chance."

While Bevens mounted his comeback, a former teammate staged one of his own. Snuffy Stirnweiss hoped to end his career in New York. He had grown up a Yankees fan. He had spurned a pro football contract to sign with the Yanks. He had won a war-years batting title and gone on to prove he was no cheese champ, teaming with Rizzuto to help the Yankees pivot from the glory days of Ruth and Gehrig to an oncoming dynasty led by DiMaggio and the next Yankee hero, Mickey Mantle. Snuffy wasn't as quick as he used to be, slipping from fifty-five steals in 1944 to eighteen two years later and three in '49, but he served as a thirty-year-old guru to the younger players. "Study the enemy," he told them. "For instance, with a runner at first, the pitcher changes his position on the mound. He grows tense, then sets himself to throw over. That's when he gives himself away. Some jerk a shoulder, some shift an arm, others inch a foot toward first. Watch close and you can read their minds."

Snuffy loved playing in his native borough, an hour's commute from his bat cave in New Jersey. "I'd leave the ballpark around five-thirty after a game," he remembered, "and be home in time to spend the evening with my family." He hoped to end his career as a Yankee. Instead, general manager George Weiss traded him to the last-place St. Louis Browns in June 1950. Weiss wanted to make room for rookie second baseman Billy Martin.

"I hate leaving home," Snuffy said, "but I've been mighty lucky. I'm only thirty. I have a long way to go before I'm through."

Later that year, when the Browns made their final road trip to the Bronx, the Yankees honored their former second sacker on Snuffy Stirnweiss Day. Thirty busloads of fans rolled in from New Jersey to see the club shower Snuffy with gifts and hip-hip-hoorays. The biggest gift was a snazzy yellow convertible that proved to be as gimpy as DiMaggio. The car conked out on the way to the ballpark and had to be towed into center field for the presentation. It was too showy for Snuffy anyway. He traded it in for a Pontiac station wagon that served for years as the Stirnweiss family car.

Managers have longer careers than ballplayers, particularly managers who win pennants and World Series. Bucky Harris led the minor-league Padres to thirteen more wins in 1949 than they'd had the year before, bringing a big-league approach to the Padres—including the Pacific Coast League's first bullpen phone—before returning to the majors as manager of the 1950 Washington Senators. Clark Griffith and his son Calvin, now the Senators' general manager, thought they owed him one more chance. They credited Harris with having rescued the franchise a quarter century before, when the Senators' 1924 pennant drive and World Series victory sold enough tickets to save the Old Fox from selling the team. As Calvin Griffith saw it, "Bucky saved our baseball lives."

Harris led the Senators to a seventeen-game improvement in 1950, lifting them from the cellar to fifth place behind Casey Stengel's Yankees. Sportswriters joked that Bucky's third term in Washington left him only one behind Franklin Delano Roosevelt.

His old rival Burt Shotton led the '49 Dodgers down the stretch against Stan Musial and the Cardinals. The New York Giants were out of the race, but that didn't keep Leo Durocher from taking every possible shot at his old team. Durocher spat every racial slur he knew at Jackie Robinson, but Jackie gave as good as he got. He called Leo old and weak, a washed-up loser. When Durocher responded by grabbing his crotch, Robinson said, "Give that to Laraine. She needs it more than I do." Durocher stewed as Jackie paced the league at one time or another in batting average, steals, and RBIs. Robinson benefited from stats guru Alan Roth's number-crunching: Roth had convinced Rickey and Shotton that their second baseman was the Dodgers' most dangerous hitter. After Shotton shifted him from second in the batting order to the cleanup spot, Robinson went on to bat .342, drive in 124 runs, and win the Most Valuable Player award.

With Durocher's New York Giants out of contention in September,

Leo hoped to knock his old team out of the race. "If we beat them," he crowed, "there will be one hundred thousand suicides in Brooklyn."

Brooklyn held a one-game lead over St. Louis on the last day of the season. The Cardinals won in Chicago. With the pennant at stake, the Dodgers and Phillies went to extra innings. Pee Wee Reese and Duke Snider scored tenth-inning runs to win the pennant. That night, twenty-five thousand fans greeted Shotton and his team at Penn Station. Maybe "next year" was here.

⚾

Another Dodgers-Yankees Subway Series.

Allie Reynolds outdueled Brooklyn's Don Newcombe in the opener, 1–0, with the only run a solo homer by Tommy Henrich leading off the bottom of the ninth. Brooklyn's Preacher Roe returned the favor in Game Two, his moist "forkball" hoodwinking the Bombers in his own 1–0 victory. The Series' key moment came in Game Three. With one out in the top of the ninth, the game was tied 1–1. Dodgers starter Ralph Branca walked Yogi Berra. He got DiMaggio on a pop-up, but allowed a single and another walk to load the bases. Clyde Sukeforth half expected to hear, "Sukey, go get him." Instead, Shotton left Branca in the game, and Johnny Mize roped a two-run single to left. The Yanks took control of the Series and never looked back.

Two days later, Shotton tempted fate by choosing Rex Barney to start Game Five. The scatter-armed Barney, making his first and only appearance of the Series, walked six and allowed five runs before Shotton sent Sukeforth to take him out of his misery. The Yankees coasted to their twelfth World Series victory. The Dodgers were still looking for their first.

Shotton celebrated his sixty-fifth birthday the week after the '49 Series. Some newsmen thought he might retire. Dick Young of the *Daily News* had spent almost three years calling for the old fuddy-duddy's head. Tommy Holmes of the *Eagle* named Shotton the goat of the Series. Holmes thought the odds were catching up with hunch-player Burt, who had skated on luck and high hopes for so long.

Shotton could have gone home to Florida and enjoyed a cozy retirement, but he had already tried that. "I used to think it would be the greatest thing if I could go fishing whenever I wanted," he mused. "But then, when I got it all arranged, I didn't want to fish anymore. And when I could play golf all day, I lost interest in golf. It's a hell of a thing when a man has good health, enough money, and nothing to do. I was wrong to ever say I was through with baseball. It's the only life for an old pepper pot like me."

He managed the Dodgers again in 1950, another eventful year in Brooklyn. Robinson hit .328 while Gil Hodges, Duke Snider, and Roy Campanella combined for ninety-four homers, and the Dodgers dueled Durocher's Giants and Eddie Sawyer's young Phillies into late September. With Shotton spurring another thin pitching staff down the stretch, Don Newcombe and Preacher Roe won nineteen games apiece. Brooklyn trailed the "Whiz Kid" Phillies by a game with one to play. Again the deciding game between the Dodgers and Phillies went to extra innings. With the score tied 1–1 Brooklyn starter Newcombe, still pitching in the tenth inning, allowed a pair of singles. Shotton left Newcombe in the game to face Dick Sisler, who already had three hits on the day. Sisler, the son of the Hall of Fame first baseman (and Dodgers scout) George Sisler, lined a three-run homer into the left-field seats, and Brooklyn was beaten again.

Philadelphia's Whiz Kids lost the 1950 World Series in a four-game sweep to the Yankees. Some observers thought the Phillies' flop reflected well on Shotton, whose Dodgers had given the Bombers a far better battle in the 1947 and 1949 Series, but the team's new owner, Walter O'Malley, wasn't one of Burt's boosters. O'Malley had won a power struggle with Rickey that spelled the end for Shotton.

"I got fired," Burt said. "And not because of my record. Walter O'Malley wanted a new organization without any Rickey men in it."

Burt and Mary Shotton packed up their rooms in Brooklyn's Hotel

St. George for the last time. After winning two pennants in three seasons and coming so close to another, he was willing to let other men debate his merits as a manager while he gave scouting, fishing, and golf another try.

Half a century later, Bill James reexamined Shotton's place in the game's recent history. James considered him underrated. "Burt Shotton, although winning the pennant in 1949, failed to replace Durocher" in the public mind, "just as Bucky Harris failed to replace Joe McCarthy despite winning the pennant in 1947," James wrote. "The parallel is precise. Joe McCarthy left the Yankees in June 1946. The team struggled through the rest of the season, but won the pennant in 1947 and finished just two games back in 1948. Leo Durocher left the Dodgers in July 1948. The team struggled through the rest of the season, won the pennant in 1949, and lost by two games in 1950. That wasn't good enough, and in both cases, the new manager was perceived as being too nice, too soft."

In eleven seasons as a major-league manager, most with the woeful Phillies of the late 1920s and early '30s, Shotton won 697 games and lost 764. But in his Dodger years his winning percentage was .603—still the best of any Brooklyn or Los Angeles Dodgers skipper who lasted as long as he did.

CHAPTER 17

Try, Try Again

A pale, persnickety corporate lawyer, the Dodgers' new owner and president parted his pomaded hair in the middle and smoked cigars through a plastic mouthpiece that kept tobacco from touching his lips. Walter O'Malley soon purged all evidence of the Branch Rickey era in Brooklyn. He fined office workers a dollar if they mentioned Rickey's name, and he removed the Pittsburgh Pirates from the Dodgers' spring-training schedule when Rickey took over the Pirates. The conversational opposite of the chatterbox he replaced, O'Malley liked to make reporters wait for him to answer a question. He would take two deliberate puffs of his cigar before pronouncing the last word on Brooklyn baseball.

His answer to the first question of 1951 consisted of two words. Who'll manage the Dodgers? "Charlie Dressen."

A veteran coach for Durocher's 1943–46 Dodgers, Dressen had assisted Bucky Harris with the 1947–48 Yankees. After George Weiss fired him along with Harris, the cocky five-foot-five Dressen led the Oakland Oaks to a Pacific Coast League pennant. When O'Malley brought him back to Brooklyn the following year, Dressen took along his third-base coach, Cookie Lavagetto.

For Cookie, returning to Brooklyn meant another spring and summer of missing Mary and their young sons in Orinda, leaving behind the lawn and rosebushes he liked to prune while listening to the radio. "But if a man offers you a big-league job, you go," he said. He knew guys who'd turned down such an offer and never got another.

Dressen's 1951 Dodgers took a thirteen-and-a-half-game lead over Durocher's second-place Giants in midsummer. Ralph Branca beat the Braves' Warren Spahn in August to boost his record to 10-3. Don Newcombe and Preacher Roe were both on their way to twenty-win seasons while Jackie Robinson, Gil Hodges, Roy Campanella, Duke Snider, and Pee Wee Reese joined Newcombe and Roe on the National League All-Star team. O'Malley scorned Robinson as "Rickey's prima donna," but Dressen saw his second baseman and cleanup hitter as Brooklyn's key man. Cookie thought about telling Jackie he was sorry for signing Dixie Walker's petition in '47 but never came right out with an apology. He figured it would make them both uncomfortable.

The Dodgers tailed off in September while Durocher's Giants, led by the former Negro Leaguer Monte Irvin, the former Dodger Eddie Stanky, and the twenty-year-old rookie Willie Mays, roared back to catch them on the season's last day. The teams split the first two games of a best-of-three playoff, with Branca losing the opener. His 10-3 start had eroded to 13–11; this was his fifth straight loss. Branca shrugged off talk of his bad luck. He wore number 13 and posed for photos with a black cat to prove he wasn't superstitious. His manager wasn't, either; Dressen told Branca to be ready to pitch, if needed, in the third and deciding game.

Brooklyn looked safe going into the ninth inning of that game, taking a 4–1 lead behind starter Don Newcombe. Two singles and a Whitey Lockman double made the score 4–2 with one out and third baseman Bobby Thomson coming up.

Dressen called to the bullpen. Out came Ralph Branca.

With first base open, the Dodgers could walk Thomson to set up a game-ending double play. They had two good reasons not to. For one, a walk would put the winning run on base—the move that backfired on Bucky Harris and Bill Bevens in the '47 Series. For another, Willie Mays waited in the on-deck circle. So Dressen made a sensible choice in having Branca pitch to Thomson.

His first pitch was a strike. His next pitch wasn't meant to be. Catcher Rube Walker wanted to move Thomson off the plate with a fastball under his chin, to set up a breaking ball down and away on the 1-1 pitch, but Branca missed his target. His fastball leaked toward the inside corner, and Giants announcer Russ Hodges followed the crack of the bat with a call that became a shout: "There's a long drive, it's gonna be, I believe . . . the Giants win the pennant! The Giants win the pennant! The Giants win the pennant! The Giants win the pennant! Bobby Thomson hits into the lower deck of the left-field stands, the Giants win the pennant and they're going crazy!"

Thomson's "Shot Heard 'Round the World" sent the Giants to the World Series and sent the Dodgers home losers yet again.

Dressen couldn't face the press after the most devastating loss in Brooklyn's long, painful history. He hid in his office, leaving Cookie Lavagetto to fulfill the manager's postgame duties. First, Cookie sat with Branca, who sprawled facedown on the steps to the Dodger clubhouse, grieving. "Why me?" the pitcher asked. "Why me?"

"I dunno," Cookie said.

Facing reporters, he offered the usual platitudes, congratulating the Giants, looking forward to next year, and so forth, but added a revealing detail. Asked how he had reacted to Thomson's shot, Cookie offered the perspective of a baseball lifer who had his head in the game at all times. "I watched his feet," he said, "to make sure he touched all the bases."

The next year the Dodgers finally won the National League pennant but lost the World Series to Casey Stengel's Yankees. A year later Dressen's 1953 Dodgers won 105 games and lost only 49. No other Brooklyn or Los Angeles Dodgers team has ever won so many. Yet once again they lost the World Series to the Yankees, led by Yogi Berra, Phil Rizzuto, and twenty-one-year-old Mickey Mantle, who had succeeded DiMaggio in center. After the Series, Dressen told O'Malley he didn't like working year to year and wanted a three-year contract. After two pennants in three years, Dressen thought he deserved a multiyear deal. O'Malley disagreed and fired him.

Lavagetto, shocked, resigned out of loyalty to Dressen. That was a step he would regret. Had he stayed in Brooklyn, he might have had a shot at the job—if not now, maybe a year or two later. As it was, O'Malley chose a malleable company man, the unknown minor-league manager Walter Alston, who signed the first of what would be twenty-three consecutive one-year contracts to manage the Dodgers.

In an ongoing game of managerial musical chairs, Dressen returned to the minor-league Oakland Oaks, with coach Cookie at his side.

⚾

In Oregon, Bill Bevens tried again. The Cincinnati Reds brought Bevens to spring training in 1952, offering a six-thousand-dollar contract if he made the team, but cut him the week before Opening Day. He joined the San Francisco Seals of the Pacific Coast League, three minor-league tiers up from the Class B league he dominated the year before, and looked lost. The thirty-five-year-old fastballer won six, lost twelve, and walked more men than he struck out. He returned to the Class B Salem Senators the following spring, heaving a few meatballs to a catcher not much more than half his age. After that he shook the catcher's hand, wished him luck, and drove home to Millie and the boys.

Bevens retired with forty major-league wins, thirty-six losses, and a sterling ERA of 3.08. In the second-to-last outing of his major-league career he pitched a complete-game one-hitter. In his final big-league appearance he threw two and two-thirds shutout innings to keep the Yankees close in the deciding game of the '47 Series. But of the thousands of pitches he delivered as a pro, all anyone seemed to remember was the one Lavagetto lined off the right-field fence to ruin what could have been the first no-hitter in World Series history.

The men who made their names in the first half of the century felt the game passing them by. Branch Rickey made his 1953 Pittsburgh Pirates the first major-league team to wear batting helmets. The aging Mahatma wanted to protect his players; he also owned stock in the company that made the helmets. Opponents snickered at the Pirates at first, as much for their record as for their "sissified" headgear. They came in last or second to last five seasons in a row.

Burt Shotton had half expected a telegram as the '52 Pirates went 42–112 to finish not only in last place but twenty-two and a half games out of seventh place. REPORT TO PITTSBURGH TOMORROW. But Rickey never asked. Instead, Shotton fished the Kissimmee River, hunted quail in the palmetto flats of central Florida, shot around par at the local golf course, and grew his own roses outside the little house he and Mary shared. One day he took their grandson to a cow pasture to gather manure for his roses. He left the boy outside the fence in case any bulls took an interest. Sure enough, Shotton was shoveling cow pies into a burlap sack when a two-thousand-pound bull came charging right at him, sending old Burt up a tree faster than you can say Jackie Robinson.

Shotton never again set foot in a big-league ballpark after managing his last game for the Dodgers in 1950. Some players, including Ralph Branca and Al Gionfriddo, griped about him for years, but they had longer memories than most. As one sportswriter wrote of Shotton, "Never was such a successful baseball man so quickly forgotten."

Al Gionfriddo slapped singles, cadged walks, and swiped bases as player-manager of the 1953 Drummondville (Quebec) Royals of Canada's Class C Provincial League, five rungs down from the majors. A fan favorite, Al was making good money for the low minors. He was a surprising second on the club in home runs when the cash-strapped Royals released him. He hooked on with the Class B Newport News (Virginia) Dodgers, a level up, and hit .315, but they released him at the end of the season. He was now thirty-two years old. "It's a dirty game," he said later. "They can do what they want with your life. We didn't have agents and lawyers. We begged."

Al and Arlene moved with their three children from Altoona, Pennsylvania, to California's San Fernando Valley. He had a drink with an old friend from the Dodgers chain, the lantern-jawed first baseman Chuck Connors, who had quit baseball to make movies with John Wayne and Burt Lancaster. Connors convinced his old friend to give baseball another shot. Al went on to bat .332 with 121 walks and a .484 on-base percentage for the 1954 Channel Cities Oilers of the Class C California League, but he found bush-league life more dispiriting by the month. "It's a great little league," he told a reporter, "but we haven't got a bus. We go around in three station wagons. The other night I had to walk two miles to a filling station after we ran out of gas."

Two years later, Al made the California League All-Star team at the age of thirty-four. He batted .354, but it was obvious that he'd never climb back to the majors. He and Arlene now had six children and he was selling cars, installing kitchen floors, and working construction in the off-season. So he retired from the game. "My big-league career was short, but I had some great years in the minor leagues and got to see an awful lot of the country," he said. "If it wasn't for baseball I might have spent my life in the Pennsylvania coal mines."

He had played only 232 major-league games, about a full season and a half. But one of those 232 games still comes up in almost every conversation about the best fielding plays in World Series history. "It came at a crucial point against a great team and a great ballplayer, Joe DiMaggio," he told an interviewer from the Baseball Hall of Fame. "I think that catch will always be remembered." Gionfriddo donated the glove he'd used to the Hall of Fame, where fans can still see it today.

Snuffy Stirnweiss spent the 1950 season in St. Louis wishing he were back in the Bronx. He hit only .218 for the Browns, who then traded him to Cleveland. Indians manager Al Lopez praised him as "an experienced man and a great competitor" but made it clear that he hoped Stirnweiss wouldn't play much. "I hope nothing happens to our youngsters on the infield. I prefer to have Snuffy around when we need him on account of an injury." In fifty games for the Indians, his nervous stomach roiling with every at-bat, Snuffy batted .216 with four RBIs. His knees ached. He tried again in 1952, riding the bench beside another thirty-three-year-old warhorse, Pete Reiser, but appeared in the field in only one game and never came to bat. Stirnweiss retired with a career batting average of .268, 134 stolen bases, his 1945 batting title, and the major-league record for best fielding percentage in a season by a second baseman. Bret Boone would break that record in 1997 (by sitting out the last day), but Snuffy had other remembrances no one could take away, including three World Series rings. Not that he ever wore them. Worrying that a stickup man might steal them, he kept his rings in a safe deposit box.

In retirement he enjoyed long afternoons in his bat-lined den at Snuff's Acre, the roomy house in Red Bank, New Jersey, where he and Jayne lived with their five kids, with another on the way. Snuffy stayed in touch with DiMaggio but was closer to another old teammate, Tommy Henrich, who was now running a brewery. His kids and Tommy's kids made Henrich's warehouse their playground on weekends. They built forts by piling up cases of beer and threw baseballs at one another.

Snuffy and Jayne were still a love match ten years into their marriage. A looker who merited second looks even from DiMaggio, Jayne made an impression at parties in her fashionable outfits and stylish hats. Her husband was proud of how pretty she was. After signing on as a mid-level executive with a Manhattan shipping company, he sent her roses when he went out of town on business trips, the way he used to do on road trips.

Like Bucky Harris, Bill Bevens, and so many others, Snuffy had what a later generation would call father issues. The consummate straight arrow, he never spoke about Patrolman Andrew Stirnweiss, busted from the force in disgrace. Jayne told him he kept things too bottled up inside; they both thought his upset stomach and ulcers came from worrying. Once his baseball career ended he threw himself into the role of doting, diaper-changing dad who drove their older children all over town in his station wagon. On a family trip to the South, he made a point of using bathrooms and drinking fountains marked COLORED. "If it's good enough for Jackie Robinson, it's good enough for me," he told the kids.

In 1954 the football coach at Red Bank Catholic High School fell ill. Boosters pressed local dad (and former All-America halfback) Snuffy to fill in. His team won the state title, but he turned down an offer to coach another year. High school football was too much pressure.

He and DiMaggio weren't as close in real life as they were in the Stadium Club at Yankee Stadium, where a mural showed Stirnweiss turning a double play inches from DiMaggio's famous swing—but Joe D still relied on him now and then. Snuffy would call Jayne: "Hi honey. Billy Martin got drunk and started a fight. I had to slip Joe out of there."

As his daughter Susan recalls, "Mommy told us Daddy would be home late because Joe was counting on him."

DiMaggio had a son with his first wife, the actress Dorothy Arnold. Marilyn Monroe tried to befriend Joe Jr. during her marriage to Joe (and their divorce and many reconciliations), but she and Joe seldom saw the boy. Snuffy always thought there was something mournful about DiMag. All Joe ever wanted was to hit, and win, get paid, get laid, and be left alone, but he also had to carry the burden of being Joe DiMaggio every minute of every day.

DiMaggio hoped to take his son to one of the Yankees' annual Father's Day games, but Dorothy Arnold kept Joe Jr. home with her that day. Snuffy was there with his brood. The Clipper didn't want to go out on the field alone on Father's Day, so Snuffy lent him a couple of his kids. "I was proud to be George Stirnweiss's daughter," Susan recalls, "but it was pretty okay to go out on that field with Joe. I can still hear the crowd!"

Snuffy was no plaster saint. He enjoyed his beer, his Cuban cigars, and his neighborhood buddies as well as his kids, sometimes all on the same afternoon. He'd take the children off Jayne's hands and drive down the Jersey shore; on the way home he'd stop for ice cream and stop again at the Wheel Club tavern in Red Bank. He'd tell the kids they could play the car radio as loud as they wanted. Then he'd light a habano, go inside for a couple of beers, and come out with a smile.

Along with DiMaggio, Henrich, and Vic Lombardi, who summered on the shore, Snuffy stayed in touch with his old double-play mate Rizzuto. He was back at Yankee Stadium for his first Old-Timers' Day in 1956 on the day the Yanks gave Rizzuto his unconditional release. Rizzuto was thirty-eight; they had Gil McDougald to play short. Storming out of general manager Weiss's office with tears in his eyes, the Scooter saw the old teammate he always called by his given name. He said, "George, I no longer have a place on the team!"

Snuffy calmed him down. He said, "Phil, let's go get Cora. You'll go to the Catskills and cool off for a couple weeks." Phil and Cora Rizzuto took his advice, and when they returned to New York the Yanks offered Phil a job in the radio booth that led to a forty-year career in radio and TV. "Seeing George that day was my luckiest thing," Rizzuto said. "Before he came along I was afraid I might drive off the George Washington Bridge. Or pop off—and if I popped off I would have made people mad and I'd never have gotten the radio job." Decades later, listeners got used to hearing the Scooter say "George Stirnweiss" when he meant to say "George Steinbrenner."

By 1957 Snuffy was working as a midlevel executive for Caldwell and Company of Manhattan, a shipping firm, when he fainted at the company's offices on Columbus Circle. What first appeared to be a panic attack turned out to be a heart attack. "A little one," he told Jayne. Within a month he was back at work. One day he received a letter from a summer camp in Connecticut, a plea from his sons Eddie and Pete: *"They spank us & beat us up. Please come save us."* Snuffy chartered a helicopter and swooped north to bring them home.

That was the year the Brooklyn Dodgers and New York Giants announced that they would move to California in 1958. Their disappearance left the Yankees alone in New York until the Mets were born in 1962. The move also effectively doomed rail travel in the majors. With the big leagues' western frontier leaping fourteen hundred miles west from Kansas City, teams now flew. Snuffy, who hated to fly, was relieved to be out of the game on that score.

He had never been happier. He enjoyed riding the ferry to Manhattan for business meetings, joining buddies for beers at the Wheel Club, dancing with Jayne at banquets and holiday parties, where the occasional fan asked for his autograph. In the summer of '58 he appeared on a TV game show, *To Tell the Truth*, posing as a jockey. When host Bud Collyer introduced the impostor as "George 'Snuffy' Stirnweiss, former star second baseman of the New York Yankees," Snuffy nodded, looking bashful but pleased to hear applause again.

In August he took the field at Yankee Stadium, playing second base for an Old-Timers' Day squad skippered by Bucky Harris. Gray-haired Al Schacht, Bucky's clown-prince coach from his Senators days, served as plate umpire, squatting lower and lower until he was calling balls and strikes from between the catchers' feet. According to the *Times*, "the nifty fielding of Rizzuto, Stirnweiss and [Bobby] Doerr drew whoops and hollers." Two weeks later Snuffy oversaw the *New York Journal-American*'s annual schoolboy all-star game. The paper ran photos of tall, fashionable Jayne Stirnweiss with their children at the Polo Grounds that night, and of the last benchwarmer chosen for the game, a Brooklyn teenager named Joe Torre.

In September 1958, a friend returning from a trip to Rome brought Snuffy a rosary with holy water inside the beads, a gift that he prized. Snuffy may have been contented as he entered middle age, but he was still a worrier. Before a speech at a high school or a Knights of Columbus meeting you'd find him sitting in a stall in the men's room, saying the rosary.

One morning in the middle of September he met a friend for coffee at the Red Bank train station. At least his friend had coffee. Snuffy, fretting about his ulcers, sipped milk. The old speedster was on his way to Manhattan for an interview with CBS TV newsman Douglas Edwards. "He almost missed the train," his son Andy recalls. "But he was pretty fast. He caught up with it and jumped on."

It was a warm, sunny morning. Snuffy found a seat in the smokers' car, where he could fire up a cigar and read the morning papers. The Yankees had clinched the American League pennant the day before, their ninth pennant in the ten years since Casey Stengel replaced Bucky Harris as manager. Snuffy may have chatted with another passenger he knew, John Hawkins, the mayor of Shrewsbury, New Jersey, who happened to be carrying $250,000 in negotiable securities in his briefcase.

The Jersey Central commuter train passed through Matawan toward Jersey City, where Snuffy would catch a ferry to Manhattan. The train rounded a bend beside a sprawling Singer sewing machine factory on its way to a mile-long trestle spanning Newark Bay. There was a drawbridge ahead.

Half a mile from the drawbridge—an old-fashioned lift-top bridge that raised the middle of the span to allow boats to pass below, leaving a gap in the rail line—a red signal warned that the drawbridge was up. Jersey Central engineer Lloyd Wilburn waved from the locomotive to a signal-tower operator to indicate that all was well. A minute or so later Wilburn's train rolled through a second warning light and then a third, speeding up to forty-five miles per hour. Snuffy and the other passengers had no reason to think there was anything wrong until the locomotive barreled through a signal known as a derailer, a last-ditch safety feature that threw the locomotive off the rails. Now the first two cars hopped and skidded over the crossties leading to the drawbridge, brakes screeching as the train flew into space over Newark Bay.

CHAPTER 18

Warning Signs

Peder Pederson, skipper of the dredging boat *Sand Captain*, was working below the bridge that morning, scooping sand from the floor of Newark Bay. He looked up in time to see a train rolling toward the open span of the drawbridge, picking up speed. Pederson threw his engines into reverse. He didn't want to be under the gap if the locomotive plunged into the bay.

Pederson set off his ship's bells and distress whistle. Seconds later the bridge's lift-house sounded its emergency siren. It was ten a.m. Whistle and siren wailed as the locomotive reached the edge of the bridge.

Passenger Paul Land of Rumson, New Jersey, remembered, "The engineer had us going like the devil. Suddenly the brakes were applied and I thought, 'We're off the track.' I could hear ties being smashed by the train for maybe a thousand feet. Then the trestle behind us disappeared." The locomotive began a forty-foot plunge to the water below, followed by the first passenger coach and then the smokers' car. The water at that point was thirty-five feet deep, which meant that the railroad cars cascading into the gray, oily bay quickly ran out of room as the locomotive struck the bottom. They banged into one another, twisting sideways and throwing passengers from their seats as the cars flooded. "I remember my wallet floating. I grabbed it," Land recalled. He escaped by crawling through a broken window.

Another commuter, Norris Fay, heard sirens and squealing brakes from his seat in the passenger car behind Snuffy Stirnweiss's. "I felt some hard bounces and then a sudden dip of the car," Fay told the Bridgewater *Courier-News*. "I was shoved forward into the seat in front of me. I knew I'd broken my leg. The car was tipping over and I felt the water rising on my legs when I started to climb, half dragging myself over half a dozen seats." Fay made his way to a providentially open door and splashed to safety.

Pederson steered the *Sand Captain* to the spot where the water foamed, boiled by the train's diesel engines. Other vessels plowed through floating chunks of wood, seat cushions, slicks of oil, and what appeared to be blood. From above came the sound of groaning metal. The third passenger car hung from bridge, swaying, its front end dipped into the bay. The car below it, the smoking car where Snuffy had joined the mayor of Shrewsbury, was underwater.

Snuffy may have been reading when the train went off the rails. Or dozing; he liked to doze on the ride to Jersey City, lulled by the hum of the wheels on the rails. But no one could have slept through the chaos of the half minute when Jersey Central 3314 barreled toward the bridge or the dizzying moment when the train began falling. Sirens, bells, the *Sand Captain*'s whistle, riders' shouts, and the weird rattle of the train derailing preceded several weightless seconds as the smokers' car went off the bridge. When it hit the bay the impact tossed riders against the coach's windows and ceiling. The two submerged passenger cars took more than a minute to fill with water. Snuffy may have been hurt; at some point he took a nasty blow to the head. Somehow he remembered his rosary, the one from Rome with a drop of holy water inside each bead, and pulled it from his pocket.

Several people jumped from the dangling third car. They swam to shore or clung to pilings until the tugboats and police launches steaming toward the bridge could pick them up. Fireboats, Coast Guard skiffs, and three helicopters soon joined the first responders. By now Snuffy, trapped in the smokers' car with more than a dozen others, was running out of time. At thirty-nine he was still relatively young and much stronger than most of the other passengers. If any of them had a chance to get out, he was the one. But perhaps the blow to his head knocked him out. Maybe he spent precious seconds trying to help the others. That would have been like him.

In the end, no one in the smokers' car survived. Police divers found Snuffy with the rosary in his hand.

A helicopter plucked Paul Land and other survivors from the water and carried them to a police boat. One, Raphael Leon of Caracas, Venezuela, had been unable to pull his wife out from under an unconscious commuter. He clung to her as long as he could. "She slipped away from me," he said. Teresa Leon died along with Mayor Hawkins, whose briefcase was recovered with its $250,000 in negotiable stocks and bonds; Veronica Jurgelowicz, who drowned with her infant son in her arms; and forty-seven others, including Snuffy. One body was found floating off Staten Island, three miles away.

"We heard this terrific roar and a hiss of water like steam, and the dredge and the bridge were both whistling distress signals," an eyewitness told the *Times*. "People in the hanging car were screaming for help, and the water was all blood." The passenger coach hanging from the bridge swayed over the wreckage for two and a half hours. Rescue workers were afraid to climb into it. At 12:31 p.m., workmen cut that car loose and it fell with a crash, sending up what the *Times* called "a spume as high as the bridge."

Thirteen-year-old Susan Stirnweiss came home from school that afternoon to find her mother sedated, a doctor and nurse tending her, reporters and policemen milling around outside Snuff's Acre. One of the first phone calls came from Phil Rizzuto, but Jayne Stirnweiss was in no shape to talk to him.

Snuffy's death shocked his old teammates, literally sobering some of them up. It wasn't just that Snuffy was a stand-up guy and loyal friend, a gamer who gave his all despite his jangled nerves and upset stomachs. It wasn't only that he left a wife and six kids behind, or even that he was one of the first of them to die. It was that Snuffy's playing days seemed to be all that mattered. One headline read STIRNWEISS, BATTING CHAMP. The Newark *Star-Ledger* identified the disaster's best-known victim as "Former New York Yankee infielder George (Snuffy) Stirnweiss" while the *Times* mentioned that "the bodies included those of George (Snuffy) Stirnweiss, former second baseman of the New York Yankees, and Mayor John Hawkins of Shrewsbury, New Jersey." There was nothing about "businessman Stirnweiss" or "husband and father Stirnweiss." If not for his baseball career, highlighted by his wartime batting title and the '47 World Series, his passing might have gone unnoticed. His old teammates, making plans to attend the funeral, sending flowers, or writing condolence notes to Jayne, couldn't help picturing their own obituaries.

Thirteen priests took turns officiating at a funeral mass at Red Bank's St. James Catholic Church on September 19, 1958. Susan Stirnweiss never forgot the Technicolor pageant of priests in their many-colored robes. Baseball commissioner Ford Frick sat in a front pew along with Yankees general manager George Weiss and former Yanks including Phil Rizzuto, Spec Shea, and Jerry Coleman. Casey Stengel sent a grand memorial bouquet from Baltimore, where the current Yankees were playing the Orioles. Joe DiMaggio was a conspicuous absentee. DiMaggio had phoned Jayne to say he was staying away so as not to "steal the spotlight." He sent flowers instead.

St. James pastor Joseph Sheehan closed the service with a eulogy written by Dr. Bobby Brown, Yogi Berra's pinch-hitting roommate, now a Texas cardiologist (and a future president of the American League). "George 'Snuffy' Stirnweiss was one of the great athletes of his day," Sheehan intoned from the pulpit, reading Brown's words. "Despite his outstanding individual skills, he was a consummate team player. He was the possessor of a great sense of humor, an outstanding person who just incidentally happened to be a great athlete." Minutes later a fifty-car procession set out for Mount Olivet Cemetery. The last five cars were hearses, one bearing Snuffy and four packed with flowers. Local storekeepers locked up their shops and followed the cortege as it proceeded up Maple Avenue.

The New Jersey Public Utilities Commission and the U.S. Interstate Commerce Commission would spend months investigating what the *Newark Evening News* labeled the Death Train of 1958. Experts concluded that the accident was the result of a bizarre chain of events. Accident reports and autopsies revealed that the sixty-three-year-old engineer Lloyd Wilburn had had a seizure or heart attack as the train approached the bridge. Some Jersey Central locomotives featured a safety device called a dead man's switch that triggered the brakes if the engineer's hand left the throttle, but train 3314 didn't have such a switch. Instead, it sped up after Wilburn collapsed. Railroad fireman Peter Andrew, the other man in the cab, must have been terrified to see Wilburn keel over with an open drawbridge ahead. At that moment Andrew had a heart attack of his own. His autopsy showed that he was dead of cardiac arrest before the train hit the water. Wilburn, however, was still alive and managed to pull an emergency cord in the last few seconds, too late. He survived his collapse only to drown as his locomotive settled to the bottom of the bay.

The Utilities Commission report on the disaster listed the cause as "human failure" and ordered that all trains operating in New Jersey be outfitted with dead man's switches.

Jayne Stirnweiss got a $300,000 settlement from the Jersey Central Railroad that sounded like a fortune until taxes and attorneys' fees cut it in half. Jayne told the children they were going to stay in the house with the SNUFF'S ACRE sign outside and the baseball bats lining Daddy's den, but it wasn't long before she wanted out. The house was so close to the Red Bank railroad line that she kept hearing train whistles. The family moved to a smaller place farther from the tracks.

In later years the Stirnweisses kept seeing DiMaggio's TV commercials pitching a newfangled kitchen appliance called Mr. Coffee.

According to Susan Stirnweiss, Joe phoned one day to ask Jayne if she'd like to be a spokesmodel for a spin-off product to be called Mrs. Tea. Jayne was flattered but said she wasn't what she used to be. "I get so tired," she told Joe. She was fighting the onset of multiple sclerosis, which would soon confine her to a wheelchair, but DiMaggio said she had nothing to worry about. "You're still beautiful," he said, "and you're such a good speaker, just like George was." Jayne thanked him but said no. This was around the time Susan Stirnweiss told her mother how she'd almost believed Joe all those years ago when he touched her chin and said that he, "not George," was her real father. Jayne laughed and then wept.

Bucky Harris sent flowers to his former second baseman's funeral. The Yankees' manager of 1947–48 had spent the early 1950s keeping the Senators respectable during his third term in Washington. With a pitching staff featuring ex-Yanks Spec Shea and Bob Porterfield, his 1952 Senators won more games than they lost despite allowing more runs than they scored—a telltale sign of good managing. Their popgun offense lacked a .300 hitter—or even a .290 hitter. Third baseman Ed Yost led the club with twelve home runs. Shortstop Pete Runnels tried ten times to steal a base and got thrown out ten times. A year later Bucky's Senators played .500 ball and came in fifth, far behind Casey Stengel's first-place Yankees. He envied Stengel, who took over a 1949 club Bucky thought of as *his* Yankees and went on to win five consecutive World Series, a feat that will never be matched.

In April 1953 Mickey Mantle walloped a towering homer at Washington's Griffith Stadium, one of the longest ever. A front-office worker used a tape measure to determine that Mantle's blast traveled a record 565 feet, giving birth to the term "tape-measure homer." The next day a sign in the upper deck marked the spot where the ball had landed. Bucky sent a clubhouse boy to "take that damned thing down." He wasn't about to showcase enemy players' feats, least of all one by a Yankee.

The aging boy wonder's mood darkened when his divorce became official. Betty Sutherland Harris, now a society divorcée, went on to marry a TV weatherman. Bucky tried to stay close to his children. He took younger son Dick to Griffith Stadium and hit grounders to him. Then, one winter, sitting alone in the Angebilt Hotel in sleepy Orlando, waiting for another spring training to begin, he wrote an anguished letter to his elder son, Stanley. Opening by thanking Stanley for sending a family photo, Bucky lamented the failure of his marriage. He said he was miserable, alone, in hell.

His confession took his son by surprise. "Dad never volunteered much, and it wasn't like him to dwell on the past," Stanley Harris said later. "He saw himself as a guy who made his living in an unusual way, that's all. But I think he was more emotional than he let on. For years he spent Christmases with Dick and our sister and me, and there were tears in his eyes when we said good-bye."

Bucky's private life improved in the mid-1950s. His second wife, Marie, twenty years his junior, joined the graying manager on Washington's social circuit. But there would be no more Christmas visits with his children. To Bucky's chagrin, Marie never got along with his ex-wife or his kids.

After the 1954 Senators slipped to sixth place with a 66–88 record, Calvin Griffith fired Harris and hired Charlie Dressen, who brought Cookie Lavagetto to Washington with him, just as he'd done with the '51 Dodgers. Bucky jumped to Detroit, where he led the 1955–56 Tigers to winning records of 79-75 and 82-72 and proved to be as good a quote as ever, an old-timer who praised young players at the expense of the immortals he'd known. He pointed out, for instance, that Rogers Hornsby and Honus Wagner often made forty or more errors in a season, twice as many as a solid 1950s infielder. "Modern players make the old-timers look like chowderheads," he said, scoffing at the thought that the old Hall of Famers towered over youngsters like Mickey Mantle and Willie Mays. "Mays and my boy Al Kaline won batting championships as sophomores in the big leagues, a fact that defied Wagner and Hornsby," he pointed out. As a prophet he batted about .600, predicting greatness for Mantle and 1954 rookies Ernie Banks and Hank Aaron, as well as Gene Conley and Billy Hoeft, who quickly faded from the scene. Yet despite the twenty-year-old Kaline's .340 average, a league-leading 116 RBIs from Ray Boone, and Hoeft's sixteen victories, Bucky's '55 Tigers finished in fifth place, a mile behind Stengel's Yankees.

Meanwhile Charlie Dressen won 53 games and lost 101 with the last-place Senators. A year later Harris and Dressen again finished far behind the world champion Yankees, Bucky's Tigers in fifth place and Dressen's Senators seventh. Anyone comparing their results, as Bucky surely did, would see that Dressen averaged 56 victories in two seasons with the 66-win Senators club he took over from Harris. In 1955 and 1956, with both men piloting American League also-rans, Dressen's Senators won a total of 112 games while Bucky's Tigers won 161. A baseball season is too full of contingencies for such comparisons to be definitive, but Calvin Griffith didn't like what he saw. In 1957, a month into yet another last-place campaign, he fired Dressen and offered the job to Dressen's loyal lieutenant Cookie Lavagetto.

Cookie said no. "What can I do better than Charlie?" he asked the owner. He was on his way home to Oakland when Dressen told him not to be stupid: "If a man offers you a chance to manage in the majors, you say *yes*."

Cookie finished out the Senators' last-place 1957 season with a better record than Dressen's, but the manager's role was a worse fit than the prewar uniforms that used to give him a rash. Among other drawbacks, he missed having a roomie. As the manager he got a suite to himself during road trips, but he got antsy reading scouting reports alone in his rooms. Sometimes he wandered down to the lobby of a hotel in Boston or Cleveland or Kansas City late at night, looking for someone to talk to. If he ran into a player breaking curfew, he'd buy the fellow a drink and keep their secret to himself.

"The Cookie Lavagetto I met was a shy man," says former *Sports Illustrated* writer Walter Bingham, who spent a week with Lavagetto for a profile in the magazine. "When I told him he was not only the subject of my story but was going to be on the cover, he squirmed and protested. He didn't want the attention." According to Bingham, Cookie took losses so hard that he broke out in hives. "He longed to be a coach again." Too good-natured to rip his last-place team in the papers or to bench a man for making errors, he took the blame himself. His approach endeared him to the players and they began to improve, fitfully. One day they made five errors in an inning. Another time they lost eighteen games in a row. Still they won ten more games in his first full season than the year before. To help them blow off steam, the manager established a kangaroo court. Before each game the team gathered in the clubhouse, where Ed Yost served as judge and jury. Players accused one another of crimes and misdemeanors from missing signs and striking out to being a rookie, having a big nose, having a pimple on your butt or a hard-to-pronounce name (sorry, Johnny Schaive and Zoilo Versalles). Cookie collected the fines and blew the money on an all-night team party at the end of the season.

His Senators finished last from 1957 through 1959, but their record got a little better each year. They crept up to fifth in 1960, twenty-four games behind the Yankees, who lost a seven-game World Series—the best since '47, people said—when the Pirates' Bill Mazeroski hit a ninth-inning shot to beat them. The Yanks were on a historic run of ten pennants in twelve seasons, but it wasn't enough to save their manager's job. A dozen years after firing Bucky Harris for winning a World Series and finishing third the next year, Yankees general manager George Weiss let Stengel go despite those ten pennants and seven World Series crowns. Weiss told reporters the Old Perfessor was past his prime. Stengel said, "I'll never make the mistake of being seventy again."

At forty-seven, Cookie was still young for a manager, still running a major-league ball club after four losing seasons in a row. He figured he was half a century into a charmed life. "Without the grace of God I'd be driving a truck," he said. Probably a trash truck like the ones his old man rode, hopping off to collect old newspapers, apple cores, fish bones, and the occasional dead dog. Instead he earned more than twenty times Luigi's wages for writing out lineups, changing pitchers, chatting with writers, and phoning his wife and sons from the road, where the club paid for his fancy suite and the ordinary meals he preferred. And not a week went by without someone reminding him of the swing he put on a Bill Bevens fastball to break up a no-hitter and win Game Four of the 1947 World Series. Never mind that his double off Bevens was Cookie's only hit of the Series, which he finished one-for-seven to drop his career postseason batting average to .118. As the years passed it meant less and less that his double off Bevens came at the end of a mediocre big-league career or that his managerial record through 1960 added up to a less-than-mediocre 248 wins and 348 losses. What mattered—what people remembered—was that he had had one charmed moment that set him apart from almost all the other fifteen thousand or so players in major-league history, All-Stars and Hall of Famers included. Cookie Lavagetto was a human highlight, hero of one of the most famous baseball moments of all.

And if you doubted that one swing could mean so much, all you had to do was ask Bill Bevens.

During World Series anniversaries of Cookie's game breaker, photographers and TV producers would sometimes arrange for the two of them to pose together. They'd shake hands and smile. It was awkward the first few times. They barely knew each other and had nothing in common except their West Coast origins and the key minute they shared a little before four o'clock on the afternoon of October 3, 1947, sixty feet and six inches apart. Bevens came in for renewed attention when the Yankees' Don Larsen threw a perfect game in the World Series of 1956, another Subway Series that was the last before the Dodgers left Brooklyn for Los Angeles. Larsen's gem was the first no-hitter in Series history—and still the only one—an everlasting distinction Bevens would have won if Cookie had struck out or even hit a bullet at somebody. Instead, Bevens and not Cookie wound up in a truck. He worked for West Coast Fast Freight, driving a semitrailer on all-night routes from Portland to Boise and back, with plenty of time to think back to 1947.

He often thought of the play just before Lavagetto broke up the no-hitter. When pinch runner Al Gionfriddo took off for second base, the no-hitter was still intact. Berra's throw almost got him. Bevens couldn't help thinking of what second-base umpire Babe Pinelli had told him an inning or two before. "Don't worry," the ump said. "You'll get the call if it's close." Then he calls Gionfriddo safe on a play that could go either way. Years later he asked Pinelli why he didn't get the call. By then, Pinelli had been the plate umpire for Don Larsen's perfect game in the 1956 Series. He refused to talk to Bevens about 1947.

Then there was the fastball Bevens threw Lavagetto. It wasn't such a bad one. Lavagetto didn't even pull it! What if Cookie's bat had met the ball a quarter of an inch lower, sending a fly to Henrich in right? Would the no-hitter have kept him in the majors another year or two? Or landed him a pitching coach's job when he retired?

One October they were shaking hands again. By then they had a routine. They'd shake and smile, then give the photographer a couple of options. Bevens might shake his fist at Cookie or aim a scolding finger at him. Cookie always smiled. Sometimes Bev looked friendly; sometimes he looked like he was grinding his teeth.

That day, after they finished posing, Bevens pulled Cookie aside.

"You knew I had a no-hitter," he said. "You coulda let it happen. Why not?"

Was he joking?

CHAPTER 19

This Is Cooperstown

Bill Bevens had a chip on his shoulder. He was proud of his three and a half years in the majors, particularly his sixteen-win season with a 2.23 ERA, fourth-best in the league, in 1946. He was proud of his work in the '47 Series, not just the one-hitter but the relief outing that kept the Yankees close in Game Seven. At the same time, he was tired of being known mainly as the Guy Who Lost the No-Hitter. Another year or two in the big leagues might have given people more to remember, but his arm let him down.

Bevens didn't gripe. He talked about his pro career only if somebody asked about it, but his three sons could tell that he missed his Yankee days. He brightened when they remembered playing tag among the outfield monuments at Yankee Stadium, and mimicked the pukey faces they made at the sight of a Wheaties box. "We *hated* Wheaties," Larry Bevens recalls. After Bill appeared in a 1946 *Boys' Life* story sponsored by the cereal, "How to Pitch by Bill Bevens," General Mills sent him cases of the Breakfast of Champions. "He kept filling our bowls, saying, 'Eat your Wheaties!'"

He turned serious when his sons began playing schoolboy ball.

He said they should bear in mind that the ball is a weapon. "They don't call it hardball for nothing." A pitcher could use that fact to his advantage, while a hitter and even catchers had to overcome their natural fear of the baseball. Watch catchers closely, he said—you'll be surprised how many shut their eyes at the instant the ball arrives. "They flinch. It's hard not to. Even big-league catchers flinch."

Larry got a lesson in hardball the day he asked his dad to throw him his best curve. "I want to catch it."

"You'll miss it," his father said. But Larry insisted, so his father showed him how to hold a catcher's mitt just under his chin. "Keep it there. It'll look like the ball's going to hit you over here"—the boy's shoulder—"but keep that mitt right where it is." With that he went to the mound.

Oddly enough for a pitcher who always struggled to throw strikes and still holds the record for most walks in a World Series game, Bevens had laser-like control during warm-ups and side sessions. "You ready?" he asked, rocking into his delivery.

"Ready!"

"Here it comes."

Larry remembers the ball spinning so fast that it hissed as it moved through the air. Halfway to the plate it looked off-target by a foot. To keep from getting plunked on the shoulder, he reached for it just as the ball darted sideways and smacked him under the chin, knocking him down. His father stood over him while Larry sucked air. "Get up, son. Be a man," he said. "I told you not to flinch."

Bevens at forty was practically unbeatable at golf, Ping-Pong, pool, horseshoes, lifting weights, rifle shooting, and Monopoly. Same thing when he was fifty. His second son, Dan, an American Legion pitcher, quit baseball soon after throwing a no-hitter because he knew he'd never measure up. "It was like growing up around a giant," Dan says. "He was twice as strong as me. It was . . . defeating."

Larry Bevens was in high school when he challenged his dad. Big Bill might still beat all their friends at almost everything, "but you could never outrun me," he said.

Bill said, "Oh yeah?"

They picked a fencepost a hundred yards away and took off for it. Each time the boy pulled ahead, his truck-driving 305-pound father found another gear and caught up. They finished neck and neck. Bevens doubled over, gasping so hard Larry thought he might be having a heart attack until he saw that his dad was laughing.

When he wasn't driving a truck, he found other work. For a time they lived on a farm, where Bill grew onions and beans. Another Bevens plot held five acres of strawberries. Another had two hundred laying hens; he and the boys collected and sold the eggs. He put on a dress shirt for a stint selling appliances at the Sears store in downtown Salem. Like the local barber who bragged about cutting his hair, customers liked being able to say they bought their fridge from Bill Bevens. He also worked on the loading dock at Seattle's Rainier Brewing Company, which had paid him six hundred dollars a month to endorse Sicks' Select Beer in his Yankee days. Now he hoisted cases of the same beer onto trucks for three hundred dollars a month.

"He did what it took to support us," Larry says. Bevens eventually worked his way into management at his trucking company, Pacific Intermountain Express, and bought a roomy house for them in Keizer, Oregon, just north of Salem. If he was sometimes hard on his sons, it was because he took fatherhood seriously. He was determined to be the opposite of the louse who deserted him and his mother in 1916. When reporters asked about his family history he said, "My father died when I was a baby." In fact, John Bevens lived until Bill's rookie year with the Yankees. A guard at the state penitentiary, he was slain in a 1944 prison break. Bill skipped the funeral.

Recalling the penniless boyhood when his Christmas gift was a single shot with a BB gun, he made the most of family holidays. He and Millie trimmed their Christmas tree with ornaments featuring the New York Yankees' logo—each year the club sent a new one to Yankee alums—and made sure there was a Flexible Flyer sled, a bat and glove, and a shiny bike or model train set for each boy on Christmas morning.

In middle age he needed ever-stronger pain pills to dull the ache in his arm. When Larry filched one to fight a headache, it knocked him out till the next day. Bill couldn't lift his right arm to shoulder height but was still strong enough to outdrive his golf buddies with an abbreviated swing, all the while telling stories about his lessons with one of the game's all-time greats. Back in the '40s the Yankees had told him that golf could help keep his weight down. It sounded easier than running laps in a rubber suit, so he turned himself over to Tommy Armour, golf's Silver Scot, a U.S. Open and PGA champion who swung a driver inscribed LFF. That was short for Armour's motto, "Let the fucker fly," which became Bevens's main swing thought. During one round he watched the slow foursome ahead with mounting frustration. When the slowpokes wouldn't let him play through, he waited for them to get 250 yards down the fairway and then airmailed a drive over their heads.

As a member of the 1947 world champions, he was sometimes invited to Old-Timers' Day at Yankee Stadium, all expenses paid. After inventing the tradition in the Ruth-Gehrig days, the Yanks saluted their matchless history with brief exhibitions between former Yankees and Red Sox, or Yankees of the 1940s and stars of other eras. Bevens flew to New York for several Old-Timers' games, wincing as he delivered batting-practice fastballs. "He was always glad when he got back home," Dan Bevens recalls. "He was still a farm boy from Oregon. New York was no fun for him—dealing with the press and slick people like Casey Stengel."

Dealing with the press meant talking about the no-hitter that never was. It meant posing for jovial photos with Cookie Lavagetto, who had such an easy smile, and why wouldn't he? As the (losing) Dodgers' hero in the '47 Series, Cookie parlayed his playing career into five (losing) seasons as a manager. Some guys were golden, some were snakebit. Bevens tried to be a good sport when they posed for hero-and-goat pictures, but inside he was growling. On the day he pulled Cookie aside to say, "I had a no-hitter. You coulda let it happen," he was being facetious. About 98 percent facetious, anyway.

There was some precedent for such a thought. They both knew of pitchers who were suspected of grooving one to an opponent—a former teammate or popular veteran—in a meaningless late-season game. Maybe the guy needed a base hit to bat .300 or a homer to lead the league. Or maybe a hitter might think about swinging and missing on purpose to help a popular pitcher set a strikeout record in a ten-to-nothing game. The difference was that nobody dreamed of such a stunt in a close game, much less a close World Series game. Cookie shrugged off Bevens's comment as sour grapes, but he remembered it.

"The idea of making an out on purpose didn't compute to him," Cookie's son Michael recalls. "He always said, 'I wasn't thinking no-hitter. I was thinking double.'" If nothing else, that moment with Bevens reminded Cookie that the other guy probably got asked about the '47 Series all the time, too, and liked it less.

While Cookie would remain in baseball as a manager, scout, and coach, Bevens would go home to his office at Pacific Intermountain Express. He made his last trip to a Yankees Old-Timers' Day in 1971. By then there was talk that his old manager might have a shot at the Hall of Fame.

⚾

Bucky Harris had led the 1956 Detroit Tigers to an 82-72 record, but his second straight winning season wasn't enough for owner Spike Briggs, who lambasted Harris as a weakling who failed to crack the whip on the spoiled, overpaid players of the 1950s. Bucky quit under pressure, saying, "I couldn't be the fiery, aggressive manager" Briggs wanted. It always played well in the press for an owner to insist on a tough-guy manager, but Bucky considered it a crock of Schlitz. He believed good managers got the most out of their rosters by treating each man differently, depending on talent, temperament, and other factors—from sex to religion to alcohol intake to the phases of the moon. He scoffed at the Tigers' press release announcing his resignation. "Don't believe it when you're told a manager has resigned," he told reporters. "A manager never resigns, he always is fired."

In 1958 he skippered the Yankees' Old-Timers against a crew of former Red Sox players managed by Joe Cronin. That was Snuffy Stirnweiss's last ballgame. A year later Harris replaced Cronin as Boston's general manager. Now a mainstay of the game's old-boy network, the onetime boy wonder was asked how he'd handle the team's touchy superstar, Ted Williams. "I'll let him handle himself," he said. One of his most significant moves was to add Pumpsie Green, the Red Sox's first black player, to the team, erasing the color line for the majors' last all-white roster.

Ted Williams heard the new GM had a drinking problem. Seeing Bucky's hands shake convinced him the talk was true. He would recall "Bucky's gorgeous young wife" and the seemingly obvious fact that "Bucky wasn't an executive. He was a falling-down drunk. By 1959, he was so far gone that the office help had to guide his hand through his signature on official papers."

Bucky had done himself no favors by lifting whiskies after Yankee victories in 1947 and '48, saying, "Gentlemen, Joe Page." There is no doubt he drank but little chance that Williams ever saw him falling-down drunk. Bucky's secret, which he never revealed to anyone outside his family, was Parkinson's disease. "His hands shook, but he was still a fierce competitor," his son Stanley recalls. "He said, 'By God, I won't let this thing beat me.'"

After two years in Boston he rejoined the Senators, but it was a different franchise from the one he had managed in the '20s, '30s, '40s, and '50s. The Griffiths had moved the team to Minneapolis after the 1960 season—taking manager Cookie Lavagetto with them—and the club had been renamed the Minnesota Twins. A new expansion franchise, also called the Senators, was installed in the nation's capital, and Bucky served as a scout for these Senators in the early 1960s. In addition to his Parkinson's, Bucky's eyesight was failing. Cataract surgery in both eyes helped, but he could no longer drive a car. Sportswriter Merrell Whittlesey drove him to ballgames at the new DC Stadium (later RFK Stadium), marveling at the old man's tight-lipped wisdom. After a Detroit Tigers club managed by Billy Martin pulled off a game-winning squeeze bunt to beat the home team, Bucky said, "I would have pitched out four straight times."

His sense of humor darkened a bit as he aged. Looking around the stadium where the Senators and Redskins played, he smiled at the thought of blowing his best chance to make millions. Back in the 1930s, when the National Football League's Boston Redskins moved to Washington, DC, the team's owner, George Preston Marshall, offered his friend Bucky an ownership stake in the team. "George Marshall wanted to borrow five thousand dollars from me," said Bucky, who was wary after several investments in Florida real estate went sour. "I couldn't see it. I didn't think Washington was a good football town. How wrong I was." By the 1970s the franchise was worth about $20 million; by 1990 the Redskins would be worth $800 million, and by 2015, $2.8 billion.

In the early 1970s, Bucky and Marie lived in Bethesda, Maryland. He could barely hold a pen to sign the photos that baseball memorabilia collectors sent him in the mail. Sometimes he signed them twice. His Parkinson's bled into early signs of dementia as his wife grew frantic with worry about their future. One night Marie left, on what she called "a family trip." He never saw her again.

His son Stanley lived nearby. As the child of a World Series hero and Washington celebrity, Judge Stanley S. Harris had advanced from fielding grounders at Griffith Stadium to the University of Virginia School of Law and a seat on the Superior Court of the District of Columbia. In 1983 Ronald Reagan would appoint him to the U.S. District Court in Washington. In his off hours, Stanley watched ballgames on TV with his father, who always had something intriguing to say. Bucky might have a hard time remembering what happened today, but his memories of his fifty-year baseball career were as vivid as ever. He could still see Walter Johnson on the mound, Ty Cobb running bases, and Babe Ruth at bat. A pop-up was a cinch play, he said, unless Ruth hit it. "Some of the Babe's pop-ups went so high they disappeared. You had to wait and pick them up again on the way down."

As his health worsened he felt doubly bereft, abandoned by his old man at the turn of the century and by his much younger wife seventy years later. His nose was bulbous, his face creased, hands shaking, watery eyes looking fishy behind oversize glasses. He moved in with his son's family, but that didn't last. "We loved him, but with our three kids all on different schedules, my wife, Becky, was cooking seven meals a day," Stanley Harris says. "And Dad fell a lot. One evening I sat him down and said we had to get him into assisted living. He startled me by refusing. Always the competitor, he said, 'I won't go.'"

Judge Harris was in chambers the next day when his phone rang. "Son," his father said, "you have never done anything to hurt me. I'll do what you want."

Bucky settled into an assisted-living facility in Bethesda. Other residents rode motorized scooters or watched TV all day. He marched outside for long walks around the grounds. After a doctor prescribed L-dopa for his Parkinson's, he felt boyish again—"I feel like I could still play second base!"—but the disease proved stronger than the drug. He got lost in the parking lot. He fell. "We'd have him over for dinner a few times a week," Stanley Harris says. "Becky would roll up his trousers and put mercurochrome on his knees where he'd scraped them."

"It's hell to grow old," Bucky said, quoting Babe Ruth.

In time, assisted living provided too little assistance. Stanley found his father a room at the Westwood Retirement Center, a nursing home, where he padded around in house slippers and a bathrobe. "It's a lonely life," Bucky told a *Washington Post* reporter who described his room with its single window and clippings taped to the wall: photos of Walter Johnson and twenty-seven-year-old Bucky Harris; a 1924 *Post* story celebrating the Senators' first and only World Series victory, headed THEY PUT WASHINGTON ON THE BASEBALL MAP; a picture of Jesus with his sacred heart circled by thorns.

Judge Harris thought his father belonged in baseball's Hall of Fame. Less deserving men had won the game's greatest honor; Bucky's problem was his reputation as a lush. "Joe Cronin and Ted Williams kept telling people he was a drunk. 'Look at Bucky with his hands shaking!'" Stanley Harris recalls. "I wrote to the Veterans Committee explaining that his tremors were due to Parkinson's. Which I could prove. I wanted to show that he belonged in Cooperstown." Stanley's appeals to the Hall of Fame's Veterans Committee, a special panel that considered managers, umpires, executives, and overlooked players, anticipated several arguments Bill James would make in *The Bill James Guide to Baseball Managers*. Not only had Bucky managed two teams to World Series titles, he'd been a player of note. His seven RBIs in the 1924 World Series matched Ruth's best total in a Series. Two of his eleven career homers helped win that '24 Series. Hall of Fame manager Joe McCarthy called Bucky Harris "the best clutch hitter I ever saw." Bucky's 2,158 victories as a manager—23 more than McCarthy won—were third on the all-time list. Just as important was the part he played in creating the role of the modern relief pitcher. After all, he was the one who sent Fred "Firpo" Marberry to the mound to save Senators games in 1924. "The term 'saves' was not used," James wrote, "but Marberry was the first pitcher aggressively used to protect leads, rather than being brought in when the starter was knocked out. Thus Marberry is, in my opinion, the first true reliever in baseball history."

Unfortunately for Firpo, fifty years passed before anyone grasped that he had been the first true reliever. Even Bucky seemed to miss the significance of what he'd done with Marberry. After using Firpo exclusively in relief for a season, he gave him more starts every year until Walter Johnson replaced Bucky as Senators manager in 1929.

Then, twenty years later, the middle-aged wonder redeemed himself. As James sees it, Leo Durocher made another key move by shifting Hugh Casey to the Brooklyn Dodgers bullpen in 1942: "Casey was the first prominent hard-throwing reliever since Marberry. The fact that a superstar manager, Durocher, did this was a factor in the 'relief breakthrough' of the late 1940s. And Bucky Harris, after twenty years of trying to act normal, converted Joe Page from a mediocre starter into a dominating closer. Harris managed the Yankees in 1947–48. He made Page a reliever. This event, more than any other one thing, brought about general acceptance of the concept of full-time relievers."

Stanley Harris pressed the Veterans Committee for years. And then, in 1975, the Hall of Fame announced a new class of inductees: Ralph Kiner, Negro Leagues star Judy Johnson, Earl Averill, Billy Herman, and Bucky Harris. The judge practically danced his way to the nursing home, where his seventy-eight-year-old father startled him again by saying he had no intention of attending his induction.

"But Dad, people are going to want to see you."

Bucky said no. Stress made his shakes worse; the 350-mile trip from Bethesda to upstate New York to give a speech with the whole baseball world listening might reduce him to a quivering wreck. He said, "I want them to remember me the way I was, not the way I am."

So the Honorable Stanley S. Harris made the trip on his father's behalf. Before setting out, he arranged for a phone line from the speakers' platform at the Hall of Fame to Room 110 in the nursing home where Bucky Harris was about to become the first man enshrined in the Hall of Fame while wearing a bathrobe.

"There's a tremor to the hands now, big gnarled hands, infielder's hands veined in the way of old age," wrote a *Post* reporter who joined him at the Westwood Retirement Center on August 18, 1975. "The left foot beats a quiet, endless tap on the blue-green rug."

Leaning toward the telephone speaker in his room, Bucky heard Commissioner Bowie Kuhn introduce him.

"The next member of the Hall of Fame we are honoring is the only one who could not be with us today," Kuhn announced. "We're going to take a moment now while we place a two-way telephone call to him." A pause, and then the commissioner said, "Bucky, this is Cooperstown." He went on to read the text on Stanley Raymond "Bucky" Harris's newly forged Hall of Fame plaque:

SERVED 40 YEARS IN MAJORS AS PLAYER, MANAGER AND EXECUTIVE, INCLUDING 29 AS PILOT. SLICK SECOND SACKER EARNED TAG OF "BOY WONDER" BY GUIDING WASHINGTON TO

1924 WORLD SERIES TITLE AS 27-YEAR-OLD IN DEBUT AS PLAYER-PILOT. WON A.L. FLAG AGAIN IN 1925. LED 1947 YANKEES TO WORLD TITLE. MANAGED DETROIT, BOSTON RED SOX AND PHILADELPHIA PHILLIES.

Then Kuhn added a personal note. "Your commissioner was a little kid in Washington, and the first manager he remembers was Bucky Harris, and there is for me special emotion and love for this man, and delight that he has been selected."

Next Kuhn introduced the federal judge who had once beaten him in a high school golf match. Stanley Harris tapped the microphone. "Dad, are you there? Good morning! Good morning and congratulations."

"I can hear you," Bucky said from Bethesda.

"Good! Is there anything you'd like to say to us, Dad?"

Bucky said, "I'm really touched." He didn't want to say much more for fear of sounding old and sick.

His son thanked the Veterans Committee and the Hall. He mentioned a few highlights of his father's long career, adding an inside-baseball tale about Bobo Newsom's reluctance to run out a ground ball. One hot day Bobo tapped a grounder to the opposing pitcher and walked straight to the dugout. Bucky barked, "If you're not on first base in three seconds, it'll cost you a hundred!" Bobo lumbered to first in 2.9 seconds to a standing ovation from the rest of the team.

Stanley Harris closed his acceptance speech by relaying his father's "best regards to the other inductees and all my friends who are there." He thanked the cheering crowd and stepped aside for Commissioner Kuhn, who spoke to his old hero once more.

"Bucky, are you still there?" Kuhn asked. "What do you think of your son's performance today?"

The newest Hall of Famer came back on the line. He said, "Tell my boy he did well, and I thank him."

CHAPTER 20

Hero and Hero

Cookie Lavagetto and Bill Bevens had little in common except for the October moment that linked them for life. Bevens was taller and stronger and less sociable, a country boy who spent most of his career in the minors and one World Series game as the focus of every baseball fan's attention. He lost that game, then faded away, working half a dozen jobs until he found a second career that had nothing to do with the game.

Lavagetto, a city boy, was a big-league lifer. A popular ten-year veteran and four-time All-Star, he spent twenty more years as a manager and coach in the majors. Even after he retired, he enjoyed near-daily pats on the back and free drinks in honor of the game-winning double that broke up Bevens's no-hitter. "In the winters he'd get up at three thirty in the morning to go duck and pheasant hunting with an old teammate Dolph Camilli and some other baseball men," his son Ernie says. "He was a happy man."

A low-key parent, Cookie never pressed Ernie and his older brother to play ball. He didn't coach or even encourage them. If his boys wanted to learn the game they could teach themselves, he said, like he taught himself swatting flies with a broomstick in his old man's wine room. "We got taunted in Little League," Michael Lavagetto recalls. "'Oh, your dad's a big star, let's see you hit a home run!' I never hit a home run and I hated baseball."

Says Ernie, "He wasn't trying to be hard on us. It's just that he wanted a break from baseball when he got home. We spent more time together later. When he was managing the Minnesota Twins I'd go meet him to keep him company. He still didn't like to be alone." In June 1961 Ernie met his father for a fishing trip. The Twins had lost five of six. They were ninth in the ten-team American League, but Cookie was in good spirits because he caught a couple of bluegills. He and Ernie were driving back to Minneapolis when the news came on the radio: the Twins had fired him.

Cookie said, "Crap. I was hoping to make it to the All-Star break."

He was collecting his things at Metropolitan Stadium when Harmon Killebrew stopped by the manager's office. "Tough break, Skip. I'm sorry," the slugger said. Cookie thanked Killebrew and retreated to his hotel suite, where the phone was ringing. The caller was the former Yankees general manager George Weiss, who had fought with Larry MacPhail and fired Bucky Harris. Weiss had moved crosstown to run New York's new franchise, the expansion Metropolitans, who would join the National League in 1962. He said he'd heard the news from Minnesota. "Would you like to join the Mets as a scout?"

Sign me up, Cookie said. He spent the rest of the 1961 season scouting lousy-to-marginal players Weiss might claim in the upcoming expansion draft. Once the Mets launched their first comical season ("Can't anybody here play this game?" manager Casey Stengel asked as his club proceeded to win 40 games and lose 120), Lavagetto coached third base and ran the club when the seventy-two-year-old Stengel was drunk. All was well until Cookie came up short of breath in a routine physical exam. An off-season X-ray showed shadows in his lungs. He was only fifty, but after thirty years of smoking two packs of Winstons a day, he suspected he was in for bad news. A doctor delivered it: "Mister Lavagetto, you have lung cancer."

They scheduled an operation to remove all or part of a lung. The surgery was a few weeks off when Cookie asked for a second opinion. A second round of tests and X-rays revealed that the initial diagnosis had been a false alarm. "There were spots on his lungs all right, but it wasn't cancer. The spots were tar from all his smoking," Ernie recalls. Cookie was still golden. "That false diagnosis scared the crap out of him, though. He quit smoking and said he wanted to get off the road, to get closer to home."

On a Mets road trip, he spoke with Wes Westrum, a coach with the Giants. "I've been traveling my whole life," Cookie said. Westrum knew the feeling. He lived in New York, a continent away from Candlestick Park in San Francisco, where his team played. "So they went to their managers and worked out what amounted to a trade of coaches," Ernie says. Stengel agreed to add Westrum to his coaching staff in 1964 while Giants manager Alvin Dark brought Cookie aboard. A year and a half later Westrum became the Mets' manager after Stengel retired. Cookie settled back into his relaxing routine of pruning roses and trimming shrubs around the ranch house in Orinda, a half hour's drive from Candlestick Park, where he served as Dark's lieutenant for a Giants team starring Willie Mays, Willie McCovey, Orlando Cepeda, and Juan Marichal.

Cookie's teenage son Ernie worked the aisles at Candlestick, hawking peanuts, while his dad coached the bases. "Vendors got a twenty percent cut, so I'd make twelve dollars on a bad night, fifteen to twenty if we had a big crowd. Good money for a kid! And we'd drive home together."

Cookie coached with the Giants until 1967, then left the game for good. "When baseball was over he didn't look back," Ernie says. "He played golf—not too well—and hiked around Orinda and Berkeley with his springer spaniel." The graying Lavagetto had such a knack with animals that he taught the family cats to do tricks. He tromped around Tilden Regional Park in Berkeley, where he'd finished last in the 1937 Professional Ball Players' Golf Tourney, hunting up lost golf balls with his spaniel, Beau. He sold the balls in the pro shop and saved the money for an occasional trip to a casino in Stateline, Nevada. Still carrying the scars of the Depression, Cookie would take a hundred dollars into the casino, not a cent more, and leave when the hundred was gone. Mary Lavagetto frowned on her husband's gambling, Ernie recalls, "but Dad kept his chin up. He had a little money in the bank and people remembered him. Strangers would come up to us in the grocery and talk about his hit in the World Series, his claim to fame. He liked that, but never brought it up himself. He said you have to be humble about baseball because the game humbles everybody."

Bill Bevens always said he wasn't bitter about the end of Game Four in 1947. He liked Cookie Lavagetto—who didn't? But his real regrets began after Game Four. He would have been better remembered if he'd gotten the win he thought he deserved in Game Seven, but the official scorer gave the victory to Joe Page. Yankee tradition allowed retired players to keep a road uniform; Bevens prized those pale gray pants and jersey with the number 16 and kept them in a closet until they got lost during a move. A bat signed by several Hall of Famers disappeared, too. He took special care of his eighteen-karat-gold World Series ring. It had a baseball on one side and an eagle on the other; the face held a white diamond centered in a baseball diamond, covering the spot where the pitcher's mound would be. Before doing yardwork one morning he took off the ring and left it in the house for safekeeping. It was gone when he came back inside. Years later his sons saw it for sale on eBay, with his name clearly visible, engraved in the band. They tried to contact the seller, but the ring was gone before they heard back.

In late middle age Bevens coached American Legion baseball. Soon his heart began acting up on him, as he put it. In 1968 Jim Ogle, the director of the Yankees' alumni association, suggested that he see his old teammate Dr. Bobby Brown. Yogi Berra's old roomie and Stuffy Stirnweiss's eulogist was now a prominent cardiologist who had helped

Whitey Ford through his own heart trouble. Bevens thanked Ogle for the idea, but he didn't want to go east again. "I'll get through it," he said.

Carotid artery surgery improved the flow of blood from his heart, and Big Bill felt stronger until complications set in. Now his right hand acted up. He could no longer grip a baseball without dropping it. "I won't be throwing anymore," he said. His coaching career was over but he still played golf, slamming half-swing drives despite his gimpy right hand, shooting around 80 with golf buddies who crowed when they won ten or twenty dollars off the local celebrity even though he was giving them strokes.

Bevens turned seventy in 1986, the year he and Millie celebrated their golden wedding anniversary with their three sons, eight grand-children, and half a dozen great-grandkids bouncing around the house. "He was a satisfied man," Larry Bevens says. "Not a hundred percent happy with his baseball years, but he figured he had a pretty good career, longer than most. He was okay with his life."

After a medical crisis in 1991—large-cell renal lymphoma—the seventy-five-year-old Bevens watched the World Series between the Minnesota Twins and Atlanta Braves from a hospital bed. His ill-nesses had whittled him down from more than 300 pounds to some-thing close to his playing weight of 210, but he still required an extra-large bed. He liked his sons to visit during ballgames so they had something to talk about besides his failing health. Like most players, he had no particular rooting interest in the Series. If asked to pick a winner, he'd take the Twins because they were the American League club and he still thought of himself as a Yankee.

His oncologist said that Bevens's kidney disease called for surgery and months or years of dialysis. The big right-hander said, "No. I won't be kept alive on a machine." The doctor told him dialysis helped thou-sands of people survive kidney failure. Bevens didn't want to hear it. He said he hoped the treatment helped others, but at his age, with his strength leaking out of him, he didn't want to start down a cor-ridor leading to a place where he was a withering body hooked to tubes and machines.

"You're going to die, then," the oncologist said.

"I know."

Bevens wasn't religious. He had always let Millie take the boys to church while he stayed home doing yardwork, which had clearer results. The longer he spent in the hospital, the more he missed working around the house and the yard.

Late in October, Larry relieved his mother at Bill's bedside. Millie kissed her husband and went home to try to nap while the men watched the World Series. It was Wednesday, October 23, 1991, another Game Four. This Game Four matched Jack Morris and John Smoltz, a pair of hard-throwing right-handers who both stood six foot three, same as Bevens. As in 1947, this one went to the bottom of the ninth and the home team won by a score of 3–2.

During the game Bevens broke with his personal tradition by reminiscing a little. He told Larry it was funny to think that he'd spent three and a half of his seventy-five years in the big leagues, and those three and a half years often seemed to mean more than the other seventy-one and a half. He'd thrown something like fifty thousand pitches as a pro, counting his thirteen seasons in the minors, but one game, one inning, *one pitch* to Cookie Lavagetto seemed to mean more than all the rest. He guessed a guy could never know how or why or if he'd be remembered.

To Millie and their sons, at least, Bevens was never the goat of Game Four in 1947. To them he was a World Series hero as well as king of the truck routes of the Pacific Northwest, the weight scales on the loading dock, the canneries, farms, sandlots, and golf courses of Marion County, the house in Keizer, and finally an extra-long bed at Salem Memorial Hospital.

"We're going to miss you," Larry told his father after the Braves won 1991's Game Four.

"I'll miss you, too," Bevens said. "It happens to everybody, I guess."

Larry squeezed his dad's hand. "See you for the game tomorrow?"

"You bet."

Cookie Lavagetto was more religious than Bevens. "He was more devout than *I was*," says his son Michael, who went on to become a Catholic priest. "He grew up in the church and loved it, but when the church made him choose between his faith and the woman he wanted to marry, he chose Mother."

Cookie and Mary Poggi, the most photographed wife of the '47 Series, had grown up together. Their families hunted mushrooms in the hills above Oakland. Then he went away to play ball, and she married the son of a University of California professor. The marriage failed, as her parents predicted—the boy's family wasn't Italian!—and Mary divorced her husband, returning to Oakland in 1945. She reconnected with Cookie when he was home on leave from the navy, and soon Cookie asked her to marry him.

They wanted a church wedding. The local pastor wouldn't allow it because the bride was divorced. They went over the priest's head to a monsignor, arguing that Mary's first marriage should be annulled, but the diocese denied their appeal. Cookie grumbled that God had a bigger heart than His priests. He and Mary wed in a civil ceremony. After that they attended mass every Sunday but never took communion or went to confession. "Dad believed in following the rules," says Michael, now known as Father Xavier Lavagetto. "He didn't take gimmes on the golf course. After committing the 'sin' of marrying a divorcée he followed the church's laws about receiving sacraments. He and Mother stayed in the pew while Ernie and I went up to take communion."

Cookie and Mary seemed perfectly matched as long as he was playing, managing, or coaching. Their marriage grew strained after he began knocking around the house in Orinda. Mary sometimes rolled her eyes at the way her husband's golf and hunting buddies treated him as a celebrity. "He was just a ballplayer," she told their sons, "not a doctor or lawyer." Cookie said she had a point. He swore he didn't mind that she wouldn't allow any baseball memorabilia in the house—no photos, no souvenirs of his career. Cookie told Michael and Ernie that fandom was a sort of false adulation. He urged them to look up to "more important men."

Two years after Cookie retired from baseball, Mary was running her own medical-supply firm. They often argued about the family business. His wife almost always won. "Mother was a smart, hard-nosed businesswoman," Ernie says.

Mary had never forgotten the reversal that wiped out her parents' Napa Valley winery in 1920. She was walking home from school one afternoon when she passed a creek the color of the grapes Cookie had stirred as a boy, the color of wine. Treasury agents enforcing Prohibition laws had dumped twenty thousand gallons of Poggi wine into the creek, destroying her parents' family business. From that day on she kept a close eye on every dollar.

She'd played happy Dodger wife in 1947, holding baby Michael up for flashbulbs and burbling to Cookie on a long-distance phone line ("I'm so proud of you! We're both so proud!"), but she soon grew tired of life as a homemaker. Mary went to work for Candido Jacuzzi, an Italian immigrant who invented a small whirlpool bath to relieve his son's rheumatoid arthritis. She worked her way up from Jacuzzi's secretary to his best sales rep, doubling local sales of Jacuzzi-brand whirlpools by focusing on hospitals and universities, including Stanford and the University of California at San Francisco. In 1956 a client gave her a tip about a new line of mechanical ventilators for cardiopulmonary patients. Mary paid the Bird Oxygen Breathing Equipment Company $5,000 for exclusive rights in Northern California. Circling back to clients who had bought Jacuzzis, "she built her own business," Ernie says. "She set up an office in a Hunter's Point slum with the shipyards on one side and a smelly slaughterhouse on the other, and in the face of fierce chauvinism, she succeeded. Doctors would say, 'What does a woman know about this?' She'd show them the research and land the account. Then comes Medicare—suddenly there's government money for medical equipment and her business goes through the roof."

Cookie worked for his wife, running the warehouse that housed the equipment she sold. She paid him more than he'd earned coaching in the big leagues. In 1971 she sold the company for $500,000. "A small fortune at the time," Ernie calls it. "She said it was enough to make us comfortable, if not rich."

That was Cookie, too: comfortable if not rich. He carried a card in his wallet, a gift from Major League Baseball entitling him to free tickets to any game that wasn't sold out. Not always the best seats, but for frugal Cookie the price was right. The commissioner's office never spelled out the requirements for this little-known lifetime pass that Cookie prized. He and Snuffy Stirnweiss got one; Bill Bevens and Al Gionfriddo didn't.

He got more sentimental as he grew grayer and paunchier. But not about everything. Cookie stayed in touch with his brother Eddie, who had given up baseball to support their parents because he was the eldest. Eddie had a long career as a firefighter in Oakland. When he was in the hospital near the end of his life, Cookie went to visit him. He took gifts, books, and baseball souvenirs, but Eddie was unimpressed. "You and I never had much in common," he told his younger brother.

That got Cookie's back up. "Fuck him," he said later, fuming. But he kept sending flowers to Ernie's hospital room.

By the time he turned seventy, in 1982, Cookie was diabetic, unable to eat his favorite desserts and too feeble to indulge other desires including sex. He scandalized his son the priest by joking that his impotence effectively annulled his marriage. "So I can take communion again!" Which he did every Sunday, amused at the thought that God would welcome him back in his current condition.

Two winters later he passed out during a duck-hunting trip. Hypothermia, doctors said. The next day he called Ernie to ask, "Were you with me?" His memory was going.

He confessed his failings to Michael, who heard Cookie's confession not as Father Xavier but as Michael Lavagetto, the littlest celebrity of the 1947 World Series. Says Michael, "He said he wished he hadn't signed the petition against Jackie Robinson. That was a big one. Dad had faced anti-Italian prejudice when he was coming up in the 1930s. 'Dago' and 'spaghetti man,' they called him. He felt ashamed that he'd signed that petition." Cookie was pleased to tell his sons that their mother had eventually made friends with Jackie's wife. Rickey liked Dodger wives to sit together, and while Mary Lavagetto wasn't much of a baseball fan, she called Rachel Robinson a beautiful woman who was always good company.

Cookie had regrets beyond signing Dixie Walker's petition. "Everybody remembered his great hit in 1947. But then he comes up in the next game with two out in the bottom of the ninth," Michael says. Cookie admitted thinking that another game-winner in the World Series might make his name forever. "He thought, *'Man, what if I do it again?'* And he struck out on a bad pitch. 'I should have laid off it. I still dream about that one,' he said." Forty years after the '47 Series, his Game Five strikeout was as vivid to him as the double that made him famous.

Bill James would call Cookie Lavagetto one of the pivotal figures of his era—a view that has nothing to do with his game-winner off Bevens. According to James, "Lavagetto is the missing link between Leo Durocher and Billy Martin. Martin is often described as a latter-day Leo Durocher, but he never played for Durocher and did not know Durocher well. Lavagetto played for Durocher for several years and became buddies with Durocher's right-hand man, Charlie Dressen. Lavagetto took Martin under his wing, roomed with him, and became one of the biggest influences of his life."

Cookie saw his stewardship of the young Billy Martin as part of a long, happy journey from Oakland to Brooklyn, Washington, Minneapolis, and a hundred other baseball towns. In one of his occasional malaprops he called his life a twist of faith.

Sometimes he watched a grainy VHS tape of 1947 World Series highlights, marveling at the swing he put on a high outside fastball and the way the other Dodgers and their happy fans mobbed him as Eddie Miksis scored the winning run. Recalling that long-ago double, how hard he hit it and how much it meant, he wondered why he hadn't hit like that more often. Maybe it wasn't so great to be known for one swing in ten big-league seasons. "They only remember me for that one hit. I should have done a lot more," he said.

Michael Lavagetto said, "Dad, most guys they don't remember at all."

It was not until the late 1980s that Mary reversed her ban on baseball memorabilia. "Mother put up photos of him: Dad with President Eisenhower and Vice President Nixon, Dad on the cover of *Sports Illustrated*. Trophies, plaques, and a rocking chair the Dodgers gave him on an Old-Timers' Day," Ernie remembers. "He liked that. And he said, 'If anything happens to me, don't cry, because God gave me a good life.'"

On August 10, 1990, Cookie settled into his favorite living-room chair. He took a few Tums to settle his stomach. Later, his wife looked in on him. Mary saw her seventy-seven-year-old husband dozing in front of the TV. Was he dreaming of some old ballgame? He looked so comfortable, she didn't have the heart to wake him.

Cookie died in his sleep that night. His *New York Times* obituary was headed, COOKIE LAVAGETTO IS DEAD AT 77; HIT IN '47 SERIES RUINED NO-HITTER.

CHAPTER 21

Back Back Back

Al Gionfriddo kept hustling. With six kids to support, he couldn't afford not to. After Branch Rickey demoted him in 1948, sixty days short of qualifying for a major-league pension, Al spent nine seasons in the minors before packing up his spikes and glove and driving home to Visalia, California.

He tried selling insurance, working the job like the gamer he was. "I would go to the county courthouse and take down names of newly married couples or those who had just become parents," he said. "I'd call them, trying to line up prospects. I would even drive around checking for yards with bicycles, to see if there were children in the house." After three years, he knew he was in the wrong line of work. "Every time I heard a ballgame on the radio I asked myself, 'What am I doing selling insurance?'"

In 1960 he joined the San Francisco Giants as a scout covering central California. Once again his prospects didn't work out. Not one of the kids he signed ever made it to the majors. After coaching a Little League team in Visalia, he used his minor-league connections to land a job as general manager of the Santa Barbara Rancheros, a low-minors club in the New York Mets' farm system. The forty-year-old GM worked with eighteen-year-old outfielder Paul Blair, the only Ranchero who would reach the big leagues. A year later, when the club joined the Los Angeles Dodgers organization, Dodgers executive Buzzie Bavasi asked him to help the franchise that had betrayed him. Bavasi wanted him to move to Idaho to run the rookie-league Pocatello Chiefs. Al said no. The job went to another obscure bush-leaguer, his old Montreal Royals roommate Tommy Lasorda, who began his Hall of Fame managerial career that year in Pocatello.

Instead of Pocatello, Al managed Petrini's Restaurant in Goleta, California, a seaside joint with chianti bottles in straw baskets on red-and-white-checked tablecloths. Eventually he bought the place and renamed it Al's Dugout. He filled the walls with baseball memorabilia, hanging blowups of his famous catch by the front door and behind the bar. Al pestered old teammates for autographed bats, balls, and scorecards, which he also displayed in the Dugout, and he kept his menu affordable to the fishermen, plumbers, and construction workers who made the place a destination on payday. "Working people eat here, the same people who are the backbone of sports," he told a *Los Angeles Times* reporter who tracked him down. "I would get to work at nine in the morning and stay until midnight six days a week. I do my own cooking, make the sauces and salad dressings." Customers asked for his autograph. Baseball fans wrote to the restaurant. "I answer each letter personally," he said, "and always enclose a postcard photo of the catch."

Sundays he played golf. Gionfriddo was a good stick, better than Cookie Lavagetto or Bill Bevens. While he won plenty of bets on the course, many of his favorite moments came before a round began, when the starter called the Gionfriddo foursome to the tee. Often as not, somebody would ask if he was baseball's Gionfriddo, the one who made the catch. He'd shake hands, sign a hat or scorecards, and send the fan away with a smile.

Like Mary Lavagetto, Arlene Gionfriddo found her husband harder to live with after he left the game. In 1971, Al and Arlene divorced after twenty-seven years of marriage. He soon fell for Sue Jacobsen, the genial first baseperson for his restaurant's coed softball team. They married in 1973. Despite his love of cooking and his devoted clientele, he eventually sold Al's Dugout and went to work as a trainer and equipment manager at a high school in Santa Barbara. "I'd do anything to get back on the playing field," he told a local sportswriter.

He got back in uniform in 1977, when the Mets staged an Old-Timers' Day to celebrate World Series past. Old Reliable Tommy Henrich came back to New York for the game along with Don Larsen, Whitey Ford, Country Slaughter, Ralph Kiner, Roy Campanella, and forty others. Early in the proceedings Mets broadcaster Lindsey Nelson, wearing an electric-blue suit that glowed in the July sunshine, nodded toward a tall, portly Yankee on the top step of the home dugout. "With us from Salem, Oregon," Nelson declared, "the man who came within one out of pitching the first no-hitter in World Series history—Bill Bevens." Bevens, now sixty, stepped forward with a pained smile and tipped his cap, revealing a fringe of graying hair. "And here is the man who stroked the dramatic pinch hit that broke up the no-hitter and gave Brooklyn a memorable victory," Nelson said. "He was later a Mets coach—Cookie Lavagetto!" Lavagetto, sixty-four and with a full head of silver hair, got one of the loudest cheers of the day. Al Gionfriddo, introduced as the man who had robbed Joe DiMaggio in 1947, got a round of applause of his own. Then came a booming ovation as the center field gate opened to reveal a trio of New York legends: Willie, Mickey, and the Duke. (Terry Cashman's 1981 hit song, "Talkin' Baseball," was inspired by a newspaper photo of that moment.) But the Mets could top even Mays, Mantle, and Snider. Moments later Nelson introduced "baseball's greatest living player." Joe DiMaggio joined the other three center fielders on a long walk to the plate, waving to the standing, cheering crowd, while Bevens, Lavagetto, and Gionfriddo found seats on the bench.

Bevens and Lavagetto didn't play in the Old-Timers' Game. They were there for curtain calls. But Gionfriddo could still cover more ground than all but a few of the retirees. In the second inning, he replaced Mays in center. When former Met Chuck Hiller drilled a hit over second, fifty-five-year-old Al got a quick jump on the ball. He went to one knee to field Hiller's single and fired the ball back to the infield.

The game lasted only two innings; Al never came to bat. Next morning he flew home to California. The Waterbury, Connecticut, *Republican* recapped his cameo: "Al Gionfriddo, 158 pounds in his prime, had a short prime," reported the only paper to pick Al out of the Old-Timers' lineups. "One game. One inning. One catch. Although he couldn't have known it then, the applause in Al Gionfiddo's life ended on that October afternoon in 1947."

He settled for satisfaction if not much applause. During the 1970s Al became an expert at tying handmade fly-fishing lures, a skill he shared with Ted Williams. His golf buddies at Sandpiper Golf Club in Goleta, California, cheered his best shots. "Pro," they called him— "Hey, pro, you're on the tee." And three months after the Mets' Old-Timers' Game, as a guest of his old roomie Lasorda, he got a hearty round of applause at the 1977 World Series between Lasorda's Dodgers and Billy Martin's Yankees. Later, when a Hall of Fame historian interviewed him, he said, "That catch . . . it was a crucial point in a World Series against a great team, against a great ballplayer, Joe DiMaggio. I think the catch will always be remembered." After fretting that "the high salaries of today" might ruin the game—the average big-league salary was then $74,000—he hit a hopeful note. "I hope baseball will stay around forever."

Like Lavagetto and Bevens, Gionfriddo and DiMaggio were linked for life. "For the longest time, Joe hated hearing about me," Al recalled. "Later on, he got nicer. We hit the banquet circuit together. We'd stand up, me five-foot-six and him six-plus, and Joe would say, 'Look at this guy, compared to me. But he made the greatest catch anybody ever made.'" It pleased DiMaggio when Al said Joe's clout would have cleared the bullpen railing if he hadn't nabbed it. Fans and historians still quarrel about that; it's impossible to tell from the video. DiMaggio must have figured that if he was going to get robbed, it was better to lose a homer than a double.

It never occurred to Gionfriddo to keep the baseball he caught. Nobody suspected it might be worth a lot of money someday. No one ever claimed to have taken the ball home or to know where it ended up. At the time, Al was thinking about getting to the dugout and the bat rack because he was up next. A minute later he grounded out, keeping his World Series batting average steady at .000.

As a prep schooler in New York's Westchester County, Chris Berman knew he wanted to be a sportscaster. "I had a vinyl album I used to play all the time, *Great Calls of Sports History*," Berman remembers. "Russ Hodges calling Bobby Thomson's shot was on there, of course, and two Red Barber bits from 1947, the Bevens game and Al Gionfriddo." By the 1980s Berman was a mainstay at ESPN, anchoring *SportsCenter*. "So I'm driving to work, listening to sports radio, and they play a clip: Barber's 'back back back' call of Gionfriddo's catch. It wasn't a home run, but I thought, 'That could be a really good way to call a homer.'" He tried it on the air that night. "Back back back" became a Berman catchphrase, uncorked so often over his thirty years of hosting the annual Home Run Derby that some viewers wish he'd never heard Barber's call. Yet Berman says his motives were pure and practical. "It was utter respect—a tip of the hat to one of the all-time greats. *And* it keeps you from screwing up. You don't want to say 'There it goes!' and be wrong. Remember how Bob Prince used to say 'Kiss it good-bye'? He was almost always right, but I never forgot the time he said, 'Kiss it . . . off the wall.'"

Al's catch lived on in other ways. When the Dodgers' Sandy Amorós stole a potential game-tying double from Yogi Berra in the seventh game of the 1955 Series, his play was instantly compared to Gionfriddo's. No highlight reel or list of great World Series catches is complete without Al's grab.

In *Portnoy's Complaint*, Philip Roth's narrator tells his psychoanalyst of "running! turning! leaping! like little Al Gionfriddo—a baseball player, Doctor, who once did a very great thing." For his part, Al preferred *Dad*, a sentimental 1989 movie starring Jack Lemmon. In one scene Lemmon, playing a cancer patient fighting senility, reminisces with his busy executive son. "The 1947 World Series!" he cries. "Joe DiMaggio, the prince of players, star of stars, and the Dodger left fielder, Al Gionfriddo." Al was impressed that Lemmon took the trouble to say his name right, *Gee-n-FREE-doe*. He wore out a VHS tape cuing up that scene for friends, family members, and visitors. Sometimes he watched it alone. "Al Gionfriddo, a second stringer," Lemmon said, "only playing that day because the regular left fielder Carl Furillo got hurt." Which wasn't true, since Furillo was playing center that day, but Al could live with a little artistic license—he'd made it into the movies.

"You know this story?" Lemmon asks in the film.

His son, played by Ted Danson, has heard the story a hundred times. "Tell it to me," he says.

"Sixth game, bottom of the sixth inning, it's eight to five Dodgers. Two on, two out. Up steps DiMaggio. He hits a smash deep to left, home run written all over it. It was perfect! But here comes this little Gionfriddo guy, racing after the ball like he doesn't realize it was hit by Joe DiMaggio. At the last possible moment he jumps, reaches over the rail, robs DiMaggio of a three-run homer! Incredible catch—it'll live forever. But then comes the really amazing thing. DiMaggio's just approaching second base when he sees Gionfriddo make this catch. He got so upset he *kicked the dirt*. Oh, this man who never showed any emotion was human after all. And it took Al Gionfriddo to bring it out! Do you know what that means to me?"

"What?"

"In America," Lemmon says, "anything is possible if you show up for work."

In 1995 the Gionfriddos moved to Solvang, California, a tidy town that sportswriter Mike Downey described as "a Denmark theme park." Founded by Danish settlers, Solvang featured a Danish Days festival, a downtown windmill, a Hans Christian Andersen museum, and revivals of *Hamlet* suggesting that nothing was rotten in Denmark. Al, now seventy-three, liked Solvang's clean streets and friendly golfers, who sometimes vied to join his foursome because he was a somewhat famous ballplayer, as the older regulars at Alisal Ranch Golf Course never failed to tell the younger ones.

One day a cousin visited him at the golf course. "Al gave me a signed photo of the catch," says Bob Gionfriddo, a Bay Area banker. "He had a few copies of that picture on him, signed *I robbed Joe D.* He signed a baseball for me, too." Soon after that, Bob ran into the Yankee Clipper at Paulo's Restaurant in San Jose, a DiMaggio hangout. When he mentioned that he was related to Al Gionfriddo, DiMaggio smiled. "Is that little son of a bitch still alive?" he asked.

Al was still a tough little SOB. Around that time, he had knee surgery. Two days later he was rehabbing in the gym, his eyes welling with tears from the pain. "The quicker I can get this knee working, the better," he said. He and Sue celebrated their twenty-fifth wedding anniversary in 1998. Snuffy Stirnweiss had been gone for forty years. Burt Shotton, the Dodger manager Al still blamed for losing the '47 Series, died in 1962. Bucky Harris passed away in his Maryland nursing home on his eighty-first birthday in 1977. Thirteen years later, Cookie Lavagetto died in his sleep, sitting in his favorite living-room chair. Al saw his obituary: COOKIE LAVAGETTO IS DEAD AT 77. Bill Bevens's 1991 obit began, "Floyd (Bill) Bevens, who pitched eight and two-thirds innings of no-hit baseball for the Yankees against the Brooklyn Dodgers in Game 4 of the 1947 World Series . . ." Even DiMaggio would prove mortal in 1999, which took some getting used to. But Al puttered on, feeding the geese and ducks in his backyard, knocking golf balls around a putting green he built in his front yard, and riding a cart around Alisal Ranch, where he shot in the 70s after turning eighty years old. The doorbell at his house played "Take Me Out to the Ball Game."

Still bitter about the abrupt end of his major-league career, he joined a class-action lawsuit contending that the game owed millions to old-timers for using their "names, voices, signatures and likenesses" without permission or payment. The California Court of Appeals ruled against the plaintiffs in *Gionfriddo v. Major League Baseball*. "He was very disappointed," Sue Gionfriddo said. Al said, "Baseball is a dog-eat-dog business." Fifty-three years after Rickey demoted him— and looked him in the eye and lied to him, Al said—the businessmen who ran the game had won again.

To his cronies in Solvang and Santa Barbara, he was good company, quick with a quip, full of baseball stories that made them laugh. And he was still hustling. In 2001 he decided to auction off the glove he'd used to rob Joe D. As a one-mitt wonder he had nothing much else to sell. He thought the glove might fetch $100,000 that he could give his children, thirteen grandchildren, and seven great-grandchildren. "It's easier to divide money than to cut up a glove," he said. But there was a catch. He had already donated his Game Six glove to the Hall of Fame. Thousands of Cooperstown visitors had seen it displayed alongside the glove Willie Mays used to rob Cleveland's Vic Wertz in the 1954 World Series. Al now claimed that the Hall's glove was a different one he had also used in the '47 Series, but experts, sportswriters, and potential bidders doubted his story. When auction day came, his glove sold for only $12,329. The buyer was Sue Gionfriddo, who didn't want a stranger to claim her husband's glove at such a discount.

On March 13, 2003, eighty-one-year-old Al Gionfriddo shot 76, four over par, at Alisal Ranch. The next morning, feeling cocky, he told his wife, "I might shoot 75 today."

He must have looked a little tired. His buddies suggested that he ride in a cart instead of walking. Al told them to forget it. He felt like a million bucks and expected to feel like a million and forty or fifty in a couple of hours, depending on how deep he got into their wallets.

On the fifth hole, a tricky par three, he missed a birdie putt and tapped in for par. He was walking off the green, feeling good about his round, when he fell over like he'd been shot. His friends called 911, but Al was gone before the ambulance arrived. The coroner called it a "massive and sudden" heart attack.

His obituary in the *Los Angeles Times* was headed AL GIONFRIDDO, 81: DODGER MADE GAME-SAVING CATCH IN '47 SERIES. It went on to quote Tommy Lasorda. "We're losing a great Dodger," Lasorda said. Later that week they buried Little Al in Santa Barbara, under a black marble headstone featuring a golf club and a baseball bat—but no glove. There shoulda been a glove.

Epilogue

The Things They Left Behind

In the fall of 1947 Red Barber wrote a story for the *New York* *Times* Sunday magazine, framing the upcoming World Series as a duel between managers who both deserved to win. "Shotton of the Dodgers and Harris of the Yankees," Barber wrote. "Long after it is forgotten who won or lost the World Series, people will remember Shotton at 62 and Harris at 50 returning to the big time and making their contributions of real greatness."

In fact, Shotton would soon be as close to forgotten as a two-time World Series manager can be. He died at the age of seventy-seven in 1962, collapsing at the dinner table beside his beloved wife, Mary, after a pleasant day at the Florida fishing camp where they lived. Good old Burt left some fishing tackle behind but few relics of his baseball days. There was a commemorative Louisville Slugger with the '47 Dodgers remembered on the barrel—*Robinson, Reese, Lavagetto,* and all the rest, including *Burt Shotten.* They spelled his name wrong on the souvenir bat.

Stanley Raymond "Bucky" Harris raised his family in Washington, DC, where his grandson Scott is currently clerk of the United States Supreme Court, the twentieth person in U.S. history to hold that position. Scott's father, retired federal judge Stanley Harris, who subbed for Bucky at his Hall of Fame induction, treasures a trophy he inherited: the eighteen-inch silver loving cup President Calvin Coolidge handed Bucky on a happy day in 1924. Its inscription reads, PRESENTED TO STANLEY HARRIS BY THE CITIZENS OF WASHINGTON D.C. IN RECOGNITION OF HIS WINNING FOR WASHINGTON ITS FIRST PENNANT OCTOBER 1, 1924. Bucky's 1924 Senators are still the only team from the nation's capital ever to win a World Series.

The glove Al Gionfriddo wore on October 5, 1947—the real one, experts believe, with its three-inch fingers and a pocket no bigger than a baseball—can still be seen at baseball's Hall of Fame in Cooperstown, New York. His widow, Sue Jacobsen Gionfriddo, became a probation officer and rose through the ranks to become chief probation officer of Santa Barbara County, California. The Susan J. Gionfriddo Juvenile Justice Center in Santa Maria is named in her honor.

After her husband died, Millie Bevens lived alone in the house in Keizer, Oregon, that Bill bought in 1966. Every December she got a Christmas card from the Yankees. She died in 2001.

The Bevens's eldest son, Larry, has a scrapbook stuffed with his father's clippings, contracts, and fan letters as well as decades' worth of Christmas cards from the Yankees, some signed by owner George Steinbrenner. One of his favorite mementoes is the framed page from *Boys' Life* on the wall of his den in Salem, Oregon: the 1946 Wheaties ad headed HOW TO PITCH BY BILL BEVENS. Larry and his brothers, Dan and Bob, are now in their sixties and seventies. They still can't stand Wheaties.

Ernie Lavagetto lives in Walnut Creek, California, ten minutes from the ranch house where his father died peacefully in his sleep and his mother, Mary, lived until her death in 2015 at the age of 102. Ernie has several boxes full of scrapbooks and photos detailing his father's long career. Sometimes he looks them over while sitting in Cookie's old rocking chair, an Old-Timers' Day gift from the Mets.

"I used to miss him when he went east for Old-Timers' games or card shows," says Ernie, "but he liked those trips. Sign his name, make a few bucks. And the longer I live, the more I appreciate who he was and what he did. Once I was checking into a hotel in Rome. I told the clerk my name and wouldn't you know it, there's an American behind me in line. He said, 'Lavagetto? Are you any relation to Cookie?' Another time, meeting someone in Mexico, same thing. 'Lavagetto like Cookie Lavagetto?' It happens a lot. And I'm so proud to say yes."

"Of the eight Yankees who have won batting titles," writes Rob Edelman of the Society for American Baseball Research, "Snuffy Stirnweiss is the least remembered, the most obscure."

Ellen Stirnweiss Pittman lives in Rumson, New Jersey. "I don't remember him," she says of her father. "I was a baby when his train crashed. I always kind of expected him to come through the door someday. 'Here I am—sorry I missed your childhood!'"

The Yankees treated the Stirnweisses as family long after Snuffy died. Snuffy's wife and children were always welcome at team functions, where Joe DiMaggio, Tommy Henrich, and Yogi Berra made them feel at home, and at the Stadium Club, where Ellen once found herself sitting on Mickey Mantle's lap. She was a pretty, blond teenager by then. "Have I got a son for you to meet!" Mantle said.

But the old Yankees died. Jayne died in 1993, and Snuffy's kids fell out of touch with his friends and their families, out of touch with baseball. They had clippings, baseball cards, and a tape of Snuffy's appearance on *To Tell the Truth* a couple of months before he died, but not much more. Ellen's older sister, Susan, still had Snuffy's rosary.

In the fall of 2015, Ellen got a call from the Museum of the City of New York. "They were clearing out some stuff they had in storage," she says, "and they found a baseball bat donated by Snuffy Stirnweiss of the Yankees. It wasn't one of his. The barrel read *George 'Babe' Ruth*. They asked if I wanted it."

Last year Ellen's doorbell rang. The FedEx man asked her to sign for a package from the museum. Inside she found the bat. Half a bat, actually—it had been sliced lengthwise like dozens of others Snuffy used to line his den. He must have sawed it in half, ruining its value on the memorabilia market, before realizing whose bat it was and offering it to the museum.

"I didn't care about that," Ellen says. "To me, seeing this weird half a bat just proved it came from him. Sixty years after my daddy died, he sent me a present."

A Note on Sources

The key sources for *Electric October* were the families of the main figures in the book. Ernie and Michael Lavagetto, Larry Bevens and his brothers Dan and Bob, Susan Stirnweiss and Ellen Stirnweiss Pittman, Judge Stanley Harris, and members of the Shotton and Gionfriddo families all contributed generously to my work. I also relied on the Giamatti Research Center at the National Baseball Hall of Fame and Museum in Cooperstown, New York, particularly Cassidy Lent, for research that affected practically every chapter.

I turned to several books again and again. In rough order of importance they include Red Barber's *1947: When All Hell Broke Loose in Baseball* (New York: Doubleday, 1982); SABR's *Bridging Two Dynasties* (Phoenix: Society for American Baseball Research, 2013) and *The Team That Forever Changed Baseball and America* (Phoenix: Society for American Baseball Research, 2012), both edited by Lyle Spatz; Peter Golenbock's *Bums* (New York: G. P. Putnam's Sons, 1984); Bucky Harris's *Playing the Game: From Mine Boy to Manager* (New York: Frederick A. Stokes, 1925); Jack Smiles's *Bucky Harris* (Jefferson,

NC: McFarland, 2011); and David Gough's *Burt Shotton, Dodgers Manager* (Jefferson, NC: McFarland, 1994).

I gleaned important details from other sources including those listed below.

Part One

In chapter 1, "Young Old Burt," many of the basics come from Gough's *Burt Shotton, Dodgers Manager* and, to a lesser degree, SABR's *The Team That Forever Changed Baseball and America*. Details on the Federal League are from Robert Wiggins's *The Federal League of Baseball Clubs: The History of an Outlaw Major League* (Jefferson, NC: McFarland, 2008) and Marc Okkonen's *The Federal League of 1914–1915: Baseball's Third Major League* (Garrett Park, MD: Society for American Baseball Research, 1989). Information on Philip De Catesby Ball comes from *The Battle That Forged Modern Baseball* by Daniel R. Levitt (Lanham, MD: Ivan R. Dee, 2012). Much of my portrait of Branch Rickey comes from Red Barber; other bits are from Lee Lowenfish's *Branch Rickey: Baseball's Ferocious Gentleman* (Lincoln: University of Nebraska Press, 2007) and *Branch Rickey's Little Blue Book* by Branch Rickey and John Monteleone (New York: Macmillan, 1995). My account of the Cardinals-Senators game during spring training 1924 is from the *Washington Post*, March 23, 1924. I got several details on spring training that year from other editions of the *Post* that month. My account of Wilbert Robinson's being felled by a grapefruit in spring training 1915 owes a debt to Alex Semchuck's Society for American Baseball Research (SABR) bio of Robinson and the front page of the *Xenia* (Ohio) *Daily Gazette*, March 9, 1915.

Chapter 2, "The Fabulous Breaker Boy," owes many details to Bucky Harris's own *Playing the Game: From Mine Boy to Manager*. Shirley Povich provided others, including the *Washington Post*'s dubbing Bucky's 1924 hiring "Griffith's Folly," in his *Post* column of October 22, 1994. I also consulted Ted Leavengood's *Clark Griffith: The Old Fox of Washington Baseball* (Jefferson, NC: McFarland, 2011) and the *Post*'s March 23, 1924, account of the Cards-Senators game.

Chapter 3, "Zenith," derives its account of the 1924 season and World Series largely from Harris's *Playing the Game* and Smiles's *Bucky Harris*. Some details, including Jacob Ruppert's boast ("Our boys will win . . ."), come from Reed Browning's *Baseball's Greatest Season, 1924* (Amherst and Boston: University of Massachusetts Press, 2003). Altrock and Schacht's antics are drawn from the Hall of Fame archives; Leavengood's *Clark Griffith*; SABR bios of Altrock and Schacht; Harry Grayson's "Altrock Wasn't Always a Clown" (*Sarasota Herald-Tribune*, June 20, 1943); "Al Schacht: Send in the Clown" by Gabriel Schechter (The National Pastime Museum, June 28, 2013); and Burton and Benita Boxerman's *Jews and Baseball: Volume I* (Jefferson, NC: McFarland, 2006). Contemporary quotes and game details come from 1924 editions of the *Washington Post*, *New York Times*, and *Boston Globe*. Judge Stanley Harris kindly quoted the wording on the trophy President Coolidge handed Bucky. Bill James's evaluation of Firpo Marberry appears in *The Bill James Guide to Baseball Managers from 1870 to Today* (New York: Scribner, 1997). Damon Runyon's report on the 1924 Series appeared in the *New York American*, October 11, 1924.

Chapter 4, "Cookie and the Flea," relies mostly on family accounts to recap Cookie's youth. My former colleague and role model Walter Bingham's May 15, 1961, *Sports Illustrated* profile of Cookie Lavagetto provided bits of Cookie's background and proved helpful later in the book. Rory Costello's SABR bio of Al Gionfriddo contributed details on Al's youth. Harold Burris's "Rickey Solves Squad-Cutting Worry by Jackpot Deal" (*Sporting News*, May 14, 1947) described the Dodgers' trade for Gionfriddo. Bob Considine's quote ("My lid's off . . .") is from Considine's International News Service column of February 3, 1942. Cal McLish's quote about his name ("I was number seven . . .") came from his August 30, 2010, obituary in the *Los Angeles Times*. The *Brooklyn Eagle* ran a letter to the editor ("*Gionfriddo— He's Our Baby* . . .") in 1947.

In chapter 5, "Bev and Snuffy," my account of Bill Bevens's youth owes many details to his sons' memories, supplemented by scrapbooks and clippings from the Portland *Oregonian* and Salem *Statesman-Journal*. Larry Bevens provided clippings from his father's high school newspaper as well as the letter his dad received from General Mills, offering an endorsement deal for Wheaties. My account of Snuffy Stirnweiss's early career derives from clippings his daughters Susan and Ellen shared with me. Details of his signing with the Yankees come from *Baseball Digest*, January 1948. His policeman father's disgrace was front-page news in the *Brooklyn Eagle* of December 1, 1930. Susan and Ellen showed me the note Snuffy sent his future wife, Jayne (*"Please don't think me too forward . . ."*). Joe DiMaggio's view of Allie Reynolds owes a debt to Reynolds's daughter, Bobbye Ferguson. My account of Snuffy's scare in the outhouse draws from Peter Golenbock's *Dynasty: The New York Yankees, 1949–1964* (Englewood Cliffs, NJ: Prentice-Hall, 1975) as well as Stirnweiss family lore.

Chapter 6, "They'll Manage," features facts and quotes from Gough's *Burt Shotton, Dodgers Manager*. Walter Johnson's outing in the rain in the 1925 World Series was described in a *New York American* column by Damon Runyon, reprinted in *Guys, Dolls, and Curveballs: Damon Runyon on Baseball*, edited by Jim Reisler (New York: Carroll & Graf, 2005). Davis Walsh of the *Philadelphia Inquirer* called Shotton baseball's "most successful failure," in an article published on September 8, 1930. The *New York World-Telegram*'s Joe Williams sized up the Yankees' front-office views in a September 12, 1946, column headed "MacPhail Discusses Manager Rumors." My account of Shirley Povich's radio play-by-play owes a debt to Jonathan Fraser Light's *The Cultural Encyclopedia of Baseball* (Jefferson, NC: McFarland, 2005) and a colorful account in the Decatur, Illinois, *Herald* of February 6, 1975. My account of Bucky Harris's firing by Phillies owner William Cox comes from the *Philadelphia Record* of July 28 and November 24, 1943.

Chapter 7, "The Year All Hell Broke Loose," owes many details to Red Barber's book and many more to the *New York Times*, *New York Herald Tribune*, *New York Post*, *Daily News*, *New York World-Telegram*, and *Brooklyn Eagle*. Jackie Robinson's quote ("And just in case . . .") appears in Jonathan Eig's *Opening Day* (New York: Simon & Schuster, 2007). Griffith's quote about black players is from a 1937 *Washington Tribune* column by Sam Lacy. My view of Rickey and Jackie Robinson amalgamates sources including Barber's book, contemporary newspapers, Robinson's *I Never Had It Made* (New York: Putnam, 1972), Eig's *Opening Day*, Golenbock's *Bums*, and Jules Tygiel's *Baseball's Great Experiment* (New York: Oxford University Press, 1983). Babe Ruth's charge that Leo Durocher stole his watch dates to Robert W. Creamer's fine *Babe* (New York: Simon & Schuster, 1974) and Golenbock's *Bums*. Durocher's midnight speech in the mess hall has been quoted many times in slightly varying forms. I triangulated the many quotes I read and presented a version I found most plausible, one that sounds like the Lip. The fact that Cookie Lavagetto signed the anti-Robinson petition, which has not been reported before, comes from Cookie's son Ernie. The quote beginning "Log of the good ship Dodger" is from Bob Cooke's *Herald Tribune* column, quoted in Glenn Stout's *The Dodgers* (New York: Houghton Mifflin, 2004). Bucky Harris's moment with Bill Bevens ("Don't worry, I'm not sending you down") comes from their families. The Phillies' and Cardinals' insults to Robinson have been retold again and again, including in Rex Barney's *Thank Youuuu for 50 Years in Baseball from Brooklyn to Baltimore* (Centreville, MD: Tidewater, 1993), which deserves a plug. Yogi Berra's "How can you think and hit at the same time?" was reported in an Associated Press story dated August 1, 1947.

Part Two

Unless noted otherwise, stories from the *New York Times*, *Daily News*, *New York Herald Tribune*, *Daily Mirror*, and *Brooklyn Eagle* quoted in Part Two are from game stories that appeared the next day. Play-by-play accounts come from those papers—particularly the *Times*, which ran next-day accounts of every Series at-bat—and Baseballreference.com, with assists from some of the players' scrapbooks. Many visual descriptions come from MLB's newsreel collection titled *Official 1947 World Series Film* from Major League Baseball Productions (2013).

In chapter 8, "Sheer Hysteria," Judge Stanley Harris provided the pregame moment between Bucky Harris and Ty Cobb. Cobb's quote ("I beat the bastards . . .") is from Al Stump's "The Last Days of Ty Cobb" in the *Los Angeles Times*, August 5, 1985. Eig's *Opening Day* was a source of information about television coverage. Other TV details come from an October 21, 2012, *Philadelphia Inquirer* article by Frank Fitzpatrick. Red Barber recorded his recollections in *1947: The Year All Hell Broke Loose* and in a *New York Times Magazine* story of September 28, 1947. Some statistics in this chapter and elsewhere in the book come from the irreplaceable Baseballreference.com.

In chapter 9, "A Horrendous Afternoon," information on TV broadcasts comes from Fitzpatrick's 2012 *Philadelphia Inquirer* story. Allie Reynolds's daughter, Bobbye Ferguson, shared details of her father's life with me. Susan Stirnweiss and Ellen Stirnweiss Pittman helped me capture their dad's experience of the 1947 Series. Rex Barney details come from Barney's 1993 *Thank Youuuu for 50 Years in Baseball from Brooklyn to Baltimore*. W. C. Heinz's moment with Yogi Berra comes from Allen Barra's *Yogi Berra, Eternal Yankee* (New York: W. W. Norton, 2009).

In chapter 10, "Bums' Rush," facts about Ebbets Field owe a debt to Ray Robinson's *The Home Run Heard 'Round the World* (New York: HarperCollins, 1991). Hugh Casey's unforgettable boxing match with Ernest Hemingway has multiple sources but is best described in Golenbock's *Bums*. Burt and Mary Shotton's routine derives from the *Eagle* and Gough's Shotton biography. Several details about Cookie Lavagetto are from Lavagetto's scrapbooks, courtesy of his son Ernie. Play-by-play accounts come from Bob Edge's CBS telecast and MLB's *Official 1947 World Series Film*. Statistics on ticket sales, World Series odds, and calls to the phone company's Series hotline appeared in the *Times*.

In chapter 11, "The Twenty-Seventh Out," my account of Bill Bevens's day comes from his sons, who heard all about it from their father and his sportswriter friend Al Lightner. SABR's Hal Gregg bio contributed details of Gregg's youth. Parts of Joe DiMaggio's experience of the 1947 Series come from Richard Ben Cramer's *Joe DiMaggio: The Hero's Life* (New York: Touchstone, 2000). Bevens's sons filled in parts of my account of the game. Snuffy Stirnweiss remembered telling the pitcher, "Don't worry, Bev . . ." My quote calling Bevens "a strong, silent man from Oregon" appeared in Dave Anderson's *New York Times Story of the Yankees* (New York: Black Dog & Leventhal, 2012). My account of Shotton's dugout challenge to Pete Reiser ("Ain't you going to volunteer?") has multiple sources but the most vivid is W. C. Heinz's story in *True* magazine, March 1958. Many clippings in the Lavagettos' scrapbooks recount Mary's happy reaction to Cookie's famous double. The never-told end of Bill Bevens's day—in a pub the barkeep closed to give Bev's party its privacy—comes from Bill's sons.

In chapter 12, "First and Second Guesses," Spec Shea's wartime experience comes from Don Harrison's SABR bio of Shea. Berra's pre-game vow to Bevens ("Bev, I'm going to get 'em back . . .") appeared in Bevens's scrapbook. Shotton's pitching choice was described by several sources, prominently including Golenbock's *Bums*. Tex Rickards's asking fans to "remove their clothes" appears in many sources, including *The Dodgers Encyclopedia* (Champaign, IL: Sports Publishing, 2001). You can hear a rousing rendition of "Follow the Dodgers" at www.youtube.com/watch?v=DNjzf8TvCVA. Cookie's memories of his game-ending strikeout come from newspaper accounts and the memories he shared with his sons.

In chapter 13, "The Robbery," information about the Society for the Prevention of Disparaging Remarks about Brooklyn comes from *Brooklyn's Dodgers* by Carl E. Prince (New York: Oxford University Press, 1996) and Jen Carlson's August 23, 2012, *Gothamist* story. Gionfriddo's memories appeared in Golenbock's *Bums*. David Halberstam's recollection of Gionfriddo's catch appears in *Everything They Had: Sports Writing from David Halberstam* (New York: Hyperion, 2008). Larry MacPhail's confrontation with Johnny Lindell was reported in the *Times* on October 6, 1947. My account of Bevens's evening comes from his family.

In chapter 14, "Battle of the Bronx," Bucky Harris's reading of Bill

Bevens's condition comes from next-day newspapers and both families' memories. My view of Harris's pitching moves owes a debt to newspaper accounts, Smiles's *Bucky Harris*, and Judge Stanley Harris. MacPhail's dramatic telling of Bucky's bringing Joe Page into Game Seven is from Gerald Holland's "Who in the World but Larry?" in *Sports Illustrated*, August 17, 1959. (Holland's profile also features a MacPhail line I prized but didn't use. Of Harris's choosing Joe Page over Allie Reynolds in Game Seven, MacPhail said, "If we had lost on Harris's gamble, Bucky would have been a discredited manager and the second guessers would have had a field day. But Bucky Harris knew his Joe Page.") My portrayal of the Yankees' victory party owes details to Smiles, Red Barber, and Cramer's *Joe DiMaggio*. MacPhail's calling Rickey a "Bible-quoting" so-and-so comes from Roger Kahn's *The Era* (New York: Ticknor & Fields, 1993). My account of Rickey's meeting MacPhail after Game Seven ("I don't like you") and MacPhail's rampage at the Yankee's postgame party comes from J. G. Taylor Spink's "Battle of the Biltmore: Victory Brawl" in the October 15, 1947, *Sporting News*, with help from Jack Mann's "The Larry MacPhail Story" in *Sport* magazine, April 1956, and Don Warfield's *The Roaring Redhead* (Lanham, MD: Taylor Trade Publishing, 1987).

Part Three

I owe much of the last part of the book to the players' and managers' families. They shared clippings, mementoes, and memories and referred me to other sources.

In chapter 15, "The Year After Hell Broke Loose," the *New York Post* reported on Al Gionfriddo Day in Dysart, Pennsylvania, on October 12 and October 13, 1947. The *New York Sun*'s Herb Goren reported on Gionfriddo's perilous position on the roster in February 1948, including his recollection of his off-season speeches ("There was no money in it . . ."). Bill Bevens's World Series bonus comes from the letter the Yankees sent along with his check, provided by Larry Bevens. Bill's quotes to the *Oregonian* about his 1947–48 off-season come from his scrapbook. Details of Snuffy Stirnweiss's post-

Series life, including his relationship with DiMaggio, come from Susan Stirnweiss. The *Sporting News* story on "Snuff's Acre" is from an undated clipping in Snuffy's daughters' collection. Details of Alan Roth's contributions can be found in Rudy Marzano's *The Brooklyn Dodgers in the 1940s* (Jefferson, NC: McFarland, 2005) and a terrific story in the July 1957 issue of *Popular Science* (forty-six years before *Moneyball!*), "How They're Using Mathematics to Win Ball Games." Roth's epilepsy is mentioned in his SABR biography by Andy McCue, who cites Roth's papers at Case Western Reserve University. Rickey's offer to Horace Stoneham—Durocher or Shotton?—has dozens of sources including Golenbock's *Bums*, Andrew Goldblatt's *The Giants and the Dodgers* (Jefferson, NC: McFarland, 2003), and Lowenfish's *Branch Rickey: Baseball's Ferocious Gentleman*.

In chapter 16, "Late Innings," the *Times* reported Harris's firing on October 5, 1948, and Casey Stengel's hiring on October 7, 1948. Stengel's quote about Elston Howard ("When I finally . . .") appears in many sources, including *Elston and Me: The Story of the First Black Yankee* by Arlene Howard with Ralph Wimbish (Columbia: University of Missouri Press, 2001) and Harvey Frommer's *New York City Baseball: The Golden Age, 1947–1957* (Lanham, MD: Taylor Trade Publishing, 1980). Judge Stanley Harris told me about his father's dinner party with Frank Sinatra; that story also appears in Smiles's *Bucky Harris*, as does an account of Harris's cross-country drive and arrival in San Diego. The line about Billy Martin's being able to "*hear* someone give him the finger" appears in Bill Pennington's *Billy Martin: Baseball's Flawed Genius* (New York: Houghton Mifflin, 2015). Martin's conversation with Lavagetto about flinching at the plate derives from my talks with Cookie's sons, Ernie and Michael, as well as David Falkner's *The Last Yankee* (New York: Simon & Schuster, 1992). Bill Bevens's arm trouble in 1949 was reported by the *Sporting News* in a clipping Larry Bevens shared with me. Bevens's comeback attempt is from an *Oregonian* clipping. Bevens's friend Al Lightner reported on his 1951 comeback in the *Oregon Statesman*. Stirnweiss's advice to base runners first appeared in *Collier's*, July 17,

1943. My account of Snuffy Stirnweiss Day at Yankee Stadium comes from Susan Stirnweiss and the *Times*, August 25, 1950. Durocher's line ("one hundred thousand suicides") appears in Goldblatt's *The Giants and the Dodgers* and Tom Clavin and Danny Peary's *Gil Hodges: The Brooklyn Bums, the Miracle Mets, and the Extraordinary Life of a Baseball Legend* (New York: New American Library, 2012). Shotton's line about retirement ("It's a hell of a thing . . .") appears in Gough's Shotton biography. Bill James's lines on Shotton come from *The Bill James Guide to Baseball Managers*.

In chapter 17, "Try, Try Again," Walter O'Malley's purge of all things Rickey can be found in Lowenfish's entry in *Jackie Robinson: Race, Sports and the American Dream*, by Joseph Dorinson and Joram Warmund (Armonk, NY: M. E. Sharpe, 1998). Lavagetto's regrets about signing Dixie Walker's petition come from Ernie Lavagetto. My account of Shotton's later life owes a debt to his grandson Burt and to Gough's biography. Gionfriddo's minor-league travails come from a story by Scott Baillie in the Hayward, California, *Daily Review*, May 20, 1954. He called major-league baseball "a dirty game" in an interview with Earl Gustkey of the *Los Angeles Times* that appeared on October 17, 1987. His reminiscences to an interviewer ("It came at a crucial point . . .") are in the Hall of Fame's Oral History Collection. The Stirnweiss family shared details of Snuffy's later life with me, including the story of his calming Phil Rizzuto down after the Yankees cut Rizzuto. Details of that incident came from Barra's *Yogi Berra, Eternal Yankee* and *Scooter: The Biography of Phil Rizzuto* by Carlo DeVito (Chicago: Triumph Books, 2010). The *Times* reported on the 1958 Old-Timers' Game on August 10, 1958. The next month's railroad crash was recounted in many contemporary newspapers as well as in *Train Wreck!* by Wesley S. Griswold (Brattleboro, VT: Stephen Greene Press, 1969).

In chapter 18, "Warning Signs," the crash's aftermath was described in the *Times, Newark Star-Ledger, Newark Evening News*, and other papers. Quotes from survivors Norris Fay and Paul Land appeared in the Bridgewater, New Jersey, *Courier-News*, September 16, 1958. Other details come from Griswold's *Train Wreck!* The text of Dr. Bobby Brown's eulogy for Snuffy Stirnweiss is from the Stirnweiss family, as is the settlement the Jersey Central Railroad provided Jayne Stirnweiss. (Several newspapers reported that Jayne received $200,000 from the railroad. I opted for the family's number.) Judge Stanley Harris shared details of his parents' marriage with me. Bucky's views on 1950s baseball ("Modern players make the old-timers . . .") appeared in the *Saturday Evening Post*, February 11, 1956. I found Cookie Lavagetto stories and quotes in Walter Bingham's Lavagetto profile in the May 15, 1961, issue of *Sports Illustrated*, and traded emails with Bingham, a former *SI* colleague of mine. Bill Bevens's memories of umpire Babe Pinelli's calls in the 1947 Series come from Bevens's sons. I heard about his somewhat facetious question to Lavagetto years later ("You coulda let it happen. Why not?") from the Bevens and Lavagetto families.

In chapter 19, "This Is Cooperstown," the 1946 *Boys' Life* story came from Larry Bevens's collection. Larry, Dan, and Bob Bevens shared information on their home life. The meaning of the *LFF* on Tommy Armour's driver (now displayed at the World Golf Hall of Fame) appeared in *Sports Illustrated*'s *The Golf Book* (New York: Sports Illustrated Books, 2008). Ted Williams's view of Bucky Harris's supposed drinking problem came from Ed Linn's *Hitter: The Life and Turmoils of Ted Williams* (New York: Harcourt, 1993). Judge Stanley Harris told me of his father's regrets about not buying into the Washington Redskins; the quote from Bucky I used appeared in the *Washington Post*, November 9, 1971. Bucky's quote to the *Post* ("It's a lonely life . . .") and other details appeared in the *Post* on August 19, 1975. Judge Stanley Harris provided a transcript of his remarks as well as those of his father and Bowie Kuhn.

For chapter 20, "Hero and Hero," Ernie and Michael Lavagetto shared their memories of Cookie's later life. Their mother's boss Candido Jacuzzi really did invent the hot tub named after him. Results of the 1937 baseball players' golf tournament came from Cookie's scrapbook. Bill Bevens's sons told me about the loss of his 1947 World

Series ring. This chapter's line from Bill James ("Lavagetto is the missing link . . .") is from *The New Bill James Historical Baseball Abstract* (New York: Villard, 2001). Cookie's calling his life a "twist of faith" comes from Bingham's 1961 *Sports Illustrated* profile.

In chapter 21, "Back Back Back," Gionfriddo reminisced about his life after baseball, from selling insurance to running Al's Dugout, in the *Los Angeles Times*, October 14, 1982. The Old-Timers' Game at Shea Stadium was broadcast by WOR-TV on July 16, 1977. (You can see it on YouTube.) The Waterbury, Connecticut, *Republican* ("One game. One inning . . .") reported on the game on July 17, 1977. Al's quote on his catch and later baseball salaries ("That catch . . .") comes from the Hall of Fame's Oral History Collection. Chris Berman's account of his "Back back back" home-run call came from my talk with Berman in December 2016. Philip Roth's line is from *Portnoy's Complaint* (New York: Random House, 1969). Lines from *Dad* appear in the 1989 film directed by Gary David Goldberg. Bob Gionfriddo shared his story of meeting Joe DiMaggio. Lavagetto's and Bevens's obituaries appeared in the *New York Times* of August 12, 1990, and October 28, 1991, respectively. Details of Gionfriddo's life in the 1990s appeared in Mike Downey's "A Fall Classic" in the August 27, 1997, *Los Angeles Times*. The New York *Daily News* reported on Al's auction of a glove he said was his '47 Series glove on November 25, 2001. Details of his later life came from the Attleboro, Massachusetts, *Sun Chronicle*, April 14, 2003. Other details and Tom Lasorda's line ("We're losing a great Dodger") are from the Associated Press obituary that appeared in the *Los Angeles Times* on March 16, 2003.

In the epilogue, Red Barber's quote about Harris and Shotton appeared in the *New York Times Magazine*, September 28, 1947. The misspelling of Shotton's name is clear on the '47 Dodgers' commemorative bat in Ernie Lavagetto's collection. Judge Stanley Harris showed me the inscription on the loving cup his father received from President Calvin Coolidge. Rob Edelman's line about Snuffy Stirnweiss ("Of the eight Yankees . . .") appears in Edelman's bio of Stirnweiss in SABR's *Bridging Two Dynasties*.

Acknowledgments

Working on this book was a pleasure thanks to the people I worked with. Ernie Lavagetto invited me to his home and shared boxes full of his father's memorabilia, and we've bounced questions and answers back and forth since then. I had the same experience with Larry Bevens. Both men encouraged my "warts and all" approach to their fathers' heroics as well as their all-too-human flaws. I also owe thanks to Father Xavier Lavagetto, a.k.a. Michael, and to Dan and Bob Bevens.

Judge Stanley Harris invited me to Washington, DC, his father's adopted hometown, for a baseball-themed lunch overlooking the Potomac. We stayed in touch as "Judge Stan" became a trusted, reliable source, fighting his balky computer all the way.

Susan Stirnweiss and Ellen Stirnweiss Pittman hosted me several times in Rumson, New Jersey, sharing clippings, memorabilia, and memories. Ellen became a friend as well as the source of one of my favorite anecdotes.

Burt K. Shotton and Bob Gionfriddo provided help for which I'm grateful. So did the indispensable Cassidy Lent at the National

Baseball Hall of Fame and Museum. And after occasional chats over the years, I went back back back to Chris Berman, who shared the story behind his famous home-run call.

No one has been more important to *Electric October* than my editor, Paul Golob, who helped choose my six protagonists and shaped the project from the proposal stage to the final page. I learned to rely on Paul's errorless counsel on everything from the book's structure to its play-by-play action and sentence-by-sentence execution. His keen intelligence, humor, and deep knowledge of the game improved my work. Anyone who likes this book should buy all the others Paul has edited.

Here's a grateful tip of the cap to publisher Stephen Rubin. I'm also indebted to his Holt colleagues Maggie Richards, Pat Eisemann, Carolyn O'Keefe, Gillian Blake, Meryl Levavi, Rick Pracher, Chris O'Connell, Muriel Jorgensen, and Fiona Lowenstein. I'd also like to thank Phil Pascuzzo for designing a terrific dust jacket.

David Halpern of the Robbins Office was pivotal to the book's conception. Many thanks to David for his smarts, good advice, and hard work on my behalf. I'm a longtime admirer of Kathy Robbins, a fandom that grows every year, and I owe thanks to Lisa Kessler and Jane Arbogast as well.

Many others supported me and my work during the research and writing of *Electric October*. Here's a round of applause for Dick Harris, Scott Harris, Pamela Thorpe, Tom and Kelly Cook, John Rezek and his *Rotarian* colleagues Jenny Llakmani and Cynthia Edbrooke, Allison Burnett, Randy Phillips, Bret and Bob Boone, Grass Roots king Ken Kubik, Bill Skrzyniarz, Matt Inman, Steve Randall, Arthur Kretchmer, Dr. Nancy O'Dell, ESPN's Allie Stoneberg, John Horne at the Hall of Fame, Bobbye Ferguson, Bob Foreman, Doug Vogel, Chris Carson, and Jim Cahillane.

No book of mine can end without major thanks to Pamela, Lily, and Cal.

Index

About the Author

KEVIN COOK is the author of the award-winning *Tommy's Honor* (now a feature film), *Titanic Thompson*, *Kitty Genovese*, and most recently *The Dad Report: Fathers, Sons, and Baseball Families*. He is a former senior editor at *Sports Illustrated* whose writing has appeared in *The New York Times*, *Men's Journal*, *GQ*, *Playboy*, *Smithsonian*, *Details*, and many other publications. He lives in Northampton, Massachusetts.